Looking Forward, Living Now

A Mission 119 Guide to Zechariah

Hutson Smelley

Looking Forward, Living Now

Unless otherwise indicated, Bible quotations are taken from The King James Bible.

Cover art by Eddie Atkinson, used with permission.

ISBN: 978-0-9861336-5-7

www.proclaimtheword.me

Other Works by the Author

Better with Jesus: A Mission 119 Guide to Hebrews
(2015)

Love, Romance and Intimacy: A Mission 119 Guide to
the Song of Solomon (2016)

Chasing Jonah: A Mission 119 Guide to Jonah (2018)

Living Hope: A Mission 119 Guide to First Peter (2019)

Deconstructing Calvinism: A Biblical Analysis and
Refutation - Third Edition (2019)

Table of Contents

Preface to the Mission 119 Series

The psalmist declares, "Thy word is a lamp unto my feet, and a light unto my path." (Psalm 119:105) The Bible is unlike all other books, not only in its grandeur and scope, but because its words are God's Words. The Bible presents to us God's special revelation of Himself, His biased view of history past and future, the reality of who we are, and a picture of all that we can be. Woven within its pages and spilling over is God's redemptive plan for humanity, with Jesus Christ as centerpiece. We do not study the Bible merely to accumulate head knowledge, but with the earnest expectation of knowing God more and drawing near to Him. Each page has something for us, sometimes encouraging us, sometimes reproving us, always revealing God, and every jot and tittle a precious morsel for our souls. Against the backdrop of a world in darkness, it is the light of truth that pierces through all the deceptions and puts reality in clear focus.

Every generation faces challenges, and the present generation is challenged about truth and whether any absolute truths are knowable. Like all the ones before it, this generation needs to hear God's Word taught boldly, with clarity, without apology, in grace and love. And this generation needs to be reminded by those who teach that the Bible was written for everyone. God has spoken with clarity so that all believers who come to the Bible yielded to what God has for them can know its truths as they grow and mature. The aim here is to strike the proper balance between too little detail to elucidate the message and superfluous detail that obscures, so that this volume is accessible and profitable to laypersons and teachers alike who seek to understand the author's original intended meaning and the continuing relevance of that message today. With this in mind, the Mission 119 Series is designed to provide guidance for the exposition of books of the Bible with depth and a commitment to a plain sense interpretation tethered first and foremost to the context and flow of argument of the book under consideration before comparison is made to other books and the perceived systematic theology of the Bible. Of a certainty, the Bible has one author and contains neither error nor contradiction, but each of the 66 books and letters in the Bible must be allowed first to speak for itself as the teacher helps learners see the message of the book in context and its application principles.

A common sentiment today is that people need only "relevant" teaching from the Bible, which suggests portions of the Bible are irrelevant, and too often means they want three steps to raising teens in place of the perfections of God, five steps to a better marriage in place of how a believer matures and walks in the Spirit, how to find blessing and wealth in place of God's demand for holy living, and so forth. May I say that every word God ever spoke was relevant and remains so today. Those who would step forward as teachers of the Word of God only do people a disservice by trying to conform God's Holy Word to the world's bankrupt self-help counterfeits when what is most needful today is the plain teaching of the whole Bible as it is. Believers engaged in the Word and yielding to the Holy Spirit will find the most practical of wisdom and grace enablement for all areas of their lives as they draw near to God in the transformative experience of knowing Him more and more. May I also suggest that while some people will flee teaching that has depth and conviction, far more people in churches today are thirsty for more depth in the teaching. They want to see that the Bible is not clichés and recycled sugar sticks but truly a light from God unto their paths. In this vein, it is my prayer that this volume of the Mission 119 Series will be a useful guide for teachers of the Bible and a special blessing for students of the Word who aspire to know God more.

Chapter 1

Introductory Matters

The book of Zechariah is nestled within that portion of our Bibles that we call the minor prophets. As one commentator of a prior generation has well said: "One of the literary ineptitudes of the centuries is the popular name given to the last twelve books of the Old Testament, namely, the Minor Prophets. The impression often gained is that these books are of minor importance. A better designation for them is that which the rabbis employed, that is, the Twelve."[1] Unfortunately, except for an occasional message from Jonah or a quick trip to Malachi for a lesson on tithing, the Twelve are rarely taught.

Indeed, the prophets as a whole do not garner enough pulpit time even though they comprise about the same amount of our Bibles as does the entire New Testament. But with careful

---

[1] Charles L. Feinberg, *The Minor Prophets* (Chicago, IL: Moody Publishers, 1990), 9.

study of the prophets, we should come to agree with one commentator's conclusion: "I am now convinced that one cannot truly understand the Scriptures without a thorough knowledge of the prophets. It is readily apparent that the New Testament authors had an intimate knowledge of these writings. Their books are filled with quotes from and allusions to the prophets. If the New Testament authors were so well acquainted with the prophets, it behooves us to give them the same attention."[2] There are perhaps many reasons some Christians do not engage in diligent study of the prophets, but the most prominent reason is that they are sometimes difficult to understand. Robert Chisholm artfully explains this obstacle in the preface to his treatise on the Twelve: "After going through the looking glass, Alice discovered a nonsensical poem called 'Jabberwocky.' Having read it, she declared, 'It seems very pretty, but it's rather hard to understand! Somehow it seems to fill my head with ideas—only I don't exactly know what they are!' Many have responded in a similar way to the strange and puzzling words of the Old Testament prophets."[3]

If the Twelve may at times be like Alice's 'Jaberwocky,' surely Zechariah most of all. The book blends narrative, poetry, and apocalyptic writing, and poses many interpretive challenges. Yet at the same time, there is an unsurpassed richness to his writings among the Twelve. Acknowledging its interpretive difficulties, Loken concludes: "Yet, it is precisely for this reason that Zechariah is among the most important books of the Old Testament. The book provides a wealth of information concerning eschatology, especially in the area of chronology."[4] But beyond what Zechariah reveals prophetically, his most prominent focus is on the coming Messiah. Indeed, "[w]ith the exception of Isaiah, Zechariah has more to say about the

---

[2] Israel P. Loken, *The Old Testament Prophetic Books: An Introduction* (Maitland, Fla.: Xulon Press, 2010), xi.
[3] Robert B. Chisholm, Jr., *Interpreting the Minor Prophets* (Grand Rapids, Mich.: Academic Books 1990), 7.
[4] Israel P. Loken, *The Old Testament Prophetic Books: An Introduction*, 356.

Messiah than any other Old Testament book."[5] He "dwells on the Person and work of Christ more fully than all the other minor prophets together."[6] Another expositor "has called the Book of Zechariah 'the most messianic, the most truly apocalyptic and eschatological of all the writings of the Old Testament.'"[7]

It is no exaggeration to say that Zechariah provides an Old Testament Christological treatise of the same caliber as the New Testament book of Hebrews. To immerse oneself in the visions and oracles of Zechariah is to see how God would encourage His people in a dark time to faith, holiness and service based primarily on the promised future blessings associated with the coming Messiah. Once we see and hear from Zechariah as they did many centuries ago, we too can get a fresh appreciation for things to come that will reorient our lives today.

The Prophet

The name Zechariah means "Yahweh remembers." This name "summarizes Zechariah's basic message to postexilic Judah: The Lord has remembered his covenant with Israel and plans to restore the fortunes of his people."[8] But who is Zechariah? There are at least 20 individuals with that name in the Old Testament. We know from Ezra 5:1 that "the prophets, Haggai the prophet, and Zechariah the son of Iddo, prophesied unto the Jews that were in Judah and Jerusalem in the name of the God of Israel, even unto them." Thus, Zechariah was born in

[5] *Ibid.*, 357.
[6] Robert B. Chisholm, Jr., *Interpreting the Minor Prophets*, 273.
[7] F. Duane Lindsey, "Zechariah," in *The Bible Knowledge Commentary: An Exposition of the Scriptures*, ed. J. F. Walvoord and R. B. Zuck, vol. 1 (Wheaton, IL: Victor Books, 1985), 1545.
[8] Richard D. Patterson and Andrew E. Hill, *Cornerstone Biblical Commentary, Vol 10: Minor Prophets, Hosea–Malachi* (Carol Stream, IL: Tyndale House Publishers, 2008), 522.

captivity in Babylon and returned to Jerusalem from Babylon with approximately 50,000 Jewish exiles. Because Haggai and Zechariah both provided date-markers in their writings, we know that "Zechariah... did not commence his ministry (as far as has been recorded) until two months after the first prophecy of Haggai, though the first prophecy of Zechariah was at least a month before the last two of Haggai."[9] The two prophets were therefore contemporaries and co-laborers to the Jewish remnant that returned from Babylonian captivity to Israel. But while Haggai focuses directly on the urgency of resuming work on and completing the construction of the Temple and provides some material on the promised Kingdom, Zechariah's ministry has a broader focus that addresses present circumstances as well as providing substantial detail about the Messiah, the Messianic Age under his reign, and the inclusion of Gentiles in the future Kingdom.

Zechariah opens the book stating that he is "the son of Berechiah, the son of Iddo the prophet." (Zechariah 1:1, 7) We know from Nehemiah 12:1-7 that Iddo was chief of one of the priestly families that returned from exile with Zerubbabel (the governor) and Joshua (the high priest). Zechariah is a Levite of priestly descent. As Keil and Delitzsch explain, Zechariah "followed his grandfather in that office under the high priest Jehoiakim (Neh. 12:16), from which it has been justly concluded that he returned from Babylon while still a youth, and that his father died young. This also probably serves to explain the fact that Zechariah is called *bar 'Iddo'*, the son (grandson) of Iddo, in Ezra 5:1 and 6:14, and that his father is passed over."[10] And as Lindsey observes, "like Jeremiah and Ezekiel before him, Zechariah was both a prophet and a priest."[11] We also know from Zechariah 1:1 that his prophetic

---

[9] Edward Dennett, *Zechariah the Prophet* (Galaxie Software, 2004), 5–6.

[10] Carl Friedrich Keil and Franz Delitzsch, *Commentary on the Old Testament*, vol. 10 (Peabody, MA: Hendrickson, 1996), 501.

[11] F. Duane Lindsey, "Zechariah," in *The Bible Knowledge Commentary: An Exposition of the Scriptures*, 1545.

ministry begins during the second year of the reign of Darius Hystaspes, "about two months after Haggai's brief, four-month ministry began."[12] While we do not know his age at that time, Zechariah is referred to as a "young man" (Zechariah 2:4). The last date marker in Zechariah is in the fourth year of king Darius (Zechariah 7:1), and the Temple construction is completed two years later (Ezra 6:14-15). Insofar as Ezra records that the people "builded, and they prospered through the prophesying of Haggai the prophet and Zechariah the son of Iddo...and finished it, according to the commandment of the God of Israel" (Ezra 6:14), we may infer that Zechariah lived to see the Temple construction completed. "Tradition makes him arrive at extreme old age, dying in Judæa, and being buried in a tomb near to the last resting-place of his fellow-seer Haggai, in the neighbourhood of Eleutheropolis. The sepulchral monument called after him on Mount Olivet is of much later date."[13]

Finally, the prophet Zechariah is not to be identified with "Zacharias son of Barachias" that was slain (Matthew 23:35). "[I]t is now well recognized that the name Barachias in the text of the Gospel is an interpolation or alteration, and that the incident mentioned has nothing to do with our prophet, but concerns the son of Jehoiada, whose murder is recorded in 2 Chron. 24:20–22."[14]

Historical Background

The nation of Israel was divided after the reign of Solomon into two separate nations—the northern kingdom (referred to as Israel) and the southern kingdom (referred to as Judah). The northern kingdom fell to the Assyrians in 722 B.C. The

---

[12] Richard D. Patterson and Andrew E. Hill, *Cornerstone Biblical Commentary, Vol 10: Minor Prophets, Hosea–Malachi*, 522.

[13] H. D. M. Spence-Jones, ed., *Zechariah*, The Pulpit Commentary (London; New York: Funk & Wagnalls Company, 1909), v–vi.

[14] *Ibid.*

Assyrians eventually fell to the Babylonians (or Chaldeans), and from about 605 B.C. to 536 B.C., the nation of Judah (the southern kingdom) was under Babylonian control with its peoples in captivity. This period of time fulfilled the seventy years of captivity foretold by the prophet Jeremiah, a time of judgment for their disobedience. Notably, the prophet Daniel was taken by Nebuchadnezzar to Babylon in 605 B.C. with other captives. The prophet Ezekiel was taken to Babylon in 597 B.C. Nebuchadnezzar later attacked Jerusalem and destroyed the First Temple (constructed by Solomon). The siege began on January 15, 588 B.C. and after some 30 months Jerusalem fell on July 18, 586 B.C.[15]

The Persian Empire was founded by Cyrus the Great, who became king of the Persians in 559 B.C. His parents were Cambyses I (the Persian king) and a daughter of Astyages (the king of the Medes). When Cyrus became the king of the Persians in 559 B.C., he was a vassal of his grandfather Astyages. But in 550 B.C., Cyrus revolted against Astyages and gained control over both nations. Cyrus later defeated the Babylonians. Daniel 5 records what happened within the city of Babylon the night it fell to the Persians (October 12, 539 B.C.). Daniel 5:1 refers to Belshazzar as "the king," but he served as the ruler of the city of Babylon in the stead of his father, Nabonidus. On the night the city fell, Belshazzar was hosting a feast in defiance of the army outside the city gates. As Daniel 5 records, God wrote on a wall inside the palace and Daniel was summoned to interpret. Those words were that the kingdom was finished. As Loken explains: "...Cyrus himself triumphantly marched into the great city of Babylon, appearing more like a liberator than a conqueror. He forbade destruction and immediately issued an edict allowing all captive peoples to return to their respective homelands. This benevolent foreign policy allowed the Jews to return to Jerusalem under the leadership of Sheshbazzar with the

---

15 Israel P. Loken, *The Old Testament Prophetic Books: An Introduction*, 281-282.

blessing of the king."[16] The return of Jews under Sheshbazzar occurred in 538 B.C.

Cyrus died in 530 B.C. and was succeeded by Cambyses II (530-522 B.C.).[17] He then died in 522 B.C. and was succeeded by Gaumata, who in turn was assassinated in Media on September 29, 522 B.C. by Darius (a cousin of Cambyses II) and other nobles. Darius the Great took the throne 522 B.C. "It was during the reign of Darius that the Jews were able to finish building the Temple thanks to the motivation of the prophets Haggai and Zechariah."[18] Sometimes Darius is referred to as Darius Hystaspes because he was the son of Hystaspes, the satrap of Parthia.[19] Zechariah's prophetic ministry begins in 520 B.C. during the reign of Darius Hystaspes. At that time, the Persian Empire was at its peak and Judea was part of the Persian Empire.

The Text

Although it is beyond the scope of this work to explore the textual issues surrounding the book of Zechariah in depth, it is important for the reader to understand that the authorship of the book has been debated since the 17th century. "Virtually all scholars accepted the claim to authorship by Zechariah until modern times."[20] Many accepted that Zechariah authored the first eight chapters, but not the balance of the book. The early critics argued that Jeremiah wrote the later chapters because Matthew 27:9-10 quotes from Zechariah 11:12-13 and attributes it to Jeremiah.[21] Eugene Merrill explains that today, multiple authors are now widely assumed:

---

[16] *Ibid.*, 284.
[17] *Ibid.*, 342.
[18] *Ibid.*, 342-343.
[19] *Ibid.*, 342.
[20] *Ibid.*, 358.
[21] *Ibid.*, 358.

There is, then, a consensus in critical scholarship that Zechariah is a composite of two or even three major works, Zechariah (1–8), Deutero-Zechariah (9–11), and Trito-Zechariah (12–14). This consensus is so deep-rooted and taken for granted that most modern commentaries, as just observed, take it as a given. Even standard introductions repeat the arguments for division raised many years ago. While this is perhaps to be lamented, it is incumbent on those who adhere to the book's unity to provide some kind of credible rationale in light of this solid wall of contrary opinion.[22]

The arguments for multiple authors primarily focuses on alleged stylistic differences between chapters 1-8 and 9-14 and alleged historical inconsistencies (e.g., references to Judah and Ephraim as if they were both still in existence as separate nations; references to Assyria and Egypt as current powers after they faded; and references to idolatry which allegedly no longer existed).[23] The difference in styles as a basis for arguing for multiple authors is precarious at best because a single author can employ stylistic differences when writing for different purposes, adopting a different genre (e.g., poetry versus prose), or when the author writes at different times (e.g., the later chapters of Zechariah were possibly written years after the earlier chapters).

The supposed historical inaccuracies are largely overstated or based on interpretive misunderstandings. As Loken explains, "These arguments...can be adequately refuted...Judah and Ephraim are used indiscriminately to express the whole nation before and after the captivity...Assyria and Egypt are used throughout the Old Testament as representative of the

---

22 Eugene H. Merrill, *An Exegetical Commentary - Haggai, Zechariah, Malachi,* Minor Prophets Exegetical Commentary Series (Biblical Studies Press, 2003), 72.
23 Israel P. Loken, *The Old Testament Prophetic Books: An Introduction,* 359.

heathen enemies of Israel...false prophets and idolatry should not be seen as totally absent in the postexilic time period—they are still condemned even during the New Testament period."[24] Beyond that, what I hope will become apparent to the reader of this commentary is that there is a substantial unity to the entire book, with a consistent focus on related topics including a future regathering of the Jewish people to a unified Israel, God's defeat of Israel's enemies, the coming Messiah, and the Messianic Kingdom to follow. Merrill is correct in his conclusion:

> Thus all the parts of the book hang closely together; and the objection which modern critics have offered to the unity of the book has arisen, not from the nature of the last two longer oracles (Zech. 9–14), but partly from the dogmatic assumption of the rationalistic and naturalistic critics, that the biblical prophecies are nothing more than the productions of natural divination, and partly from the inability of critics, in consequence of this assumption, to penetrate into the depths of the divine revelation, and to grasp either the substance or form of their historical development, so as to appreciate it fully.[25]

Purpose of the Book

While Haggai and Zechariah are contemporaries who "both alike laboured for the encouragement of the children of the captivity in building the temple,"[26] the content and focus of their preaching is considerably different. Hartman is correct that both prophets minister during a time of discouragement:

---

[24] *Ibid.* at 359-360.
[25] Carl Friedrich Keil and Franz Delitzsch, *Commentary on the Old Testament*, vol. 10 (Peabody, MA: Hendrickson, 1996), 503.
[26] Edward Dennett, *Zechariah the Prophet*, 5-6.

"The Prophet Zechariah's day was a time of deep discouragement for the Jewish people who had returned from the Babylonian captivity. They were so deeply troubled that many had lost their will to continue the daunting task of reclaiming the land. It seemed that God Himself had turned His back on them. The future was so clouded by what appeared to be impending disaster that the national spirit was at a very low ebb. If God was not prepared to intervene, where could they turn?"[27] Haggai's messages speak to the present spiritual condition of the audience and urge the rebuilding of the Temple, with a modest focus on things future. In contrast, Zechariah's preaching has a pervasive future orientation that is not far in the background even in those portions of the prophet's writings directed at current conditions. Thus, while the preaching of Haggai and Zechariah differs in their overall focus, each complements the other.

The primary purpose of the book of Zechariah is found in his first message (1:1-6), which functions as a prologue and purpose statement for all that follows. There, the prophet calls upon the people to remember that their ancestors were taken into captivity in Babylon because they rejected God's Word through His prophets. Against the background of this relatively recent history of God's people, the prophet reminds them of a simple but critical spiritual concept: "Turn ye unto me, saith the LORD of hosts, and I will turn unto you, saith the LORD of hosts." (Zechariah 1:3) Thus, the heart of Zechariah's ministry is a call to spiritual renewal. It would not be enough merely to rebuild the Temple, but they should be spiritually prepared for proper worship in the new Temple.[28] But more than that, they should be the people of God not only in name, but in their experience of faith, service, and worship. To urge the people to spiritual renewal, the prophet whose name means "God

---

27 Fred H. Hartman, *Zechariah: Israel's Messenger of the Messiah's Triumph* (Bellmawr, NJ: Friends of Israel Gospel Ministry, 1994).

28 Richard D. Patterson and Andrew E. Hill, *Cornerstone Biblical Commentary, Vol 10: Minor Prophets, Hosea–Malachi*, 522.

remembers" encourages the people with the confirmation that, in fact, God does remember His promises to His people. In the first vision in chapter 1, Zechariah is provided "good words and comfortable words" for the people and "the LORD of hosts [says], I am jealous for Jerusalem and for Zion with a great jealousy...I am returned to Jerusalem with mercies: my house shall be built in it...My cities through prosperity shall yet be spread abroad; and the Lord shall yet comfort Zion, and shall yet choose Jerusalem." (Zechariah 1:13-17)

What sets Zechariah apart is his eschatological and Messianic focus that dominates most of the book. David Baron well summarized this two-fold emphasis: "There are some reasons why this portion of Old Testament Scripture should especially be precious to Christians. I will mention only two. First— because of the clear and striking manner in which it testifies of our Lord Jesus... Indeed it seems to be the special aim and mission of Zechariah to condense and concentrate in small compass, and in his own peculiar terse style, almost all that has been revealed to the 'former prophets' about the person and Mission of Messiah—His Divine and yet truly human character, and of His sufferings and of the glory that should follow...Secondly, on account of the light it throws on the events of the last times preceding the great and terrible 'Day of the Lord,' which is fast approaching."[29] Whereas many other prophets, including to a large degree Haggai, speak directly to the current behavior of the people with specific criticisms and instructions, Zechariah encourages their renewal based on God's promised future blessings.

One of the difficulties faced by modern Christian readers of prophetic writings like those in Zechariah, is that too many of us have been told and perhaps convinced that what God has to say about the future is non-essential. This is largely rooted in the fact that Christians are historically divided in their

---

[29] David Baron, *Zechariah: A Commentary On His Visions And Prophecies* (Grand Rapids, MI: Kregel Publications, 2005), 5-6.

interpretations of eschatological matters and cannot even agree if Jesus will rule and reign over a literal Davidic Kingdom on this earth. The frequent response has been to downplay the significance of the roughly 25% of the Bible that is prophetic to support the view that the differences of interpretation do not matter. How often have we heard, "don't major on the minors." The view is that we can grow to spiritual maturity just fine without God's Word about future events and at the same time avoid all those inconvenient disagreements. Pastors in local churches, especially the large and mega churches, take no formal position at all in the name of unity. After all, "reasonable people can differ" on all matters of prophecy. This, of course, is a choice to disregard a significant portion of Scripture. Still others have convinced themselves that studying "end times" is for the seminarians but not the average person in the pew.

As we begin the wonderful journey through Zechariah, we need to re-assess the place for the prophetic Scriptures in our lives based on the Biblical compass and not our current church culture. We know from our Biblical compass that prophecy is practical and necessary for our spiritual walk. The author of Hebrews says, "Now faith is the substance of things hoped for, the evidence of things not seen." (Hebrews 11:1) The "faith" at issue in Hebrews is *not* believing the gospel, for the author assumes his audience is comprised of believers. Rather, the "faith" looks to the greater content of God's Word that Christians are expected to believe and live by. The author of Hebrews especially has in mind prophetic matters, as the various lives he uses as illustrations in Hebrews 11, the famous hall of faith, demonstrate. The author of Hebrews says to his audience, and us by application, that we are to so trust in God's promises about the future that our present lives are reoriented around them. The examples he provides bear this out. God told Noah about a coming flood and Noah jumped into action building the ark. (Hebrews 11:7) We read that Abraham was told to leave Ur of the Chaldees for a promised land but packed up everything and began the journey "not knowing whither he went" because he trusted in God's promised future blessing. (Hebrews 11:8) Indeed, Abraham "looked for a city which hath foundations, whose builder and maker is God" (Hebrews 11:10), a reference to the New Jerusalem or heavenly city (Hebrews 11:16). All of this is to say that we need to approach Zechariah with the mind of a Noah or Abraham and let God's promises about the future reorient our lives today, as these promises were intended to reorient the lives of the remnant of God's people in Zechariah's day.

The specific future promises of God that Zechariah preaches to encourage his audience to reorient their lives include future blessings on Israel and the Gentile nations associated with the coming Messiah and his Kingdom. Zechariah speaks to the coming Messiah and king, his rejection, a future evil shepherd (the Anti-Christ), a future regathering of Jewish people to the Holy Land, God's overthrow of Israel's enemies, a time of national revival in Israel when they turn to the Lord Jesus, and the Messianic Kingdom to follow when the Lord will be physically present ruling from Jerusalem and believers from all nations will travel to Jerusalem to see the Lord. Indeed, Zechariah paints across the broad canvas of time and space a portrait of Messiah and a fairly comprehensive timeline of things to come.

Zechariah's future-oriented approach has provided a continuing fountain for future generations to drink from. Hartman is correct in his assessment: "Even as his message met the immediate need of the returned Jerusalemites, it went far beyond the immediate context to encompass the ages and give an enduring message of hope to troubled people across the centuries. Of even greater significance is the fact that this *minor prophet* delivered a *major message*, the essence of which portrays the glorious prophetic future of Jerusalem and end-time events."[30] The Jewish people, long after Zechariah's ministry ended, continued feasting in his book with expectations of a coming Messiah. They saw fulfillment of

---

[30] Fred H. Hartman, *Zechariah: Israel's Messenger of the Messiah's Triumph.*

Zechariah's words at the Triumphal Entry of our Lord Jesus. The New Testament writers frequently quote and allude to the great prophet:

> Whereas Haggai's vision encompassed, for the most part, his immediate, temporal situation, the range of his contemporary and colleague was much more expansive; for Zechariah not only shared Haggai's burden about the inertia of the postexilic community, but by vision and dream saw the unfolding of Divine purpose for all of God's people and for all the ages to come. Rich in apocalyptic imagery and packed with messianic prediction and allusion, Zechariah's writings became a favorite of the New Testament evangelists and apostles. The glorious hope expounded by the prophet was viewed by them as being fulfilled in the saving work and witness of Jesus Christ. No Minor Prophet excels Zechariah in the clarity and triumph by which he looks to the culmination of God's program of redemption.[31]

With this background in mind, an outline of the book is provided below.

I. PROLOGUE (1:1-6)

　　A. God was displeased with Israel before the exile (vv. 1-2)

　　B. God calls the Jewish remnant to spiritual renewal (vv. 3-4)

　　C. God warns the Jewish remnant not to be like their ancestors, on whom all His warnings came true (v. 5-6)

II. EIGHT VISIONS ABOUT MESSIAH

　　A. First Night Vision – Renewed Blessings (1:7-17)

---

[31] Eugene H. Merrill, *An Exegetical Commentary - Haggai, Zechariah, Malachi*, 59.

i.   Messiah is the man on the red horse protecting the Jewish remnant and commanding angels who survey the earth (vv. 8-10)

ii. Messiah is the angel of the Lord to whom the angels report that the earth is at rest (v. 11)

iii. Messiah provides good and comfortable words that God will bless Israel once again (vv. 12-17)

B. Second Night Vision – Israel's Enemies Defeated (1:18-21)

i.   Israel's enemies throughout history are pictured as four horns (vv. 18-19)

ii. Messiah's defeat of Israel's enemies is pictured as four carpenters fraying the horns (vv. 20-21)

C. Third Night Vision – Glorious Future (2:1-13)

i.   The vision – Messiah measures Jerusalem for reconstruction and future blessings when he will dwell in and protect it (vv. 1-5)

ii. The oracle – Messiah and a united people of God (vv. 6-13)

1. The Jewish people in exile are exhorted to return (vv. 6-7)

2. When he comes, Messiah will avenge Israel on the nations (vv. 8-9)

3. The Jewish remnant is exhorted to rejoice when Messiah dwells in Jerusalem and there is a unified people of God comprised of Jews and Gentiles (vv. 10-11)

D. Fourth Night Vision – Joshua is Cleansed (3:1-10)

i.   The vision – Messiah the Priest (vv. 1-7)

1. The high priest Joshua, representative of the remnant, is accused by Satan (v. 1)

2. Messiah is the angel of the Lord who rebukes Satan and clothes him in clean priestly garments (vv. 2-5)

3. Messiah exhorts Joshua to righteousness as he will be in charge of the new Temple to be finished soon (vv. 6-7)

ii. The oracle – The coming servant Branch (vv. 8-10)

1. Joshua is a type for the coming priestly Messiah called "my servant the BRANCH" (v. 8)

2. Messiah will be the sovereign stone on which the Kingdom is established (vv. 9-10)

E. Fifth Night Vision – Messiah the Priest-King (4:1-14)

i. The vision (part 1) – The special candlestick and two olive trees

1. Zechariah sees a golden menorah supplied by two olive trees (vv. 1-3)

2. The message for Zerubbabel is that his successful leadership will not be in his resources or the nation's strength, but by God's Spirit (vv. 4-6)

3. Zerubbabel will by the Spirit overcome obstacles and lead the people to complete the Temple (v. 7)

ii. The oracle – The coming Temple builder (vv. 8-10)

1. Zerubbabel is a type for the coming king Messiah who will build a Temple (vv. 8-9)

2. Zechariah's audience needs to see their role in God's unfolding plan for the ages (v. 10)

iii. The vision (part 2) – Messiah as Lord of the whole earth (vv. 11-14)

1. Zechariah's questions for an explanation (vv. 11-12)

2. The offices of king and priest serve and typify Messiah, the Lord of the whole earth (vv. 13-14)

F. Sixth Night Vision – The Flying Scroll (5:1-4)

i. Zechariah sees a large opened flying scroll (vv. 1-2)

ii. The scroll is God's righteousness enforced in the Kingdom (vv. 3-4)

G. Seventh Night Vision – The Bucket of Evil (5:5-11)

i. Zechariah sees the wickedness in Israel, personified and captured in a ephah (vv. 5-8)

ii. Wickedness is exiled to Babylon and worshiped there (vv. 9-11)

H. Eighth Night Vision – The Chariots of God (6:1-8)

i. Zechariah sees four chariots coming out from between two bronze mountains, with different colored horses (v. 1-3)

ii. Messiah deploys chariots to subdue the enemies of Israel thus bring rest to his spirit (vv. 4-8)

I. The Symbolic Crowning of Joshua (6:9-15)

i. Zechariah directs four men to create a crown and the prophet symbolically crowns Joshua the high priest (vv. 9-11)

ii. Joshua is a type for Messiah the Branch, who will build a temple and rule from it as the priest-king (vv. 12-13)

    iii. The crown is to be placed in the Temple as a memorial (v. 14)

    iv. When Messiah builds the Millennial Temple, the people will acknowledge him as Messiah (v. 15)

III. FOUR MESSAGES ABOUT MESSIAH – Fasting to Feasting (7:1-8:23)

  A. First Message – Shall We Fast? (7:1-7)

    i. Bethel sends a delegation to Jerusalem to ask if they should continue fasting as they did in exile (vv. 1-3)

    ii. God responds rhetorically that they fasted only for themselves and not because of the sin that resulted in the exile (vv. 4-7)

  B. Second Message – A History Lesson (7:8-14)

    i. Before the exile, God exhorted Israel to righteousness in how they treat vulnerable people (vv. 8-10)

    ii. Israel refused and hardened their hearts (vv. 9-12)

    iii. Because they would not listen, when they cried for help God did not listen but scattered them (vv. 13-14)

  C. Third Message – Renewed Blessings (8:1-8)

    i. God is again jealous for Israel and will bless Israel (vv. 1-2)

    ii. Jerusalem has a glorious future in the Kingdom as a safe and secure city of truth where Messiah dwells (vv. 3-6)

    iii. In the Kingdom, God will bring His scattered people back to Israel to be His people in truth and righteousness (vv. 7-8)

iv. God exhorts the remnant to recall how it was before the exile when the people were disobedient (vv. 9-10)

v. In contrast, the remnant will enjoy blessings (vv. 11-15)

vi. God exhorts the remnant to righteousness in how they treat one another as He had exhorted the nation before the exile (vv. 16-17)

D. Fourth Message – You shall feast (8:18-23)

i. The fasting will be turned to feasting in the Kingdom (vv. 18-19)

ii. Because Messiah will dwell in Jerusalem and believing Jews and Gentiles will go to pray before him (vv. 20-23)

IV. TWO BURDENS ABOUT MESSIAH (9:1-14:21)

A. FIRST BURDEN – Two Advents of Messiah (9:1-17)

i. God is pictured as an invader from the north marching to Israel and destroying her enemies along the way (9:1-6)

ii. This judgment on Israel's neighbors eliminates their idolatrous practices and refines these nations to a believing Gentile remnant (9:7-8)

iii. Messiah the king brings spiritual deliverance to Israel at his first advent (9:9)

iv. Messiah returns and destroys Israel's enemies who invaded the land and Messiah implements his global Kingdom (9:10)

v. Messiah calls the Jewish people in exile to return home (9:11-12)

vi. Messiah empowers the people to defeat the Gentile invaders in Israel (9:13-17)

B. FIRST BURDEN – Messianic Kingdom Blessings (10:1-12)

    i. In the Kingdom, Messiah blesses the land with rain (10:1)

    ii. In contrast to the bad shepherds, God empowers His people and sends them Messiah to lead them victoriously against their enemies (10:2-7)

    iii. God will regather the Jewish remnant to Israel in a new exodus (10:8-12)

C. FIRST BURDEN – Messiah, the Good Shepherd, Rejected (11:1-17)

    i. Israel will fall under judgment for rejecting Messiah at his first advent (11:1-3)

    ii. God will send the good shepherd Jesus Christ who will be rejected by Israel (11:4-8)

    iii. God will allow Israel to be punished by a Gentile invasion (11:9-11)

    iv. Messiah the good shepherd is valued at 30 pieces of silver (11:12-13)

    v. After rejecting Messiah, Israel is internally destabilized and then relegated to a series of bad shepherds (11:14-16)

    vi. God will kill the ultimate bad shepherd, the Anti-Christ (11:17)

D. SECOND BURDEN – Turning to Messiah Jesus (12:1-14)

i. In the day of the Lord, the Creator God will deliver Israel from invading Gentile armies (12:1-4)

ii. In the day of the Lord, God will empower the Jewish people and leadership to defeat the invaders (12:5-8)

iii. In the day of the Lord, God will pour out His Spirit and there will be a national revival as a Jewish remnant mourns over murdering Messiah at his first advent (12:9-14)

E. SECOND BURDEN – Messiah Takes Away Sins (13:1-9)

i. In the day of the Lord, a fountain will cleanse the Jewish remnant of sin and uncleanness (13:1)

ii. In the day of the Lord, Messiah will remove idolatry and false prophets from Israel (13:2-6)

iii. God will smite His good shepherd, the Messiah (13:7)

iv. In the day of the Lord, two thirds of the Jewish people will die leaving a refined believing remnant (13:8-9)

F. SECOND BURDEN – Messiah is Victorious (14:1-21)

i. In the day of the Lord, an invading international military force will have initial success in taking Israel (14:1-2)

ii. In the day of the Lord, Jesus returns and fights the invaders (14:3)

iii. Jesus splits the Mount of Olives in two, providing an escape for the remaining Jewish remnant in Jerusalem (14:4-5)

iv. Jesus' return will be marked by a cosmic sign (14:6-7)

v. Jesus will change the topography of the land and create two new rivers to irrigate it (14:8-11)

vi. Messiah will destroy the invaders by a flesh-eating plague and a plague of confusion so they turn on one another (14:12-15)

vii. The Gentiles that survive the Tribulation will join the Lord in the Kingdom and pilgrimage to Jerusalem to worship (14:16-19)

viii. The Kingdom will be characterized by holiness (14:20-21)

Chapter 2

Looking Back

One of the most inspiring chapters in the Bible is Hebrews 11. There, the author of Hebrews exhorts his audience by historical examples of real people to live out their Christian faith, by which he means having their lives in "the now" wholly reoriented around God's promised future blessings. Indeed, he writes that "faith is the substance of things hoped for, the evidence of things not seen." (Hebrews 11:1) God's promises in the heart of faithful Christians are so real and tangible in the present that their lives are lived out on the basis of God's eternal blessings and not present, momentary gratification. They live as pilgrims on this earth with one foot firmly in heaven's door, focused on Jesus Christ as the chief example of faithful living ("who for the joy that was set before him endured the cross"), with many saints of the past as witnesses that the enduring Christian life can be attained by faithful believers. Thus, we are exhorted in Hebrews 11 to learn from the positive examples of those in the hall of fame of faith.

The book of Zechariah is all about looking forward to God's promises and living now in a manner consistent with believing those promises. But the preparation for that is a look back. The prior generations in Israel failed to live in obedience to God's Word, but instead characteristically spurned His Word delivered through His prophets. As the book of Zechariah calls upon a small remnant of Jewish people that returned to Israel and to Jerusalem to embrace being the people of God and engage in the physical and spiritual reconstruction that is necessary, God would have them learn from the negative examples of the past and implore them not to repeat the disobedience of the prior generations. Being the people of God begins with hearing God's Word and volitionally choosing to embrace it and live it by the enabling power of the Holy Spirit. God's Word is always a call to action. If they will do this, God will return His blessing upon them and they will take their place in His greater redemptive program for humanity.

Scripture and Comments

The first six verses of the book of Zechariah form the introduction or prologue to the entire book. The book will end climactically in Zechariah 14 with the coming Messiah's triumph over Israel's enemies and the implementation of Messiah's Kingdom populated by a people of God that includes Jews and Gentiles. The book throughout will stress eschatological promises and blessings, especially those associated with the coming King-Priest-Messiah-Deliverer. Just as John the Baptist in the first century called upon Israel for repentance as the Kingdom was at hand (e.g., Matthew 3:2: "...Repent ye: for the kingdom of heaven is at hand."), so also God's re-affirmation to Israel of His ancient promises to this nation begins with a clarion call for a turning back to Him in obedience, including His command to rebuild the Temple. As Ralph Smith aptly puts it: "Zechariah was a prophet of unrealized hopes, and although work on the temple had already started when he began his ministry, he placed his work against the background of the exile and its causes. The exile had been due to the father's rejection of God's word to turn from their evil ways. Now Zechariah addresses another generation and asks them to learn from the past."[32]

> **Zechariah 1:1** In the eighth month, in the second year of Darius, came the word of the LORD unto Zechariah, the son of Berechiah, the son of Iddo the prophet, saying, **2** The LORD hath been sore displeased with your fathers.

The name **Zechariah** means "Yahweh remembers." As the book unfolds, we will see that the message is that Yahweh remembers His people and His promises to them. In particular, God promised Abraham He would make a nation from his lineage, provide that nation a permanent dwelling place (real estate), and that Abraham's seed would be a blessing to the families of the world. (e.g., Genesis 12:1-3) As a group of exiles returned from Babylonian captivity, their outlook is likely one of despair. The promises to the Fathers, the blessings Moses spoke of, and the glory of the nation Israel under King David, were now in their distant past. And perhaps for many of them, so was God. But at this critical moment, the God that made the promises to the Fathers, that gave the Law to Moses, and that selected David as King, intercedes into their lives and the message is that He remembers. And that means the promises stand and they will realize the benefits of those promises if they return to Him.

We are given very little information here about **Zechariah**. While his identification has engendered a great deal of debate, it is important to keep in mind that the inspiration of Zechariah's prophecy, its proper interpretation, and its relevance to our lives does not depend on how much or little

---

[32] Ralph L. Smith, *Micah–Malachi*, vol. 32, Word Biblical Commentary (Dallas: Word, Incorporated, 1984), 184.

we know about the prophet. We do know that **Zechariah** is **the son of Berechiah** and grandson **of Iddo**. Additional background on the prophet is found in the prior chapter. Note that Jesus' statement in Matthew 23:35 is also a focus of debate: "That upon you may come all the righteous blood shed upon the earth, from the blood of righteous Abel unto the blood of Zacharias son of Barachias, whom ye slew between the temple and the altar." As Loken cautions: "One should be careful to distinguish the writing prophet (and priest) Zechariah from the priest Zechariah (also the son of Berechiah) who was killed by King Joash, an infamous event referred to by the Lord (2 Chron. 24:20-22; cf. Matthew 23:35; Luke 11:51)."[33]

Importantly, **Zechariah** is specific in giving a time marker for his first message. It is the **second year of** the reign of the Persian king **Darius** Hystaspes (521-486 B.C.), which means it was late October or early November of 520 B.C. That he dates his message in relation to the Persian ruler **Darius** reminds us of the precarious state of affairs for Israel, which remains under Gentile rule. Zechariah's contemporary, Haggai, preaches his third and fourth messages on December 18, 520 B.C., and so there is a one to two month overlap. What we read in the first instance is that Zechariah's message is God's message. It is **the word of the LORD**. This is emphasized in the first six verses of the book, which form the prologue to the book and set forth the practical purpose for the book—to turn them back to God that they would not merely be God's people by label but by their faithfulness to His Word.

The Bible claims for itself over and again to be **the word of the LORD**. The mistake of the generation in Judah that God exiled into Babylonian captivity, and indeed several rebellious generations before them, was that they rejected the Word of God. God's prophets spoke for God and offered His divine commentary on their conduct, but time and time again they

---

[33] Israel P. Loken, *The Old Testament Prophetic Books: An Introduction*, 358.

refused to listen to a message that did not tickle their ears. Certainly few of them would have said, "I reject God's Word," but the veneer of their spiritual faces and empty rhetoric meant nothing against the backdrop of their rebellion to God's revelation through His written Word and the prophets. Because of their past disobedience, God was **sore displeased with** the prior generations—**your fathers**.

It is important that we understand that these were not atheists, but people who considered themselves to be religious or spiritual, much like our culture today. If I may put it into the context of today, these are church going folks or at least folks that culturally identify themselves as Christians or "evangelicals" when it is convenient. Probably many of them attend the popular Third Baptimethopresbutheran Assembly. They are emotional during the song service, shout to God and occasionally congratulate the pastor on his messages. But their worship rings hollow because they reject the Word of God (refuse to obey) spoken through the prophets. And they do so because they do not like the message. The message from God requires them to change, and change always requires us to give something up.

Now that the 70 years of Babylonian captivity is over, God returns a refined remnant (see Ezra 2 for a listing) to Israel to reconstitute the nation, through whom God will fulfill His covenant promises (particularly as to Messiah). This remnant must be reminded of their ancestors' rebellion and the resulting judgment so that history is not repeated. This is preparatory to all that God has for them through **Zechariah**.

> **3** Therefore say thou unto them, Thus saith the LORD of hosts; Turn ye unto me, saith the LORD of hosts, and I will turn unto you, saith the LORD of hosts.

God gives Zechariah the words that he is to deliver to the remnant of Israel. Here again, it is emphasized that this is not

Zechariah's message, but rather he is only the messenger: **Thus saith the LORD of hosts**. This is all the credibility the message needs. This is why we can take the teachings of the Scriptures as words to live by, words to parent by, and words to guide our marriages, our social behavior and every facet of our lives. Skeptics sometimes ask why a Christian spends so much time learning the Bible. The reason is simple, for in it, "Thus saith the LORD of hosts." The Bible is not a prop with which to furnish our carnal house. Recall what Peter said to Jesus at the end of John 6: "Lord, to whom shall we go? thou hast the words of eternal life." (John 6:68)

Notice that it is not just the **LORD**, but the **LORD of hosts**. The **hosts** are God's angelic armies. God is the general in charge of armies of angels and more than capable of accomplishing His sovereign will, both in the lives of individuals and nations, a point that will be made abundantly clear as the book unfolds. Notice also what God says, **Turn ye unto me ... and I will turn unto you**. This is no doubt both a call to repentance (a change of thinking especially in light of recent history) and a concomitant turning to God. This is the prerequisite to restoration as a people. In the New Testament, James similarly says, "Draw nigh to God, and he will draw nigh to you." (James 4:8) The principle here is simply stated, but simply stated does not always translate into simply executed. Surely this turning to God means listening to, believing and caring about what He says, and then honoring Him with our thoughts, words and actions in light of His Word. It is the reorientation of our lives around His truth. The problem is that we have a great capacity to see ourselves as ok, taking this message to be for other people or another time. We have Ph.D's in seeing other people's faults, but often a pre-school education in seeing our own. It is far easier for us to look out the window than in the mirror.

Making application to our own lives, the message to turn to God requires a balanced, realistic self-inspection so that we can see areas where we have not given ourselves over to God and then make the change God requires by the grace enablement of His Spirit. The standard is God's Word. What a fitting message for our culture today. We often want the blessings of God but we outlawed praising Him in our schools and many other public places. We want His favor but refuse to evangelize like we believe Christ is the exclusive means of salvation. We want to see God's hand moving in our lives, our marriages, our relationships with our kids, in our workplaces, and on and on, but we also want to pursue our love affair with worldliness. When we do that, we reject God's Word and settle for the empty promises of sin that are no more valuable now than they were in Genesis 3. In return for immediate gratification we give up the blessing of growing closer to God and the transformative experience of Him drawing nearer to us. We must catch hold of the implications of this passage. This is a radical paradigm for living in reality as God says it is.

God is **sore displeased** with Israel's prior generations, and His appeal through Zechariah to the generation is to not be like their "fathers." They committed treason against the One with whom they contracted through the mediator Moses. In Deuteronomy 28, the blessings and cursings are specified. As a nation, they breached the agreement with God and suffered the consequences exactly as God told them they would: "But it shall come to pass, if thou wilt not hearken unto the voice of the LORD thy God, to observe to do all his commandments and his statutes which I command thee this day; that all these curses shall come upon thee, and overtake thee." (Deuteronomy 28:15). God specifically warned about using a foreign nation as a tool of judgment:

> **Deuteronomy 28:49** The LORD shall bring a nation against thee from far, from the end of the earth, *as swift* as the eagle flieth; a nation whose tongue thou shalt not understand; **50** A nation of fierce countenance, which shall not

regard the person of the old, nor shew favour to the young: **51** And he shall eat the fruit of thy cattle, and the fruit of thy land, until thou be destroyed: which *also* shall not leave thee *either* corn, wine, or oil, *or* the increase of thy kine, or flocks of thy sheep, until he have destroyed thee. **52** And he shall besiege thee in all thy gates, until thy high and fenced walls come down, wherein thou trustedst, throughout all thy land: and he shall besiege thee in all thy gates throughout all thy land, which the LORD thy God hath given thee.

Authentic turning to God leads to real life change. As Christians, we must keep in mind that the appeal of Scripture to be Christ-like (2 Corinthians 3:18) entails a radical change in who we are as we grow in our relationship to God, a true inward reality and not a veneer of externalities.

4 Be ye not as your fathers, unto whom the former prophets have cried, saying, Thus saith the LORD of hosts; Turn ye now from your evil ways, and from your evil doings: but they did not hear, nor hearken unto me, saith the LORD. **5** Your fathers, where are they? and the prophets, do they live for ever? **6** But my words and my statutes, which I commanded my servants the prophets, did they not take hold of your fathers? and they returned and said, Like as the LORD of hosts thought to do unto us, according to our ways, and according to our doings, so hath he dealt with us.

God is explicit here. The remnant should not follow the example of their **fathers**, those prior rebellious generations whose continued disobedience resulted in the Babylonian exile. The prior generations are a negative example to all of us. The single greatest lie Christians believe today is that "I know the truth and therefore I experience it." They were given extensive revelation from God through **the former prophets** but they did not live it out. They were told to **turn ...from** their **evil ways** and **evil doings**, and they were warned to do so **now** or immediately, but they refused to **hear** the message, that is, to respond in obedience or **hearken unto** God. At the root of their rejection of God's Word through **the former prophets** was sin. If we had a crystal ball showing us what each decision contrary to God's Word will cost us in the future, I think we would surely rethink many of our decisions. This turning to God and change of heart would seem to be the underlying prerequisite for the myriad blessings God will pronounce to Israel through Zechariah. If they choose to continue in the way of their **fathers**, they should expect exactly the same response from God that the prior generations received.

In verse 5, God poses two piercing rhetorical questions: **Your fathers, where are they? And the prophets, do they live forever?** Their **fathers** and the **prophets** they ignored are dead and gone. And of course **the prophets** do not **live for ever**. In contrast, the Word of God endures. Even though the prior generations rejected God's Word, their rejection did not change the fact that the words **which** God **commanded** His **servants the prophets** were vindicated as truth when they **took hold of** their **fathers**, that is, when the terrible judgment they were warned about came to pass. The resulting destruction of Jerusalem in 586 B.C. and the displacement of Judah's inhabitants was undeniable testimony that the people are mortal but God's Word endures.

Zechariah records his audience's response to the message the LORD **of hosts** spoke through him: **Like as the LORD of hosts thought to do unto us, according to our ways, and according to our doings, so hath he dealt with us.** This is a wonderful response, a response that takes responsibility and signals hope, a response that says, "Yes, we want to be the people of God." This response gives way for the marvelous restoration God has for them, the rebuilding of the Temple, the Holy City, the priesthood, and the nation from whom Messiah will come.

Most Christians would surely say, "I want to grow in my relationship with God. I want to be used by Him for the extraordinary." But those are just words. James says, "But be ye doers of the word, and not hearers only, deceiving your own selves" (James 1:22) about your maturity. Our maturing in the Lord means that we are radically changing from who we were the day we first placed faith in Christ into the likeness of Christ. We should be able to look back 5 years ago and see that we are not the same person we were then because we have turned over more and more of our lives to Him. Of course, we cannot do that of our own resources. The apostle Paul explains that our Christian life starts in the Spirit and continues in the Spirit. (Galatians 3:3) The Christian walk is not a list of rules and practices that through determination and discipline we keep until we mature. Rather, it is walking in the Spirit that is the key to our sanctification in the Lord. (Galatians 5:16, 25) In the prologue to his wonderful book, Zechariah simply says, turn to God. But for this we need God's resources. As we shall see, Zechariah confirms: "Not by might, nor by power, but by my spirit, saith the LORD of hosts." (Zechariah 4:6)

Closing

Charles Ponzi became so infamous as a conman and swindler before he died in 1949 that still today pyramid-structured money-making schemes are known as *ponzi* schemes. He promised profits too good to be true, then used the money from new investors to pay prior investors, giving the illusion that his promises were good. Sin promises people so much but in the end delivers so little. The Bible calls sin out for what it is and warns us against it. Nevertheless, the magnitude of the promises that sin makes—like the *ponzi* schemes—always finds new "investors" willing to give up so much for it. Judah pursued the fleeting promises of sin rather than God, and for that they suffered a terrible judgment at the hands of the Babylonians and 70 years of captivity. In the final analysis, sin did not deliver on its promises, but only led them to despair. But God, through the prophet Zechariah, promises restoration to the remnant that returned from captivity, appealing to them to not only be His chosen people in name, but to be the people of God by the faithful testimony of their lives. God's intent is to physically and spiritually restore the nation.

The message of Zechariah is fitting for most cultures today, and especially in the United States. Over a relatively short period of time, our nation has fallen further and further from God pursuing fleshly indulgence and an insatiable materialism. We are a prodigal nation, just like Judah. God's message through Zechariah rings through the centuries to us, with God imploring us, "Turn ye unto me...and I will turn unto you." The same message is fitting for many churches today that embrace worldliness in the garbs of being relevant. And the message for us individually is to turn to God. If we are already faithful in our walk, we are reminded to stay the course.

Application Points

- **MAIN PRINCIPLE:** Examine your life against God's Word, knowing that as you draw closer to Him that He will draw closer to you.

- Accept that God's Word is His biased view of reality, and regardless of whether we accept it or agree with it, God's Word will endure and should therefore be the objective grounding for our lives.

- We should learn from the example of those generations in ancient Judah that rejected God's Word spoken through His prophets and not expect God to wink at us if we individually or as a nation engage in the same conduct.

Discussion Questions

1. What parallels can you draw between the culture in which Zechariah preached his message and our culture today?

2. In practical terms, what does it look like in a person's life when he turns to God and God draws near to him?

3. What can a person do to make sure that they are aware of any areas in their lives where they need to affect change? How can others help us?

4. What do you think their fathers thought about God's Word revealed through the former prophets? Why didn't they properly respond and how did they justify their disobedience?

5. What are some "hot button" issues where our culture has departed from God's standard? How should churches address these issues?

6. What should we do if we hear a message preached in church that makes us feel guilty or uncomfortable?

7. What is the implication from this passage about the proper role of God's Word in our lives? Does it matter if we do not agree with God's viewpoint on an issue or if obedience will require radical life change on our part?

8. On a scale of 1 to 10, 1 being worldly and 10 being completely turned over to God, where do you stand on the following issues, and if you are not a 10 what can be done about that? movies, music, literature, friends, eating / gluttony, giving, integrity in all aspects of life, being active in and consistently attending church, submissiveness, sexual purity, prayer, serious Bible study, instructing your children in God's Word, evangelism, spiritual leadership in the home.

9. What is the difference between engaging the culture around us with the gospel in a relevant way and being changed by the culture? What are the symptoms of both of these?

10. What do think of when you consider the phrase "authentic Christian"?

Chapter 3

Good and Comfortable Words

How far do you trust God?

God told Abraham, "Get thee out of thy country, and from thy kindred, and from thy father's house, unto a land that I will shew thee: And I will make of thee a great nation, and I will bless thee, and make thy name great...and in thee shall all families of the earth be blessed." (Genesis 12:1-3) But centuries later in 520 B.C. when Zechariah speaks, he speaks to a discouraged people who did not see these blessings. Instead, they see their circumstances. The nation did not look great and did not bless the families of the earth. Jerusalem lay in ruins. The Temple that was once one of the architectural marvels of the ancient world was destroyed decades earlier.

But if God can be trusted, the promises remain. It is especially fitting that Zechariah's name means "God remembers." No matter how the circumstances appear, God remembers His promises. The good news for Israel through the prophet Zechariah reminds them that God remembers and God will fulfill His promises. That means that despite how things look, Israel has a glorious future and will be a blessing to the families of the earth.

Scripture and Comments

As will be seen, the series of eight night visions that Zechariah records in chapters 1 thru 6 form a single unit of thought. In a single evening, God shows the prophet a series of visions that provide him insight into what God is doing at the present time, especially through Israel's leadership, and take him to the distant future when the promised Messiah literally dwells in Jerusalem and all the nations of the world enjoy the Messianic Age. Accordingly, these are not eight unrelated visions, but eight visions tightly woven together to form the unified message calling the nation to spiritual renewal largely through confirming that the nation has a glorious future. I note that the ordering of the eight visions is also not arbitrary. The visions are organized in a chiastic pattern, as shown below:

A – Vision 1: The Angel of the LORD sends angelic scouts to do worldwide reconnaissance and they report that the world is at rest.

B – Vision 2: God removes Israel's enemies from the land.

C – Vision 3: Jerusalem is measured for reconstruction and the Messiah of nations will dwell in Jerusalem.

D – Vision 4: Joshua is fit for priestly service but God will bring a future servant, the Branch, to remove sin and bring lasting peace.

D' – Vision 5: Zerubbabel will lead the people to finish the Temple, and he and Joshua will be enabled by the Spirit.

40

C' – Vision 6: God's righteousness is enforced in Israel.

B' – Vision 7: God removes wickedness from Israel.

A' – Vision 8: The Angel of the LORD sends angelic warriors to Israel's enemies to quiet God's spirit.

FIRST NIGHT VISION

> **Zechariah 1:7** Upon the four and twentieth day of the eleventh month, which is the month Sebat, in the second year of Darius, came the word of the LORD unto Zechariah, the son of Berechiah, the son of Iddo the prophet, saying,

The day is the **four and twentieth day** of the **eleventh month**, or **Sebat**. Once again, we are told that it is the **second year of** the reign of the Persian king **Darius** (521-486 B.C.). In our calendar, it is February 15, 519 B.C. This means that about 3 months passed since the oracle found in verses 1-6. What follows is the first of eight visions commonly referred to as Zechariah's "night visions." In a single night, **Zechariah** sees eight spectacular visions, which he subsequently records in writing. As in verse 1, we read that **Zechariah** is **the son Berechiah** and grandson **of Iddo** the priest.

Note that what follows are not simply the man Zechariah's words. For on that day some 2500 years ago **came the word of the LORD unto Zechariah**. The next verse will clarify that the **word** of God **came** to the prophet in a vision. **Zechariah** refers to the **word** of God nineteen times, and another twenty times **Zechariah** will say "thus saith" or "thus speaketh" the LORD. For this reason, we know that everything **Zechariah** writes is "given by inspiration of God, and is profitable for doctrine, for reproof, for correction, for instruction in righteousness." (2 Timothy 3:16) As I indicated in the introductory notes in the prior chapter, there are those who would downplay the significance of the prophetic portions of the Bible for

Christians today, but may I say, there is perhaps no more dangerous road for the Christian to travel than the one that begins with setting aside portions of God's Word.

> **8** I saw by night, and behold a man riding upon a red horse, and he stood among the myrtle trees that were in the bottom; and behind him were there red horses, speckled, and white. **9** Then said I, O my lord, what are these? And the angel that talked with me said unto me, I will shew thee what these be.

We should note at the outset that much of what we will read in the night visions are what is known as *apocalyptic literature.* This is highly symbolic literature where God uses symbols to convey His thinking and perspective to us. While some readers may be intimidated by this type of literature, and others may suggest that the symbols are beyond knowing, we must keep in mind that God is not trying to "hide the ball." Instead, the symbols enhance God's explanation of events as He presents on the canvas His biased perspective on events past, present and future. And to the extent that any of the symbolic meanings seem hidden, God either provides the answers through an interpreting angel to Zechariah, who then records what he has seen and heard, or through later revelation in the book or in the Bible. We will see that one unique aspect of Zechariah's visions is that he does not merely see the vision, but participates in it.

Zechariah sees this first vision at **night**, and in particular, he sees a **man riding upon a red horse** standing by **myrtle trees** at **the bottom,** by implication, of a ravine or valley. Myrtle trees are common in Israel, and they are very small trees, closer to what we might consider a large shrub. Such trees have a special significance for the Jewish people as they were used in the construction of booths for the Feast of Tabernacles. (Nehemiah 8:14-17) In keeping that feast, the people remembered their time of fellowship with God in the wilderness, and I note that the feast finds eschatological fulfillment in the Messianic Kingdom as Zechariah will explain in the fourteenth chapter. But as the vision unfolds it will become apparent that this first vision does not directly concern the future Kingdom, but the present state of the world during Zechariah's ministry. Without being dogmatic in identifying the significance of the **myrtle trees**, Feinberg's view best fits the context: "The myrtle because of its fragrance and lowliness typifies and symbolizes Israel; the deep place speaks of her degradation."[34] The vision pictures Israel, even in its present state, in the care and protection of God.

Although God permitted great calamities to fall upon the nation as a judgment (see Deuteronomy 28:49-57, 29:26-28), He preserved the faithful remnant through the captivity (see, e.g., Deuteronomy 30:1-3; Jeremiah 21, 29; Ezekiel 9:3-4) and the rider now stands guard over them (cf. Zechariah 12:8). At this point in time, some 50,000 people had returned from the 70 years of Babylonian captivity (see Ezra 2), but Jerusalem lay in ruins, and indeed would continue in ruins for several decades before the rebuilding of the wall and city would begin in earnest under the leadership of Nehemiah. Many of the surrounding cities were also in ruins and the once glorious nation had been taken away into captivity (see further background in the preface), and so it is fitting that in this scene the **myrtle trees** do not picture an elevated status for the remnant of Israel as they might if they were on a high mountain, but instead, they are humbled and the prophet looks down at them. But critically, God is not through with Israel. And may I say, God is not through with Israel today either: "I say then, Hath God cast away his people? God forbid. For I also am an Israelite, of the seed of Abraham, of the tribe of Benjamin. God hath not cast away his people....Even so then at this present time also there is a remnant according to the election of grace." (Romans 11:1-5)

---

[34] Charles L. Feinberg, *God Remembers: A Study of Zechariah* (Eugene, OR: Wipf and Stock Publishers, 2003), 20.

Beside the **trees**, Zechariah saw **a man riding upon a red horse.**
The **man...stood among the myrtle trees that were in the
bottom**, as a century at his guard-post, and he is not alone. But
what becomes apparent is that he is no mere guard, but the
captain. For **behind him were there red horses, speckled, and
white**, and apparently there are riders on the other horses
since **they** will answer to the **man** on the **red horse**. Many
expositors assume that there are four horses, but the text does
not say that and so some caution is warranted. However, based
on the similar imagery of Zechariah 6:1-7 and the interpreting
angel's explanation that the horses (and chariots of chapter 6)
are "the four spirits of the heavens, which go forth from
standing before the Lord of all the earth" (Zechariah 6:5), it is
reasonable to understand there to be four chariots in the
parallel vision and thus four scouting horses in this first vision,
plus the **man** on the **red horse** watching over the **myrtle trees.**

Zechariah's reaction is much as ours would be. He does not
know what to make of what he sees, but there is an **angel**
standing by, to whom the prophet asks, **O my lord, what are
these?** The term **lord** here is not "Yahweh" (written in the
KJV as LORD), and is used here as a term of respect (e.g.,
Genesis 18:12). Zechariah's interpreting **angel** is referred to as
the angel that talked with me. The presence of an **angel** to
explain visions to Zechariah will be a common element in the
night visions, similar to some other apocalyptic literature (e.g.,
Daniel 7:16; Revelation 7:13-14). The pronoun **these** Zechariah
asks about refers to the colored horses since that is the part of
what he sees that is out of the ordinary and they are explained
by the interpreting **angel**, who responds that he will **shew**
Zechariah **what these be**, that is, that he will identify for
Zechariah the **horses.**

> 10 And the man that stood among the myrtle
> trees answered and said, These are they whom
> the LORD hath sent to walk to and fro through
> the earth. 11 And they answered the angel of

> the LORD that stood among the myrtle trees,
> and said, We have walked to and fro through
> the earth, and, behold, all the earth sitteth still,
> and is at rest.

However, the interpreting angel is not the one to provide the response to the prophet's inquiry. Rather, **the man that stood among the myrtle trees**, namely the man on the red horse already introduced in verse 8, speaks directly to Zechariah. As indicated before, a unique feature of Zechariah's visions is that he participates in them. **The man** on the red horse identifies **these**, in reference to the other horses and riders, as **they whom LORD hath sent to walk to and fro through the earth** like scouts sent out by their commanding officer to observe and report back. **The man** does not include himself in the description and does not appear to have engaged in the scouting mission, but instead, will receive their report. By implication, then, **the man** sent out the scouts on their mission. The concept of walking **to and fro through the earth** is an expression of God's dominion over it. In Job 1:7, Satan uses similar language to express his belief in his own dominion over the earth (a belief God challenges): "And the LORD said unto Satan, Whence comest thou? Then Satan answered the LORD, and said, From going to and fro in the earth, and from walking up and down in it." Similarly, in Genesis 13:17, God tells Abraham to walk the Promise Land that God had given him; Abraham's walking over it would establish his ownership and dominion over it.

God is called the LORD of hosts 53 times in the book of Zechariah, including eight occurrences in the first chapter. God is pictured as a general in charge of His angelic army. And in this first vision, the General through **the man** on the **red horse** dispatches scouts to survey the planet and report back to **the man**. That God can do this affirms His complete dominion over the planet against all competing claims. Zechariah states that the scouts report to **the angel of the LORD**. This identifies **the man** that is speaking to Zechariah as

the angel of the LORD. This phrase is used elsewhere in the Old Testament and the identification is frequently interchanged with LORD. (see, e.g., Genesis 22, Exodus 3) Recall that in John 8, Jesus claims to be the "I AM" that spoke to Moses from the burning bush in Exodus 3, thus providing a strong case that at least in the instance of Exodus 3, **the angel of the LORD** is the pre-incarnate Jesus Christ. There is good reason, especially based on Zechariah 3, to take **the angel of the LORD** here to be the pre-incarnate Jesus. Indeed, He will be called in these night visions the "stone," "servant," "Branch" (3:9), and "Lord of the whole earth" (4:14). And as we shall also see, the reference to **the man** is most likely a deliberate distinction of **the angel of the LORD** from the other angels in the night visions.

To identify who **the angel of the LORD** is, we must keep in the mind that in the immediate context (and in the book in general), God is presented as the **LORD of hosts.** The **man** guarding the myrtles is in immediate command of the hosts, who here and in chapter 6 answer to him. There is prior Biblical precedent for **the angel of the LORD** being referred to as a "man." Moses wrote in Genesis 32:24 of the incident of Jacob wrestling with a "man" for a blessing: "And Jacob was left alone; and there wrestled a man with him until the breaking of the day." Jacob received the blessing and "called the name of the place Peniel: for I have seen God face to face, and my life is preserved." (Genesis 32:30) Centuries later, the prophet Hosea commented on this episode, confirming the "man" was an angel: "Yea, he had power over the angel, and prevailed...." (Hosea 12:4) There is likewise prior precedent for **the angel of the LORD** acting in the capacity of captain of hosts. In Joshua 5, as Joshua contemplated the coming siege of Jericho, he learned that in reality God is leading the attack through His captain:

> **Joshua 5:13** And it came to pass, when Joshua was by Jericho, that he lifted up his eyes and looked, and, behold, there stood a man over

against him with his sword drawn in his hand:
and Joshua went unto him, and said unto him,
Art thou for us, or for our adversaries? **14** And
he said, Nay; but *as* captain of the host of the
LORD am I now come. And Joshua fell on his
face to the earth, and did worship, and said
unto him, What saith my lord unto his servant?
15 And the captain of the LORD'S host said
unto Joshua, Loose thy shoe from off thy foot;
for the place whereon thou standest *is* holy.
And Joshua did so.

As we see from Joshua's experience, the one he met is also
described as "a man" as well as the "captain of the host of the
LORD." Moreover, when Joshua worshiped the "man," Joshua
identifies the captain as "my lord" and is not rebuked for
worshiping the captain (cf. Revelation 19:10), and Joshua is
informed that he is standing on holy ground. This alludes to
the similar experience in Exodus 3 when "the angel of the
LORD" commissioned Moses from the burning bush (see
Exodus 3:5) and where Moses was told to remove his shoes
because he was on holy ground. In both instances, it is not the
soil but the presence of God himself that makes the ground
(the space in His immediate presence) holy. In both Joshua 5
and Zechariah 1, the angel of the LORD is the captain of the
Lord's angelic armies and presents the divine presence of the
God of hosts himself.

While a robust study of the doctrine of "the angel of the
LORD" is beyond the scope of this book, it is important to
note that the Bible presents "the angel of the LORD" as deity,
and thus it is fair to conclude that "the angel" is none other
than Jesus Christ, the Son of God. Several passages affirm the
angel's deity: Genesis 16:7-14 (Hagar calls the "angel" Lord and
the angel promises the same blessing God promises to
Abraham concerning "seed"), Genesis 21:16-19 (angel speaks
from heaven in the first person as God), Genesis 22:11-18 (angel
swears by himself), Genesis 31:11-13 (angel claims he is God),

Genesis 32:24-30 (Jacob wrestles with the angel and remarks that he saw God "face to face"), Genesis 48:16 ("angel" interchanged with "God"), Exodus 3:2-6 ("angel" interchanged with "God" and calls the place "holy ground"), Exodus 14:19-24 (angel goes before them like God), Exodus 23:20-23 (angel can pardon sin and God's "name is in him"), Joshua 5:13-15 (Joshua worships the angel on holy ground), Judges 2:1-4 (angel brought them out of Egypt to the land he promised them), Judges 6:11-16 (angel is present with Gideon but "the LORD looked upon" Gideon), and Acts 27:21-25 (Paul says he belongs to and serves "the angel of God"). I would also point out that within Zechariah 3:1-7, we find "the LORD" interchanged with "the angel of the LORD," again establishing the deity of "the angel of the LORD" in view here. Yet more must be said than pointing out the deity of "the angel of the LORD." As John commented of Jesus in John 1:18: "No man hath seen God at any time; the only begotten Son, which is in the bosom of the Father, he hath declared *him*." Since "the angel of the LORD" is deity and visible, He must be none other than the Son of God, the pre-incarnate Christ. And, indeed, throughout Zechariah's book we will see the actions of God carried out by the coming Messiah, as they are here.

Note that the angelic riders answer **the angel of the LORD** with their report, as reporting to their commanding officer, or more fitting, the captain of the LORD'S hosts. They first confirm that they scouted the planet, having **walked to and fro through the earth**. Their report is a global report regarding the status of the planet, namely that **all the earth sitteth still, and is at rest**. The point of their report is that the nations are **at rest** or peace. The question to be answered is why the Gentile nations are at rest, for this is the central idea in this vision. Loken is partly correct in his assessment that "[t]his tranquility was the direct result of the Persian peace brought about by Cyrus and strengthened by Darius."[35] But it also seems that the Gentile nations are **at rest** relative to Israel,

35 Israel P. Loken, *The Old Testament Prophetic Books: An Introduction*, 368.

which seems the obvious point of the scouts' information gathering. Relative to Israel, the nations are at rest because by all appearances the nation is defeated and gone.

> 12 Then the angel of the LORD answered and said, O LORD of hosts, how long wilt thou not have mercy on Jerusalem and on the cities of Judah, against which thou hast had indignation these threescore and ten years? 13 And the LORD answered the angel that talked with me with good words and comfortable words.

In response to the report, the **angel of the LORD** (who is also the rider on the red horse) intercedes on behalf of Judah, asking **the LORD of hosts** (armies) **how long wilt thou not have mercy on Jerusalem and on the cities of Judah, against which thou hast had indignation these threescore and ten years?** What he is asking the LORD is, in view the current state of affairs resulting from the seventy years or **threescore and ten years** of Babylonian captivity that has now ended (e.g., Jeremiah 25:11-12, 29:10; Daniel 9:2), when will the LORD reverse His judgment? When will God again have mercy on Judah? This is reminiscent of Daniel's prayer as he saw the 70 years coming to a close: "O Lord, hear; O Lord, forgive; O Lord, hearken and do; defer not, for thine own sake, O my God: for thy city and thy people are called by thy name." (Daniel 9:19) God's response is **good words and comfortable words**, but quite probably it is **the angel of the LORD** in Zechariah's presence that Zechariah refers to when he writes, **the LORD answered the angel that talked with me with good words and comfortable words**, which will follow in the night visions. Because **the angel of the LORD** asked the LORD **of hosts** the question, it is natural to assume the LORD of hosts answered **the angel of the LORD**, who in turn told the interpreting **angel**. This is also consistent with Zechariah 3, where the high priest is accused by Satan of being unworthy of service, and it is **the angel of the LORD** that speaks for God.

LOOKING FORWARD, LIVING NOW

This means not only that Judah is no longer under the thumb of Babylon (that had changed almost 20 years prior) but also that Judah is being reconstituted as a nation in its own land and with God's Temple reconstructed, the focal point of Jewish worship. God's message of the restoration of His people is a primary theme of Zechariah's prophetic ministry, which again is consistent with the meaning of Zechariah's name ("Yahweh remembers").

> 14 So the angel that communed with me said unto me, Cry thou, saying, Thus saith the LORD of hosts; I am jealous for Jerusalem and for Zion with a great jealousy. 15 And I am very sore displeased with the heathen that are at ease: for I was but a little displeased, and they helped forward the affliction. 16 Therefore thus saith the LORD; I am returned to Jerusalem with mercies: my house shall be built in it, saith the LORD of hosts, and a line shall be stretched forth upon Jerusalem. 17 Cry yet, saying, Thus saith the LORD of hosts; My cities through prosperity shall yet be spread abroad; and the LORD shall yet comfort Zion, and shall yet choose Jerusalem.

Imbedded between some of the "night visions" are oracles that build on the visions, and these four verses comprise the first such oracle. In verse 13, the interpreting **angel** shares with the prophet "good words and comfortable words" but those words are not recorded there. Now, Zechariah is to provide that encouraging message to the people: **So the angel that communed with me said unto me, Cry thou, Thus saith the LORD of hosts, I am jealous for Jerusalem and for** my holy mount **Zion with a great jealousy**. We need to understand that God's jealousy for Jerusalem is not sinful jealousy as the word infers when it speaks of negative human behavior (i.e., according to Merriam-Webster, **a:** intolerant of rivalry or unfaithfulness **b**: disposed to suspect rivalry or unfaithfulness). Rather, it speaks of God's love in action for the good of His people. It is significant that God is again referred to here as **the LORD of hosts**, being pictured as a warrior ready to defend His people with his armies. Note that mount **Zion** is a hill in Jerusalem just outside the walls of the Old City (the early Jerusalem) but the term is often used in the Bible as a metonymy to refer to the entire city or even the Temple Mount. This indicates that God is about to change everything and bring about a reversal of fortune for Israel. To the person on the outside looking in, there is no hope for Israel. But nothing is impossible with God.

The report from the four scouts is made to the angel of the LORD and then to the LORD of Hosts, who is **very sore displeased**. God's response helps us better understand Zechariah's vision. The seemingly insignificant myrtle trees in the preceding vision represent Israel in its present state, while the **heathen** or Gentile nations **are at ease**. The Hebrew translated **are at ease**, according to the NET translation notes, "has the idea of a careless, even arrogant attitude...it suggests that the nations take for granted that God will never punish them just because he hasn't already done so." When the Babylonians were defeated in 539 B.C. by the Persians, Judah's affliction was somewhat relieved, but Judah is still under the thumb of a foreign power. And of course, other Gentiles oppressed Israel throughout history (e.g., the Egyptians, the Assyrians, the Edomites). We might ask why God would be angry at the nations since God judged Israel for its disobedience through **the heathen**. The reason God gives is that **I was but a little displeased, and they helped forward the affliction**. The Gentile nations made the situation worse than it should have been. This likely indicates that while God allowed certain Gentile nations to be a tool of judgment against His people, they went too far.

God's response to this situation is that He is **returned to Jerusalem with mercies** (i.e., compassion in action). Moreover,

God says that **my house** or Temple **shall be built in it**. The original Temple, sometimes referred to as Solomon's Temple because it was constructed during his reign as the third king of Israel, was destroyed in 586 B.C. by the Babylonians under Nebuchadnezzar's command. Like his contemporary Haggai, a purpose of Zechariah's ministry is to encourage the rebuilding of the Temple. The implication from God's return to Jerusalem is that He left at some point prior to this time (see Ezekiel 10-11). Of course, God is omnipresent, but He previously withdrew His protection from Jerusalem enabling the Babylonians to overtake it. Now, God is back, meaning His protection and blessings are returned to His people. As a result, the Temple will be rebuilt, which is vital to the spiritual restoration of Israel. The remnant of people returned to Judah will be safe. Indeed, **a line shall be stretched forth upon Jerusalem**. This is a reference to an engineer's measuring line used in preparation for building projects. The point is that the Temple and the city will be restored, which pictures physical and spiritual renewal for Israel.

This is good news and comforting news. Moreover, God will again prosper the nation so that its **cities** will overflow with **prosperity**. God reminds them that He **shall yet comfort Zion** and **shall yet choose Jerusalem**, that is, that they are still His people and the promises to the fathers will still be honored. And that remains true. Paul expresses a similar thought in Romans 11:1: "I say then, Hath God cast away his people? God forbid...." As we will see in Zechariah 2, the present blessing on **Jerusalem** in Zechariah's day is a foretaste of blessings to come in the Messianic Kingdom.

SECOND NIGHT VISION

18 Then lifted I up mine eyes, and saw, and behold four horns. **19** And I said unto the angel that talked with me, What be these? And he

> answered me, These are the horns which have
> scattered Judah, Israel, and Jerusalem. **20** And
> the LORD shewed me four carpenters. **21** Then
> said I, What come these to do? And he spake,
> saying, These are the horns which have
> scattered Judah, so that no man did lift up his
> head: but these are come to fray them, to cast
> out the horns of the Gentiles, which lifted up
> their horn over the land of Judah to scatter it.

These four verses contain Zechariah's second night vision. Again, keep in mind that the sequence of eight visions all occur during the same (perhaps restless) evening. The prophet **lifted...up mine eyes, and saw, and behold four horns**. The imagery of horns is often used in the Bible to symbolize power, strength, kings and kingdoms. (See, e.g., 1 Samuel 2:1, 10; Psalm 18:2, 75:10, 89:24, 132:17; Jeremiah 48:25; Daniel 8; Micah 4:13) Zechariah does not understand the vision, and so he asks **the angel that talked with me, What be these?** As noted earlier, this sort of imagery is not God hiding the ball, and often the image is shown to the prophet followed by his questions being answered. Here, the interpreting angel **answered** Zechariah's question, explaining that **these are the horns which have scattered** or dispersed abroad the people **Judah, Israel, and Jerusalem**. While we might attempt to identify **four** specific Gentile powers that scattered God's people (e.g., the Assyrians scattered the northern kingdom or **Israel**, the Babylonians scattered **Judah**), that there are **four horns** does not mean that God had four distinct Gentile nations in mind. Consistent with the vision in Zechariah 6 and the concept seen in several places in Scripture of the earth having four directions or four corners (e.g., Isaiah 11:12, Revelation 7:1), that there are **four horns** seen here pictures a complete scattering of Israel by Gentile oppressors. It refers to "the universal character of the persecution of God's people by the nations."[36] Viewed this way we should not take the **four**

---

[36] *Ibid.*, 369.

horns as a merely historic reference, but one that would include oppressors after Zechariah's time. Later in the book will see that Israel will fall under the attack of Gentile invaders after Messiah is killed and again prior to his return.

In contrast to the **four horns** that destroy, spoil and enslave, **the LORD shewed** Zechariah **four carpenters**. The **four carpenters** or artisans are people who build and restore. Zechariah asks of the interpreting **angel, What come these to do?** The question apparently inquires of both **the horns** and the **carpenters**. As before, the interpreting **angel** responds, **saying, These are the horns which have scattered Judah, so that no man did lift his head**. This pictures oppression of the people, and consistent with the earlier reference to the **horns** having **scattered Judah, Israel, and Jerusalem**, we should understand the same is inferred here. But the **angel** continues: **but these** artisans **are come to fray** or terrify the **horns** and **to cast out the horns of the Gentiles, which lifted up their horn over the land of Judah to scatter it**. In other words, the **carpenters** rid the nation of its Gentile oppressors. By implication and consistent with the earlier reference to the **horns** having **scattered Judah, Israel, and Jerusalem**, we may take the carpenters as liberating Israel also.

To some extent this already happened historically. For instance, the Babylonians were a **horn** as to **Judah**, and to some degree the Persians were then a **carpenter**. But such events were incomplete and temporary. There would still be more **horns** to come, including the Greeks, Romans and others. The point of the vision is to contrast the scattering of God's people by Gentile nations at all times with a coming complete and permanent routing of Israel's enemies and restoration of the God's people in their land. The critical question raised by this vision is how God will bring about this reversal of circumstances. The answer, as Zechariah will unfold for us in the balance of the book, is that God will do so in relation to the coming Messiah and the implementation of his Kingdom.

Good and Comfortable Words

But if God still has plans for glory and blessing for a unified Israel in the Promised Land, the remnant in Zechariah's day should be encouraged to action.

Closing

I watched an interesting film several years ago called *The Truman Show*. The basic plot of the film was that a man named Truman, played by Jim Carrey, had been raised from infancy in a fake reality created by Hollywood inside a large dome while the world watched him on television 24/7. Everyone he interacted with was a paid actor or actress. Everything about his daily life was fabricated. The director and scriptwriters created his town (all props), job, friends, family and even his wife. The climax of the film was when he finally discovered what happened and escaped the dome, but until that discovery, all of his decisions were based on what he believed to be reality.

Like Truman, we make all of our decisions based on our perception of reality, and unfortunately, there are forces at work to shape our perception and give us a distorted view of reality. We make decisions and respond to reality as we believe it to be based on our worldview. A technical definition of "worldview" provided by Professor Harry Leafe would be as follows: "Worldview is an orderly and related set of beliefs (presuppositions about life) that form the basis of evaluating and integrating into our thinking what we come to believe and by which we consciously or subconsciously interpret or judge reality." The challenge for Christians is to have a Biblical worldview, to see reality through eyes of faith in what God's Word says. God said in Isaiah 55:8: "For my thoughts *are* not your thoughts, neither *are* your ways my ways." A cornerstone of our worldview as Christians must include what God's Word says about the future, and especially what He says about the coming Messiah and the Messianic Age or Kingdom and His future blessings for Israel. Our response to life now, including how we prioritize the things that matter most to us, is shaped by our understanding of things future.

Application Points

- **MAIN PRINCIPLE:** God is not finished with Israel and the unified nation will prosper under God's blessings and protection.

- Develop a Christian worldview that is primarily informed by God's special revelation in the Bible including what God's says about the future.

- Understand that God exercises His sovereignty in global events, especially as they relate to judgment and blessing for His people.

Discussion Questions

1. What is a Biblical worldview? How does this concept relate to Zechariah's first two night visions?

2. Should Christians desire to have a Biblical worldview, and if so, what should be done to develop a Biblical worldview?

3. Why does God use apocalyptic literature as He does in the first two night visions? Is it to "hide the ball" from us?

4. Based on the first night vision, or any other passages in the Bible, who do you think the angel of the LORD is? And why does it matter?

5. What is the "jealousy" of God? Can that "jealousy" be a positive trait for believers?

6. If God raised the Babylonians as a tool of judgment against Judah, why is God angry with the Babylonians after the fact?

7. When God makes a promise, how far can you truth Him?

8. What does counting on God look like in the life of a believer? What about in the life of a church?

9. Why do the horns oppress Judah? To this day, have the horns stopped oppressing Israel? And what is to be the Christian's attitude toward Israel today?

Chapter 4

Living without Walls

The Bible calls us to look forward but live now. We see this exemplified by so many in the hall of faith recorded in Hebrews 11. They reoriented their lives (living now) around God's Word about the future (looking forward). Their confidence in God's promises was so real and strong as to be tangible in their lives so that those around them could see their confidence reshape their lives. The apostle Paul exclaimed, "For we walk by faith, not by sight." (2 Corinthians 5:7) He means that we walk—think, speak and act—**by faith** in God and His Word. We live and respond to life on the basis of God's written revelation to humanity, including especially what He says about the future.

We find in Zechariah 2 a specific application of the principle of looking forward with eyes of faith at God's promised future blessings and living now on that basis. God blessed the Jewish people during their exile to Babylon. Many adjusted to their new lives there, had children, and prospered. Babylon was no longer punishment, but comfort. Yet God called upon His people to return home, to move from a place of comfort to a place that lay in ruins, from a place of depending on their resources to a place of depending on God again. God shows them a glorious future for Israel so that they will live now on the basis of what they can only see looking forward with eyes of faith.

Scripture and Comments

In the first night vision, God said, "I am returned to Jerusalem with mercies: my house shall be built in it...and a line shall be stretched forth upon Jerusalem." In a very real sense, those "mercies" were experienced in Zechariah's day, but what we will see in this third vision is that the current blessings on Jerusalem were a foretaste of glorious future blessings for Jerusalem during the Messianic Kingdom.

THIRD NIGHT VISION

> **Zechariah 2:1** I lifted up mine eyes again, and looked, and behold a man with a measuring line in his hand. **2** Then said I, Whither goest thou? And he said unto me, To measure Jerusalem, to see what is the breadth thereof, and what is the length thereof. **3** And, behold, the angel that talked with me went forth, and another angel went out to meet him, **4** And said unto him, Run, speak to this young man, saying, Jerusalem shall be inhabited as towns without walls for the multitude of men and cattle therein: **5** For I, saith the LORD, will be unto her a wall of fire round about, and will be the glory in the midst of her.

Using similar language to the words in 1:18 that opened the second night vision, Zechariah writes, **I lifted up mine eyes**

again. We are to understand that the prophet reports to us what he sees in a vision from God. He sees **a man with a measuring line in his hand**. But who is the **man**? Just as the **measuring line** takes us back to the first night vision (see 1:16), so also does the reference to a **man**. In 1:8, Zechariah sees "a man riding upon a red horse" who in 1:10 speaks to the prophet and explains the actions of the other riders / horses. Then the "man riding upon the red horse" is identified as "the angel of the LORD." After the eight night visions, Zechariah will crown the high priest Joshua as a symbol or type of the promised Messiah and explain, "thus speaketh the LORD of hosts, saying, Behold the man whose name is The BRANCH; and he shall grow up out of his place, and he shall build the temple of the LORD." (Zechariah 6:12) The coming Branch, the Messiah, will build the future temple, just as we also see foretold by the prophet Ezekiel:

> **Ezekiel 40:1** In the five and twentieth year of our captivity, in the beginning of the year, in the tenth *day* of the month, in the fourteenth year after that the city was smitten, in the selfsame day the hand of the LORD was upon me, and brought me thither. **2** In the visions of God brought he me into the land of Israel, and set me upon a very high mountain, by which *was* as the frame of a city on the south. **3** And he brought me thither, and, behold, *there was* a man, whose appearance *was* like the appearance of brass, with a line of flax in his hand, and a measuring reed; and he stood in the gate. **4** And the man said unto me, Son of man, behold with thine eyes, and hear with thine ears, and set thine heart upon all that I shall shew thee; for to the intent that I might shew *them* unto thee *art* thou brought hither: declare all that thou seest to the house of Israel. **5** And behold a wall on the outside of

the house round about, and in the man's hand a measuring reed of six cubits *long* by the cubit and an hand breadth: so he measured the breadth of the building, one reed; and the height, one reed.

Ezekiel devotes chapters to the construction of the future temple that will be constructed when Messiah implements his Kingdom. It seems probable that the **man** in Zechariah's third vision is Messiah, the Branch. This view finds further confirmation in the heavy Messianic focus in the balance of Zechariah 2.

Zechariah interacts with the **man** in his vision just as he did in the first night vision. Here, Zechariah asks him, **Whither goest thou?** The prophet is naturally curious and wants to know what the **man** is going to measure. In response, the **man** speaks directly to Zechariah as he did in the first vision (1:10), explaining that he will **measure Jerusalem, to see what is the breadth thereof, and what is the length thereof.** At one time, Jerusalem had walls, the **length** and **breadth** of which could be readily measured, but those walls were destroyed by the invading Babylonians and probably subsequent scavengers. Zechariah is living in a Jerusalem without adequate security. In that historical context, a city with inadequate walls was a "sitting duck" for invasion and plunder, a point that will come up again in verse 4. One would expect that the **man** is measuring the ancient boundaries so that the walls can be reconstructed, but that is not the case. Rather, the point is that the city will prosper beyond the boundaries of the prior walls, and when that happens, the security provided by walls will no longer be necessary.

Zechariah is privy to the discussion between **the angel that talked with me,** which is the interpreting **angel** from the first two night visions, and **another angel** that **went out to meet him.** It seems that the **man** dispatched **another angel** to speak to the interpreting **angel,** to in turn speak to the prophet. This follows the pattern from the first vision where the "angel of the LORD" (1:12) spoke to "the angel that talked with me" (1:13) who then provided a message to the prophet (1:14). This lends support that the message in verses 4-5 to Zechariah is from the **man**, who as argued already, is probably the angel of the LORD. We read that **another angel** directs the interpreting **angel** to **run** and **speak** to Zechariah, who is referred to as **this young man**. The reason for his running is that the message is urgent. And the message is comprised of "good words and comfortable words" (Zechariah 1:13) that **Jerusalem shall be inhabited as towns without walls for the multitude of men and cattle therein.** The good news God has for Zechariah is that **Jerusalem** will be restored and inhabited by so many people that it cannot be contained by walls. What a contrast this must have been to the city's present circumstances with only a small remnant returned from Babylonian captivity.

Despite how some expositors take all judgments in the Bible against the Jewish people literally, but none of the blessings, it is indisputable that **Jerusalem** never achieved the blessings in view here. This unfortunate reality was affirmed when **Jerusalem** was destroyed in the first century. The prophecy looks forward to the state of **Jerusalem** in the future Messianic Kingdom, which interpretation finds support in the next verse and in the closing verses of the chapter. But for the moment, we do well to be reminded that the life of faith is one that is reoriented around God's Word, and especially His promised future blessings. Thus, this promised glorious future for **Jerusalem** was to spur a return to rebuild the city. In the near term, as a result of Zechariah's and Haggai's ministries, the Temple construction will be complete. Some 75 years after Zechariah's visions in the time of Nehemiah (445 B.C.), Nehemiah records the disarray of Jerusalem, particularly the absence of walls. (Nehemiah 1:3) This prompts Nehemiah, as governor of Judah, to journey to Jerusalem and supervise the rebuilding of the walls. (Nehemiah 2:9-6:19) God's people are spurred to action in view of the promised future blessings on

Jerusalem. That the walls are rebuilt under Nehemiah's leadership confirms that the city without walls in the present vision looks to the distant future.

In verse 5, **the LORD** promises both his protection (**I... will be a wall of fire round about**) and his presence (**and will be the glory in the midst of her**). It is significant that Zechariah does not say **the LORD** of hosts but just **the LORD**, likely referring to the "angel of the LORD" as the similar language in 1:13 did. At the end of the Steven Spielberg film *Back to the Future*, the characters Doc, Marty and Jennifer are about to take a trip in a time machine (aka Doc's Delorean) to the year 2015. Marty is concerned there is not enough road to get the car up to 88 miles per hour as required for time-travel, but Doc had already been to the future and made alterations to the car. Doc famously responds: "Roads? Where we're going, we don't need roads." Then the car takes flight like a plane, zooms to 88 miles per hour and travels forward in time. Here, God says, if I may paraphrase: "Walls? Where we're going, we don't need walls." The reason is that **the LORD...will be a wall of fire round about** the city providing divine protection.

When will this take place? After Zechariah's time, **Jerusalem** would see violence and destruction again and again (e.g., from Antiochus IV Epiphanes in the time of the Maccabees, from the Romans in 70 A.D. and again in 135 A.D.). Indeed, even to this day, **Jerusalem** is at risk of attack and its politicians must address avowed enemies like Iran. Simply put, **Jerusalem** never achieved the status of being a city with no need of walls. The fulfillment of this promise will only come when God **will be the glory in the midst of her**. These words cannot be spiritualized away. God promises a future time when the city is more prosperous than ever before, has a larger population than ever before, and enjoys total security because He is literally in the city. While Zechariah does not provide all the details within this one vision, he continues in the balance of the chapter and the entire book to fill in those details. The fulfillment will be in the Messianic Kingdom when Jesus literally rules and reigns from **Jerusalem** and will **be the glory** of God **in the midst of** the city. Note that Zechariah repeatedly emphasizes this future reality of God and His people dwelling together. (e.g., 2:10-11, 8:3, and 14:16)

> **6** Ho, ho, come forth, and flee from the land of the north, saith the LORD: for I have spread you abroad as the four winds of the heaven, saith the LORD. **7** Deliver thyself, O Zion, that dwellest with the daughter of Babylon. **8** For thus saith the LORD of hosts; After the glory hath he sent me unto the nations which spoiled you: for he that toucheth you toucheth the apple of his eye. **9** For, behold, I will shake mine hand upon them, and they shall be a spoil to their servants: and ye shall know that the LORD of hosts hath sent me.

Zechariah provides in verses 6-13 an oracle that draws from the first three night visions. The phrase **Ho, ho, come forth** is a call to immediate attention. God is calling His people to **flee from the land of the north**, a reference to Babylon. Note that **the LORD** says, **I have spread you abroad as the four winds of the heaven.** The phrase **as the four winds of the heaven** is a simile to express God's control over the events. But we understand that God used the Babylonians to **spread** His people **abroad**. The Babylonian captivity technically ended and the Jewish people were free to return, but most did not. Now God is calling for their return to the land. More Jewish people would return to Israel and by the time of Jesus' earthly ministry, Judah would be well populated again with Jewish people. Despite this partial return, however, a substantial portion of the people remain scattered (the Diaspora) up to the present day. But there awaits a future regathering together for Israel that Zechariah will further develop later. (10:6-12) Just as the **four winds** are used to describe the scattering of God's people, they are also used to describe their regathering during the Tribulation, "And he shall send his angels with a great sound of a trumpet, and they shall gather together his elect from the four winds, from one end of heaven to the other." (Matthew 24:31) Thus, Israel's full obedience to the command to return will not happen until the Messianic Kingdom.

The invitation to return to the Promise Land continues in verse 7, but is more narrowly focused on those taken captive to Babylon. God addresses the invitation to **Zion**. Although technically a mountain in Jerusalem near the Temple mount, the word is often used figuratively for all of Jerusalem, and promises to Jerusalem are representative of promises to the entire nation. Similarly, the phrase **daughter of Babylon** is an expression that simply refers to its inhabitants. To His scattered people in **Babylon**, God says, **Deliver thyself**. The command to return presents a test of faith that parallels their earlier exodus from Egypt. God did not make it look easy, nor did He supernaturally rebuild Jerusalem for them, but God made the way for their safe return to Judah. The choice to return is theirs. They can remain where they no longer belong (from God's perspective) or they can take a faith journey home in reliance on God's promise of provision and safety. This is what looking forward and living now looks like. When God calls us as Christians to a particular ministry or task, it also requires a faith journey, often from a place of comfort to a place of uncertainty standing beside a God of certainty. But that does not mean that stepping out in faith is easy.

Next, **the LORD of hosts** says, **After the glory hath he sent me unto the nations which spoiled you: for he that toucheth you toucheth the apple of his eye**. This passage is typically misinterpreted to reference God sending the prophet Zechariah **unto the nations** in some symbolic sense. But this misses the point entirely. The word **glory** refers to the **glory** of God. The moving agent in taking action against **the nations** is the angel of the LORD that guarded Israel, represented by the myrtle trees, in the first night vision. As Feinberg writes, "the Messiah is sent by the Father for the vindication of His glory on the nations that have spoiled Israel."[37] This judgment on **the nations** that **spoiled** Israel builds on what God previously said about being "jealous for Jerusalem and for Zion with a great jealousy" (1:14), being "very sore displeased with the heathen that are at ease" (1:15), and the vision of the "four carpenters" (1:20) that "fray them, to cast out the horns of the Gentiles" (1:21). This is the first of several references to **sent me**, all of which point to Messiah as the moving agent for the LORD of hosts. (Zechariah 2:8, 9, 11; 4:9; 6:15)

There is a warning here to the nations that those who touch Judah (**he that toucheth you**) are like those who would dare to place their finger on the pupils of God's own eyes (**toucheth the apple of his eyes**). This, of course, is a figure of speech called an anthropomorphism in which God is viewed as having human characteristics in order to more clearly express a truth about God. We know from our experience that our eyes are perhaps the most sensitive part of our bodies, and if someone tries to touch our eyes, they will draw our immediate response or retaliation. This is a vivid picture of how God will be stirred to a forceful retaliation for His people. And this verse should be a solid reminder to the **nations** today in their dealings with Israel. There will be a day of reckoning. While as Christians we are not required to support every policy of the Israeli government, we dare not individually or as a nation oppose Israel.

Continuing in the first person, Zechariah speaks for the Messiah, **For, behold, I will shake mine hand upon them** in judgment, **and they shall be a spoil to their servants**. The Gentile nations **shall be a spoil to their servants,** the Jewish people, just as Egypt was **a spoil** to Israel when God brought His people out of Egypt. (see, e.g., Exodus 12:35-36) As further confirmed in Zechariah 14:14, this will occur in association

---

[37] Charles L. Feinberg, *God Remembers: A Study of Zechariah*, 39.

with the return of Jesus Christ and His judgment on the Gentile invaders in Israel. At that future time, when **the nations** experience the judgment of God, Messiah says **ye** (Israel) **shall know that the LORD of hosts hath sent me**. We cannot fail to acknowledge how frequently Jesus refers to the Father sending Him, especially in John's Gospel. (e.g., Matthew 10:40; John 4:34, 5:24, 6:38, 9:4) And we must also remember John's words: "And the Word was made flesh, and dwelt among us, (and we beheld his glory, the glory as of the only begotten of the Father,) full of grace and truth." (John 1:14) At the time when God judges Israel's enemies through His Son Jesus Christ, there will be a national revival in Israel and, in contrast to the first advent, a Jewish remnant will characteristically recognize Jesus as the Christ, the **sent** One. Zechariah will address these issues in later chapters as he continues his portrait of Messiah. (e.g., Zechariah 12)

> **10** Sing and rejoice, O daughter of Zion: for, lo, I come, and I will dwell in the midst of thee, saith the LORD. **11** And many nations shall be joined to the LORD in that day, and shall be my people: and I will dwell in the midst of thee, and thou shalt know that the LORD of hosts hath sent me unto thee. **12** And the LORD shall inherit Judah his portion in the holy land, and shall choose Jerusalem again. **13** Be silent, O all flesh, before the LORD: for he is raised up out of his holy habitation.

In the third vision, God promises a glorious future for Jerusalem when he "will be the glory in the midst of" Jerusalem. This passage gives further confirmation that these promises will be fulfilled by Jesus Christ. Continuing in the first person for the coming Messiah, Zechariah calls upon the city of Jerusalem (the **daughter of Zion**) and by implication the entire nation to **sing and rejoice**. The stated reason for celebration is that God is going to **dwell in the midst of** Jerusalem. Zechariah

2:10 has parallels to Zechariah 9:9, which reads: "Rejoice greatly, O daughter of Zion; shout, O daughter of Jerusalem: behold, they King cometh unto thee: he is just, and having salvation; lowly, and riding upon an ass, and upon a colt the foal of an ass." We know from John 12:14-16 that Jesus fulfilled Zechariah 9:9 at the Triumphal Entry. The similar call in the present oracle to **sing and rejoice** is, like that of Zechariah 9:9, a call to celebrate the arrival (**I come**) of Messiah to **dwell in the midst of** Jerusalem.

Zechariah continues, **and many nations shall be joined to the LORD in that day, and shall be my people.** First, note the time-marker, **in that day.** References to **that day** are frequent in Zechariah and other prophets as a shorthand for "the day of the LORD," referring to the future tribulation and the time of Messiah's return. (see, e.g., Joel 2-3, Malachi 4:5, 2 Peter 3:10) Not only will Messiah dwell in Jerusalem, but at that future time (**that day**), Gentiles will also **be joined to the LORD,** enjoying the blessing of knowing God, for they **shall be my people.** This is in sharp contrast with 2:8-9 where Messiah brings judgment on the **nations.** But this fulfills the promise to Abraham in Genesis 12:3 that "in thee shall all families of the earth be blessed." (see Galatians 3:8) Other prophetic texts also look forward to this future time of unity of all of God's people composed of Jews and Gentiles. (e.g., Isaiah 2:2-4, 25:6-10, 56:1-8, 66:18-24; Jeremiah 3:17; Daniel 7:14; Micah 4:2) Thus, from Zechariah's perspective, both were true—God would bring judgment on Israel's Gentile enemies and at the same time Gentiles **shall be my people.** We know from New Testament revelation (see, e.g., Romans 9; Ephesians 2) that the death of Jesus Christ as a substitutionary atonement for sins opens the way for a new humanity of all peoples who place faith in Jesus Christ.

Moreover, we read that when the Messiah **will dwell in the midst of** Jerusalem, Israel **shalt know that the LORD of hosts hath sent me unto thee.** As already noted, the phrase **sent me** is a reference to God sending the Messiah, not Zechariah. But more than that, Israel **shall know**, which points to their faith in Jesus Christ as the One God **sent**. This is important because Zechariah will in chapters 9, 11, and 12 address the fact that when Messiah comes the first time, He will be largely rejected by Israel and killed. We find confirmation in the New Testament that at the first advent, Israel characteristically rejects Jesus as the Christ, the Son of God. They reject Jesus as the **sent** One. But Zechariah looks beyond that time at the second advent when Jesus is physically present in Jerusalem and a refined remnant of the nation will accept Jesus (**shalt know** Him) as the **sent** One from the Father, **the** LORD **of hosts**. (see also 13:8-9)

In **that day** when Messiah dwells in Jerusalem, he **shall inherit** or take possession of **Judah his portion in the holy land, and shall choose Jerusalem again**. The "good words and comfortable words" in Zechariah 1 include that "the LORD shall yet comfort Zion, and shall yet choose Jerusalem." (Zechariah 1:17) By sending the Messiah, God will fulfill to Israel all that was promised. Messiah will take possession of the Holy Land against all other claims to it, and he will bless Israel. When these events take place (in **that day**), the world must **be silent... before the** LORD. This is a picture of the entire world's submission to the will of God, particularly the future blessing of God's people (Jewish and Gentile) outlined in this chapter of Zechariah. Nothing can stop God, **for he is raised up out of his holy habitation**. God is viewed here as moving out of heaven to protect and take what is **his portion**. We know God's Word will be honored in all creation: "I have sworn by myself, the word is gone out of my mouth in righteousness, and shall not return, That unto me every knee shall bow, every tongue shall swear." (Isaiah 45:23) And we know from New Testament revelation that all of this is fulfilled in Jesus Christ: "That at the name of Jesus every knee should bow, of things in heaven, and things in earth, and things under the earth." (Philippians 2:10) That God provides the people such assurance through Zechariah is encouraging to them to live in faith that Israel has a glorious future.

Closing

A missionary friend of mine spent most of his years in the field ministering in Africa. After realizing the call to missions as a young man, he decided that his ministry in Africa would be greatly helped if he acquired a medical degree so that he could bring physical healing and spiritual healing to the mission field. After completing his education and raising funds for their work, he and his wife spent many fruitful years on the mission field in Africa. When asked about the dangers of the mission field he and his wife worked in, his response was that the only safe place in the world is right in the middle of God's will, whether that places you somewhere in the United States or someplace in Africa. What a simple reminder about looking forward while living now. God's promises stand, and if we accept by faith what God says about the future (e.g., that all nations will be joined to him), then that should dramatically affect how we think and live now. In Zechariah 2, the people still in Babylon were called to leave their comfort place for a city without walls and a nation in ruins based on God's promises, and most of them never did it. Those who returned formed a faithful remnant with which God began rebuilding the nation physically and spiritually. As Christians who aspire to lead a life of faith, we may be called to leave behind what we think is "safe" for a city without walls where our sense of safety is rooted only in the God who is there with us.

Application Points

- **MAIN PRINCIPLE:** In the Messianic Kingdom Jerusalem will prosper without walls and be completely secure because of God's divine protection as the promised Messiah will bring judgment on Israel's enemies, physically dwell in the Holy city, and His people shall be comprised of Jews and Gentiles.

- We need to reorient our lives now around God's promises, including His promises about the future.

- Sometimes the life of faith requires us to leave what is safe and comfortable for a place where we must rely entirely on God's promises and provisions.

Discussion Questions

1. What does it mean to live by faith and not by sight (consider Habakkuk 1:2-4 and 2:4; 2 Corinthians 5:7)? Give examples you have experienced or witnessed.

2. Can God's blessings toward you be measured? What are some of God's blessings toward you promised in the Bible?

3. What is the eternal destination of the believer?

4. What can a person do to feel safe and secure (physically, emotionally, spiritually)?

5. What does the regathering of Israel in the future, notwithstanding their rebellion, say about the character of God (see Genesis 17:1-8)?

6. What does it mean for a child of God to "step out in faith"? What is the difference between faith and presumption?

7. Has Israel ceased being the apple of God's eye (see Romans 11:1)? What does this verse say to those nations in our day that support or oppress Israel?

8. How does God ultimately bring many nations together as one people (see Ephesians 2:11-18)?

Chapter 5

Evaluated

It requires no keen intellect to tear down people. If you grade another person on the basis of their failures, they will fail every time. In fact, in recent years, it has become increasingly common with the polarized political banter for people to grade the United States by her failures. The evaluation strings together some low points in our nation's history and ignores the successes to arrive at an evaluation of failure. Some people evaluate Christianity that way, grading it by some negative experiences they had in some church or with some Christian, and they give Christianity an F on the basis of those failures.

Satan does the same thing. Satan speaks the language of criticism and ridicule. He tears down people. In his assessment, every believer is graded with an F and every believer is unworthy of God. But God knows the worst about His own and still loves them. He sees His people through the lens of the righteousness of His Son. He says they are worthy.

Not only that, God makes it possible for us to live out our new righteousness in Christ. Critical to being the people of God is moving beyond our past failures and reckoning that we are children of God, worthy because the Son is worthy.

Scripture and Comments

This is the fourth of Zechariah's eight night visions. To this point we have seen that God announces his displeasure at the Gentile enemies of Israel, His decision to bless His people again, His promise that Jerusalem will have a glorious future, His call to the scattered Jewish people to return to their homeland, and His promise of a coming Messiah to Israel and the nations that will usher in an age of peace as Messiah physically dwells among His people. Being the people of God is all about experiencing changed lives now based on God's promises, and in this fourth vision that principle will come to bear in the life of the high priest Joshua.

FOURTH NIGHT VISION

Zechariah 3:1 And he shewed me Joshua the high priest standing before the angel of the LORD, and Satan standing at his right hand to resist him.

The text says **he showed** Zechariah the next night vision, but it does not specify who **he** is. Clark and Hatton explain that most scholars believe **he** is the LORD: "Some scholars (Petersen, NLT) think it refers to the interpreting angel. However, most take it to refer to the Lord, especially as a similar clause occurs in 1:20 with the Lord as subject."[38] The better view, however, is that **he** is the interpreting angel. If we read chapter 3 as a continuation of chapter 2, the interpreting

---

[38] David J. Clark and Howard A. Hatton, *A Handbook on Zechariah*, UBS Handbook Series (New York: United Bible Societies, 2002), 119.

angel brought Zechariah a message in 2:3-4, that message is set forth in 2:5-13, and therefore it is natural to take 3:1 to pick back up with the interpreting angel. The antecedent for **he** is not the reference to the Lord in the oracle contained in 2:5-13, but the interpreting angel in 2:3-4. In this way, the interpreting angel brought Zechariah a message in chapter 2, then **showed** him the vision in the opening of chapter 3, then "came again, and waked" Zechariah for the next vision in 4:1.

Zechariah sees **Joshua the high priest** in a courtroom setting, although it a heavenly scene that parallels the setting in Job 1:6-12 and 2:1-7. In Job 1, Satan claims dominion over the earth and all it contains. (Job 1:7) God disputes Satan's claim and offers as a counter-example to Satan's asserted dominion the man named Job, "a perfect and an upright man." As is his character, Satan then accuses Job of only serving God because of God's protection and material blessings toward him. God rejects Satan's assessment and gives Satan authority to test Job in order to establish that Satan is not only wrong about Job but does not have unfettered dominion because of men like Job. Of course, there is a stark contrast between Job who is righteous and Joshua who (as we will see) is defiled, as is Judah for whom he stands in as representative. Note that **Joshua** is **standing before the angel of the** LORD in the posture of a defendant before the presiding Judge. Like the adulteress of John 8:1-11 before Jesus, **Joshua** is guilty, but the judge is righteous. Recall Jesus' words, "my judgment is just; because I seek not mine own will, but the will of the Father which hath sent me." (John 5:30)

Joshua is really the name "Yeshua," which means "Yahweh saves." In the New Testament, Jesus' name is the Greek form of Yeshua. Many Jewish Christians today refer to Jesus as Yeshua. This **Joshua** is also mentioned in Haggai 1:1, 12, 14, 2:2, 4, Zechariah 3:1 and 6:11, Ezra 2:2 and Nehemiah 12:1, 26. **Joshua** is a descendant of Aaron through Zadok, the line of priests established by David and Solomon. (1 Chronicles 6:3-15)

He is the son of Jehozadak (2 Kings 25:18; 1 Chronicles 6:40-41) and grandson of Seraiah, who was the High Priest in 587 B.C. at the beginning of the exile into Babylonian captivity. Seraiah was executed by the Babylonians. As Merrill remarks, "it is likely that Joshua was already advanced in years when he returned to Jerusalem in 538, nearly fifty years later. Certainly by the year of Zechariah's night visions (519) Joshua was an old man."[39]

Others present in the courtroom scene are the **angel of the LORD** and **Satan**. The text does not say that the LORD of hosts is present. Instead, **the angel of the LORD** acts on behalf of the LORD of hosts as the judge, as he is the moving agent for the LORD of hosts in the prior visions and most of the rest of the book. As we have shown in the prior notes, **the angel of the LORD** is the pre-incarnate Son of God. In the New Testament, Jesus claims the role of judge: "For the Father judgeth no man, but hath committed all judgment unto the Son... And hath given him authority to execute judgment also, because he is the Son of man." (John 5:22, 27) Note that the word **Satan**, translated here as a proper noun, is a generic word used elsewhere to mean an adversary or opponent. (e.g., Numbers 22:22, 2 Samuel 19:22, 1 Kings 11:23) **Satan** is a deceiver and for the present time has limited access to God. Ultimately, Satan will be eliminated from the earth (Revelation 20:2), but for the time being Christians need to have a sober awareness of who Satan is and how he works. (see e.g., 2 Corinthians 2:11, 11:14; 1 Peter 5:8) This episode gives us great insight into the father of lies (John 8:44), namely that one of his methods of attack against the children of God (especially those who would serve God) is to **resist** or accuse them before God. Whereas **Joshua** stands as the accused before the judge, **Satan** takes the role of prosecutor, **standing at his** (i.e., the defendant, **Joshua**) **right hand to resist** or charge **him**. We can infer that what **Satan** does in accusing **Joshua** (and Job) he does also to other believers. When Peter

---

[39] Eugene H. Merrill, *An Exegetical Commentary - Haggai, Zechariah, Malachi*, 118.

speaks of **Satan** seeking people to devour like a roaring lion, we understand that his methodology will often involve false accusations and deceit.

An accusation is obviously made here in Zechariah 3, but the precise accusation is not specifically stated as it is in Job. **Joshua** is the high priest of the remnant of Judah. If Judah is to regain its former glory as a nation whose people obey, serve, and worship the living God, it needs a qualified spiritual leader. God selects Joshua for this position. We can infer from this context and the statement that Satan is there to **resist** Joshua, that Satan accuses him of being inadequate and unqualified for the task of being the high priest. We need to also note that if **Joshua** is unfit, by implication the remnant is spiritually unfit to reconstitute Judah. In the first night vision, the Gentile nations used by Satan are at rest because of the deplorable condition of Judah. Now that God is restoring Judah, Satan is vigorously working in opposition to God.

> **2** And the LORD said unto Satan, The LORD
> rebuke thee, O Satan; even the LORD that hath
> chosen Jerusalem rebuke thee: is not this a
> brand plucked out of the fire?

Zechariah uses the first LORD to refer to the **angel of the LORD** as the speaker. Again, as indicated in the notes in chapter 3 of this commentary, this is the pre-incarnate Jesus, the Son of God. Viewed this way, God the Son pronounces the ruling of God the Father (the LORD of Hosts), rebuking Satan's accusations (**The LORD rebuke thee**). We should not miss the severity of this **rebuke**, as it is repeated, **even the LORD that hath chosen Jerusalem rebuke thee**. Although in the form of a rhetorical question, the point is that Joshua is **a brand** or burning stick that God has **plucked out of the fire** and thus rescues, much as he rescued Lot from the destruction of Sodom and Gomorrah. But here, Joshua is representative of the remnant God brought back to the Land from exile. (Amos 4:11) Remember that Joshua, in his role as high priest, stands in for the people. God initiates blessing toward Joshua and indeed toward Judah as a whole, and Satan opposes that blessing. Satan has not changed! Where God is working, Satan will attack. Remember that God uses crooked sticks to hit home runs and we should not be surprised or dismayed when the Satan attacks our adequacy and motives.

In every age and with every generation, being the people of God requires godly leadership. Today, God is spreading the gospel throughout the earth through local churches (and their members), and in those churches He establishes leadership. The spiritual leadership for national Israel was different than for churches today, but many of the principles are the same. A first principle that we see here is that the leader is the man God selects. Committees and congregations may subsequently confirm what God has done, but they dare not supplant God's role in this matter by relying on secular principles to find a CEO rather than godly principles to recognize God's shepherd.

> 3 Now Joshua was clothed with filthy garments, and stood before the angel. 4 And he answered and spake unto those that stood before him, saying, Take away the filthy garments from him. And unto him he said, Behold, I have caused thine iniquity to pass from thee, and I will clothe thee with change of raiment. 5 And I said, Let them set a fair mitre upon his head. So they set a fair mitre upon his head, and clothed him with garments. And the angel of the LORD stood by.

We are again told that **Joshua... stood before the angel** of the LORD (as in verse 1), in the posture of a defendant before the judge, but this time Joshua's clothing is described. He is **clothed with filthy garments**, and this is the basis for Satan's charges. The phrase literally means that Joshua's **raiment** is covered with excrement. This is symbolic of the fact that

Joshua sinned, and so did the nation he represented. In the Bible, clothing is often symbolic of a person's sinfulness or lack thereof. (see e.g., Luke 9:29; Revelation 3:5, 18, 6:11, 7:9, 19:8) This does not mean that Joshua is unsaved, but that he is stained with sin. He needs to be ritualistically clean for his office (e.g., Leviticus 22:6-7), which requires new clothes. This parallels the cleansing of the high priest's clothing (and the high priest himself) as part of the celebration of the Day of Atonement. The difference is that this cleansing is not for the feast, but for keeping the office of high priest. Also, we must continue to bear in mind that Joshua's defilement is Judah's defilement. Zechariah's contemporary, Haggai, presents the problem in Haggai 2:10-14, where God concludes by saying, "The people of this nation are unclean in my sight."

The irony of the situation is that "the father of lies, was telling the truth on this occasion!"[40] It is not as if Joshua might prove his innocence. He is "red handed" guilty and the stains and vile stench of his raiment puts that beyond doubt. Like the trial of the adulteress that opens John 8, the guilt of the accused here cannot be denied, and the accused can do nothing to fix the problem. As Ellsworth exhorts, this is as much a vision about us as Judah: "This is also a vision about us! Not one of us is free from sin. Not one is fit to serve the Lord. And Satan is ever eager to remind us of our failures. When it comes to our sins, Satan has a very long memory, and, if we let him, he will make sure that we have very long memories as well."[41]

In verse 4, **he answered and spake unto those that stood before him** and ordered that Joshua be fitted with new, clean clothing. The **he** is the LORD that spoke in verse 2, whom we have identified as the angel of the LORD. Note that it was **those that stood before him**, i.e., **stood before** the angel of the LORD, that were ordered to **take away the filthy garments**

---

[40] Roger Ellsworth, *Opening Up Zechariah*, Opening Up Commentary (Leominster: Day One Publications, 2010), 34.
[41] *Ibid.*

from Joshua. We are not told who **those** are, and so this has been the cause of some debate. The two most common options are that they are angels or Joshua's fellow priests as witnesses to God's pronouncement. It seems more likely that **those** refers to angelic witnesses to the heavenly courtroom scene. The reason for this identification, first, is that they are ordered to carry out the change of raiment. If they are Joshua's fellow priests, then surely their garments are just as defiled as his own since Joshua's defilement is not merely his own personal defilement but representative of the nation, including the priests. This is all to say that it is improbable that a group of defiled priests would be summoned to this task before their own defilement is dealt with, and we also note that Zechariah makes no mention of their garments, an unlikely omission if they are priests. Second, the emphasis of this scene is that a change of clothes is an act of divine grace on the part of the LORD. It is incongruent with this picture of divine grace that the actual dispensing of the grace would be accomplished by sinful men rather than the LORD'S angelic servants. Third, there are three references to those that stand by (in 3:4; in the reference to "them" in 3:5; and "these that stand by" in 3:7). These references are in contrast to "thy fellows that sit" in 3:8, which almost certainly refers to Joshua's peers, i.e., his fellow priests. Throughout the scene, the angelic servants stand, not only as witnesses, but as servants ready to execute the instructions of the angel of the LORD.

In any event, there is no question about the symbolism of what occurs, for the angel of the LORD states to Joshua that **I have caused thine iniquity to pass from thee**. Joshua is **clothed... with [a] change of raiment** representative of God having declared Joshua cleansed. Only God can do that:

> **Isaiah 61:10** I will greatly rejoice in the LORD,
> my soul shall be joyful in my God; for he hath
> clothed me with the garments of salvation, he
> hath covered me with the robe of righteousness,

as a bridegroom decketh *himself* with ornaments, and as a bride adorneth *herself* with her jewels.

It is interesting to note here that the phrase **change of raiment** employs a Hebrew term used only here and in Isaiah 3:22, which means "especially fine, white garments" or "rich apparel."

There is yet another aspect to all of this. **Joshua** is a Levitical high priest, but Jesus is the coming priest-king after the order of Melchizedek. In this courtroom scene, Jesus fulfills a priestly function in cleansing **Joshua**. Satan accuses Joshua of inadequacy to be high priest because he is a sinner and the angel of the LORD makes him clean. The angel of the LORD recognizes His future redemptive work as Messiah, not only to save sinners, but to provide a continual cleansing for them. This parallels the New Testament teaching in John 13:8-10 and 1 John 1:9 regarding the cleansing from sin in a believer's life, which is done on the basis of Jesus' shed blood. At this point, Joshua is not only the man God selected for leadership, but he is qualified because of the cleansing **change of raiment** that the angel of the LORD provides in his priestly role. "Just as Joshua formerly bore the collective iniquity of the people, now he carries the grace and forgiveness the LORD had just imparted both to Joshua and to Judah."[42] I also note that this cleansing is by grace, for there is no personal merit here.

Upon hearing God's ruling through the angel of the LORD, Zechariah speaks up for Joshua and participates in the vision, also taking on a priestly role. He understands that Joshua will receive new clothing and calls out to make sure that the new clothing includes a **fair mitre upon his head** (a head-dress like a turban). The new headdress is fitting to the dignity of Joshua's position as high priest, whose mitres typically bore the inscription, "Holy To The Lord." (Exodus 28:36; 39:30)

---

[42] George L. Klein, *Zechariah*, vol. 21B, The New American Commentary (Nashville, TN: B & H Publishing Group, 2008), 140.

Zechariah's participation shows he understands and supports what God is doing, even if he does not see all the implications, and it may be that God allows his participation for this reason. As previously indicated, **they** most likely refers to angelic servants. They **set a fair mitre upon** Joshua's **head, and clothed him with garments.** Zechariah mentions almost in passing that **the angel of the LORD stood by.** This reminds us that what was done—even the addition of the **fair mitre** by Zechariah—is with His approval and at His direction as the judge and priest, consistent with His leadership role in the earlier visions.

> **6** And the angel of the LORD protested unto Joshua, saying, **7** Thus saith the LORD of hosts; If thou wilt walk in my ways, and if thou wilt keep my charge, then thou shalt also judge my house, and shalt also keep my courts, and I will give thee places to walk among these that stand by.

The text says that **the angel of the LORD protested**, but we should not take **protested** to indicate opposition. Rather, it is a charge, direction, or exhortation given **unto Joshua.** The **angel of the LORD** speaks on behalf of **the LORD of hosts.** This verse must be understood in its covenant context. Israel was covenanted with God under what is often referred to as the Mosaic Covenant. God made promises to Israel, but these promises required Israel's obedience (e.g., Deuteronomy 10:12-22, 28:9). Likewise here, Joshua is promised three things:

1) That he will **judge** or govern **my house**, that is, the Temple (this means the Temple will be reconstructed in Joshua's lifetime while he is still high priest);

2) He will **also keep** or govern the **courts** or courtyards around the Temple (this indicates the completion of the courtyards under Joshua's leadership). As Clark and Hatton observe, "This was an increase in his privileges, since before the exile it was the king who had ultimate

responsibility over at least the physical aspects of the Temple. See for instance 1 Kgs 2:27; 2 Kgs 16:10–16; 22:3–7."[43]; and

3) He will have **places to walk among these that stand by**. Most likely, and consistent with verse 8, **these** refers to the angelic witnesses. The point would be that Joshua will have access to God. Satan accuses Joshua of being unqualified to lead as high priest, but God qualifies him and promises him access. We must remember that in a very real sense, once a Temple is built, Joshua in fulfilling his role as High Priest will annually enter the Holy of Holies and enjoy access to God's presence. But there may be more here as the imagery suggests access to the heavenly, and not merely the shadow of the heavenly. What is clear is God's promised blessing on the ministry and life of Joshua, and this is good news for the nation of Judah that desperately needs spiritual restoration.

In order for Joshua to retain this authority, however, he must keep God's ways (**If thou wilt walk in My ways**) and must diligently carry out his priestly duties (**if thou wilt keep My charge**). This explains the reason **the angel of the LORD** gives Joshua the new raiment symbolizing his cleansing; it is preparatory for Joshua's role as high priest and the promises God has for him that require his obedience and therefore continued cleansing.

> **8** Hear now, O Joshua the high priest, thou, and thy fellows that sit before thee: for they are men wondered at: for, behold, I will bring forth my servant the BRANCH. **9** For behold the stone that I have laid before Joshua; upon one stone shall be seven eyes: behold, I will engrave the graving thereof, saith the LORD of hosts, and I will remove the iniquity of that

---

[43] David J. Clark and Howard A. Hatton, *A Handbook on Zechariah*, 125–126.

land in one day. 10 In that day, saith the LORD
of hosts, shall ye call every man his neighbour
under the vine and under the fig tree.

The angel of the LORD continues speaking, but now addresses
both **Joshua the high priest** and his fellow priests (**thy fellows
that sit before thee**), as He turns to future events. That the
priests **sit before** Joshua indicates they are of lower rank and
are under his instruction; it "was customary for pupils to sit
before their masters when receiving advice or instruction from
a senior person. Compare 2 Kgs 4:38; Ezek 8:1; 14:1; 20:1; 33:31;
Acts 22:3."[44] The phrase **for they are men wondered at** means
that God is using them as a sign to Judah that God is bringing
about a spiritual restoration. Of course, it would not make
sense to have a high priest and priests serving under him
without a Temple, nor would Judah's spiritual restoration be
possible without the Temple. The presence of **thy fellows**
surely indicates that the Temple will be completed. But
probably, in view of the rest of the verse and the reference to
the BRANCH, thy fellows signifies more. They are a type for
a future priestly order, consistent with the Old Testament
promise to Israel and the New Testament teachings about all
those that identify with Jesus Christ by faith being a priestly
nation. (Exodus 19:5-6; 1 Peter 2:9) And similarly, **Joshua the
high priest** is a type for another high priest, which Zechariah
now introduces.

God promises to **bring forth my servant the BRANCH**.
Packed into these words are two Messianic titles, **servant** and
BRANCH. We find the Messianic title **servant** in passages
such as Isaiah 42:1; 49:3, 5; 52:13; 53:11 and Ezekiel 34:23-24.
Charles Feinberg's comments on these two titles are
enlightening:

> What was the thought of the Spirit of God in
> designating the Messiah in this twofold
> manner? He is called My Servant, because He

---

came into the world to do the will of the
Father. The will of the Father was His perfect
and holy delight always. It is through the
service of Messiah that God's world-wide
redemption plan is executed. The name
Zemach (a proper noun in our text) conveys
several truths. First, it brings out the lowliness
and humiliation of the Messiah (Isa. 11:1).
Second, it reveals His eminence (Isa. 53:2). He
grows up before the Lord Himself. Third, it
directs our attention to His humanity. He is
connected with the earth, and more
particularly the land of Palestine (Zech. 6:12).
Fourth, it relates Him to the Davidic dynasty
(Jer. 23:5,6). Fifth, it focuses our thought upon
the deity of the Branch (Isa. 4:2). Sixth, it
conveys the truth of His fruitfulness in
comparison with the barrenness of all others
(Isa. 11:1; 53:10). Seventh, it speaks of his
priestly work and character; for being touched
with the feeling of our infirmities, He is a
becoming and fit High Priest for sinful men
(Zech. 6:12). How unspeakably full are the
designations of God for His only-begotten and
much-beloved Son! When God introduces His
Son to our admiring and reverent gaze, we do
well to prostrate ourselves at His feet and
there abide.[45]

The translation capitalizes **BRANCH** because the term is
understood to be a proper noun referring to a specific person.
It is a frequent messianic title that speaks of the one that
would come in the line of David as the Messiah, namely Jesus.
(Psalm 132:17; Isaiah 4:2, 11:1; Jeremiah 23:5-6, 33:15-16; Ezekiel
17:22-24) The words of Jeremiah are illustrative:

---

[45] Charles L. Feinberg, *God Remembers: A Study of Zechariah*, 51.

Jeremiah 23:5 Behold, the days come, saith the
LORD, that I will raise unto David a righteous
Branch, and a King shall reign and prosper, and
shall execute judgment and justice in the earth.
6 In his days Judah shall be saved, and Israel
shall dwell safely: and this *is* his name whereby
he shall be called, THE LORD OUR
RIGHTEOUSNESS.

Zechariah will use the term again in 6:12 to indicate the
Messiah. Thus, Joshua, and by extension all of Judah, are given
this prophecy to encourage them to live in view of what God is
presently doing among them in the restoration of the
priesthood and rebuilding of the Temple and in how that
present work fits in with the future eschatological plans of
God. But as David Baron observes, "The climax of the
Messianic references in this great prophecy is reached in the
9th verse...."[46]

The speaker in verse 9 is **the LORD of hosts**. He says **behold**,
calling special attention to the importance of the
announcement—**the stone that I have laid before Joshua**.
Identifying **the stone... laid before Joshua** with **seven eyes** has
caused much debate, as explained by Klein:

> A brief list of suggestions for the stone's
> meaning in this context includes a capstone, a
> jewel in a priestly breastplate, a gem set in a
> crown, building materials for the temple, a
> metaphor referring to the temple itself, a rock
> in the holy of holies, an altar, the holy
> mountain, the Messiah, the kingdom of God,
> and the nation of Israel—and these are only a
> few of the more prominent interpretations. In
> the search for a solution, one must ask several
> initial questions. Is the stone a metaphor for a

---

[46] David Baron, *Zechariah: A Commentary On His Visions And Prophecies*, 114.

historical person, and if so, who is he? If the stone represents an actual stone, did Zechariah intend a cornerstone used in a construction project? Did the stone have some ritual significance? After determining the significance of the stone proper, interpreters must next attempt to determine the meaning of the "eyes" on the stone and the significance of the inscriptions written on it. [47]

Before honing in on a likely interpretation of this announcement, we do well to remember that Zechariah does not write on a blank prophetic slate. The Psalmist announced: "The stone which the builders refused is become the head stone of the corner." (Psalm 118:22) Isaiah prophesied that "he shall be for a sanctuary; but for a stone of stumbling and for a rock of offence to both the houses of Israel, for a gin and for a snare to the inhabitants of Jerusalem." (Isaiah 8:14) And again: "Therefore thus saith the LORD God, Behold, I lay in Zion for a foundation a stone, a tried stone, a precious corner stone, a sure foundation: he that believeth shall not make haste." (Isaiah 28:16) This "stone" will be the foundation for the building of God's Kingdom on earth:

> **Daniel 2:44** And in the days of these kings shall the God of heaven set up a kingdom, which shall never be destroyed: and the kingdom shall not be left to other people, *but* it shall break in pieces and consume all these kingdoms, and it shall stand for ever. **45** Forasmuch as thou sawest that the stone was cut out of the mountain without hands, and that it brake in pieces the iron, the brass, the clay, the silver, and the gold; the great God hath made known to the king what shall come to pass hereafter:

---

[47] George L. Klein, *Zechariah*, vol. 21B, The New American Commentary, 145–146.

and the dream *is* certain, and the interpretation thereof sure.

Daniel looks forward past all human kingdoms to a "stone...cut out of the mountain without hands," that is, not by human hands but by God, an Eternal Kingdom. We need also to be mindful that Jesus claims Messianic import in these passages:

> **Matthew 21:42** Jesus saith unto them, Did ye never read in the scriptures, The stone which the builders rejected, the same is become the head of the corner: this is the Lord's doing, and it is marvellous in our eyes? **43** Therefore say I unto you, The kingdom of God shall be taken from you, and given to a nation bringing forth the fruits thereof. **44** And whosoever shall fall on this stone shall be broken: but on whomsoever it shall fall, it will grind him to powder.

In Matthew's Gospel, Jesus lays claim to be king and Messiah, the son of Abraham and the son of David. Yet the "builders" (the Jewish leadership of his day) reject Him. But God makes this "stone which the builders rejected" into "the head of the corner," who will be the foundation of the coming "Kingdom of God" and destroyer of His enemies. The apostle Peter builds on these concepts as well, when he speaks of Jesus as the "living stone," and those joined to Him by faith as "lively stones" being "built up a spiritual house, a holy priesthood, to offer up spiritual sacrifices, acceptable to God by Jesus Christ." (1 Peter 2:4-5)

> **1 Peter 2:6** Wherefore also it is contained in the scripture, Behold, I lay in Sion a chief corner stone, elect, precious: and he that believeth on him shall not be confounded. **7** Unto you therefore which believe *he is* precious: but unto them which be disobedient, the stone which the builders disallowed, the

same is made the head of the corner, **8** And a stone of stumbling, and a rock of offence, *even to them* which stumble at the word, being disobedient: whereunto also they were appointed. **9** But ye *are* a chosen generation, a royal priesthood, an holy nation, a peculiar people; that ye should shew forth the praises of him who hath called you out of darkness into his marvellous light: **10** Which in time past *were* not a people, but *are* now the people of God: which had not obtained mercy, but now have obtained mercy.

In short, Jesus is the "stone" that becomes the corner stone of a new humanity joined to him by faith, which God will build into a "royal priesthood" and "holy nation, a peculiar people." They are the "the people of God." Commenting on the use of the term "stone" for Messiah, Feinberg writes:

> Why is the Messiah called the Stone? It relates Him to Israel. To them He was the stumbling-stone and rock of offense (Isa. 8:14). But to those in Israel who trusted Him, He was a never-failing refuge (Isa. 28:16). The Stone relates Christ to the nations. He will be the Destroyer of the godless world-monarchies (Dan. 2:35). The Stone connects the Christ to the Church. He is her foundation and top-stone (Psa. 118:22; Eph. 2:20-22). The designation relates the Messiah to God. He is the Stone made without hands, the One who is called the Tabernacle which God pitched, not man (Dan. 2:34). The Stone speaks of the beauty of the Son of God (Zech. 3:9). The engravings (*mephatteah* used of engraving precious stones, as well as gold, carved work, and sculpture—Exod. 28:9; 28:36; II Chron. 2:13; Psa. 74:6) are those

conducive to its beauty... The Stone reveals Him to be the dependable Rock, Fortress, High Tower of the trusting soul. Compare the many passages in the Psalms. The Stone relates Him to the Spirit of God, for the seven eyes are symbolic of manifold intelligence and omniscience (Isa. 11:2; Rev. 5:6).[48]

With this background in mind, we turn back to the text of Zechariah 3:9. Central to the messages of both Zechariah and Haggai are the rebuilding of the Temple. This chapter confirms the qualifications of Joshua as High Priest and promises that, with his obedience, he will see the Temple completed, as would Zerubbabel (Zechariah 4:7). But there is another construction project afoot, and God is the builder. The cornerstone of large construction projects in the ancient world had inscriptions, typically to the ruler that ordered the construction. God says that He **will engrave the graving thereof**, but we are not told what the inscription will say. The point is not what words God **will engrave** (if any), but the fact that it is God doing the engraving, just as He etched the Ten Commandments with His finger. (Exodus 31:18) God is the architect and builder of this project, and His **servant the BRANCH** will be its cornerstone or foundation, and his defining work will be to remove sin from the **land in one day**. In a sense, that is one of the purposes of the Temple. The High Priest would annually enter the Holy of Holies as part of the Day of Atonement (or Yom Kippur) and in that one day Israel's sins were atoned until the Feast had to be repeated the next year. But what Zechariah sees in this vision is much superior as it is the removal of sin or **iniquity** from Israel with finality. Feinberg explains concerning that **day**: "Most Christian expositors claim it is the day of Calvary, but it must look beyond that to a day when Israel in a time of national atonement and repentance will have ratified for her in her

---

[48] Charles L. Feinberg, *God Remembers: A Study of Zechariah*, 52.

national life actually, that which was wrought out potentially and provisionally at Calvary."[49] That **day** will be detailed later in Zechariah's prophecies, notably in Zechariah 12:9-14, where Messiah cleanses the land of her enemies and sin.

Note that this **stone** has **seven eyes**, identified later in Zechariah 4:10 as "the eyes of the LORD, which run to and fro through the whole earth." In Revelation 5:5-6, God combined the ideas of Jesus as the **BRANCH** or Root of David, as well as having on Himself the **seven eyes** of God:

> **Revelation 5:5** And one of the elders saith unto me, Weep not: behold, the Lion of the tribe of Juda, the Root of David, hath prevailed to open the book, and to loose the seven seals thereof. **6** And I beheld, and, lo, in the midst of the throne and of the four beasts, and in the midst of the elders, stood a Lamb as it had been slain, having seven horns and seven eyes, which are the seven Spirits of God sent forth into all the earth.

In Revelation 5, the image is that of Jesus, with whom the Holy Spirit dwells ("seven eyes, which are the seven Spirits of God"), receiving from God the Father His inheritance of all creation. Messiah's description as a **stone** with **seven eyes** confirms he is not earthly rock, but a living, omniscient stone imbued with the essence God, i.e., deity. Of course, through the lens of the New Testament, unquestionably the **stone** is the Son of God, Jesus.

The result of Jesus' removing Israel's sin will be a time of blessing, peace and security for God's people **in that day**. References to **that day** or "the day of the LORD" are common in the prophets, referring to the future tribulation and the time of Messiah's return. (see, e.g., Joel 2-3, Malachi 4:5,

---

[49] *Ibid.*, 53.

2 Peter 3:10) Here, the focus is particularly on the blessings to Judah in **that day**, when they can **call every man his neighbor under the vine and under the fig tree.** This is a picture of peace and tranquility where **every man** is a **neighbor** and not an enemy, something Israel has yet to enjoy. Note that trees are similarly referred to elsewhere because their shade is a picture of blessing. (see 1 Kings 4:25; Micah 4:4) Moreover, from this verse and Micah 4:4, the **fig tree** pictures the blessings provided by Messiah when he comes. This is why, in John's Gospel, that Nathanael (whom Jesus said had "no guile") is at the fig tree. (John 1:47-51) Nathanael is most probably praying there for Messiah to come and deliver them, which explains his profound response to Jesus' statement that He witnessed him there. Zechariah will later address in detail how the fulfillment of this promise comes about, but for the moment, we see again that this looks forward to the Kingdom when Jesus Christ rules and reigns on the earth and beckons its audience (and us) to look forward with hope and live now in expectation.

Closing

This chapter in Zechariah ends with a profound promise of the coming servant and Branch. As Christians, we know this speaks of Jesus Christ, the Son of God. He is not only the One through whom we obtain eternal salvation, but the One through whom we continue our spiritual walk. As Jesus says in John 15:5: "I am the vine, ye are the branches: He that abideth in me, and I in him, the same bringing forth much fruit: for without me ye can do nothing." And we are part of the priesthood prefigured by Joshua's "fellows." Peter says we are "a chosen generation, a royal priesthood." (1 Peter 2:9) Everyone who is willing to yield to God's leading can be used in extraordinary ways by God. And none are disqualified by past failures or even present failures. As John writes, "And if any man sin, we have an advocate with the Father, Jesus Christ the righteous." (1 John 2:1b) We have the same advocate Joshua had those centuries ago.

Application Points

- **MAIN PRINCIPLE:** We are qualified for service to God by grace through His Son.

- The old priesthood was a type for the new priesthood, of which the servant and Branch is the head or high priest.

Discussion Questions

1. What is Satan's role in the passage and do you think his role is different toward God's people in general than it was toward Joshua?

2. What did Joshua do to earn his change of clothes? Did he have to engage in some behavior, make a commitment of obedience, promise not to sin, or anything else to get his change of clothes?

3. Given that Joshua was clothed with excrement before Jesus gave him a change of clothes, what does our sin really look like?

4. What is Joshua promised if he obeys God's requirements in verse 7? Could he lost what was promised there?

5. What New Testament passages confirm the servant and Branch is Jesus?

6. When will God remove the iniquity of Israel in one day? How could God possibly do that?

Chapter 6

By My Spirit

A man spends hours installing a large new refrigerator in the house but it does not work. He breaks down and reads the instructions while his wife is not looking. He reads the trouble-shooting section. He reads the FAQs. He googles it. He tries everything, and then in desperation, gives it a swift kick. Nothing happens. Then his wife walks by and says with a smirk on her face, "Have you tried plugging it in?" The thing about that new refrigerator is that you can fill it with food and cover the doors with your favorite magnets so that it looks like it is supposed to look, but if you do not plug it in, it has no power to fulfill its design function of cooling and preserving the food. And that is how it is as Christians. We can try our very best to do what we think we must do to look the part, but if we are not plugged in, we will never live out God's purpose for our lives. Our ability to accomplish all that God has for us is rooted in God's enablement by His Spirit. If we try to do it our way, or in reliance on our resources, mustering all of our discipline and determination, we will fail. But when we are plugged in, God will accomplish the extraordinary through us, not as passive bystanders but yielding servants.

Scripture and Comments

It is easy in our Bible study to get so focused in on a verse or passage that we lose sight of the bigger picture. Every book of the Bible has a structure, a primary theme and a flow such that all the pieces fit within and further the larger whole. The book is a single unit of thought that itself fits into the larger unit of the whole of the cannon, but is also composed of subunits in an orderly and compelling way. This is true in spades of the book of Zechariah, and especially of the prophet's eight night visions. As noted in chapter 2, the visions are organized in a chiastic format, which means that the fourth and fifth visions correspond. Scholar Eugene Merrill explains:

> Vision five forms a matching pair with vision four, both in terms of its juxtaposition to it and its subject matter. Both deal with cultic persons or objects (the high priest and the menorah respectively), both mention historical persons contemporary to the prophet (Joshua and Zerubbabel), both refer to temple building, and both reach their climax on a strong messianic note. For all these reasons it is to be expected that the two visions are mutually interpretive. In addition, because there is a clear process of theological development in the series of night visions, all that has gone before will need to be kept in mind as this fifth vision is unfolded.[50]

---

[50] Eugene H. Merrill, *An Exegetical Commentary - Haggai, Zechariah, Malachi*, 131.

So as we embark on our study of Zechariah 4, not only the immediate context, but all that preceded and especially the vision of Zechariah 3, as well as the balance of the book, must be our guide. In Zechariah 3, Joshua the High Priest is assured of his place in the blessings to come to the nation. And what is implied there—that the Temple construction will be completed—is explicitly stated in the next night vision. Joshua and Zerubbabel, anointed and empowered by the Spirit of God, are assured of their place in God's purposes. And more than that, following on the promised servant and Branch in Zechariah 3, "the two of them represent the two great messianic offices, priest and king, that are central to the sovereign rule of YHWH over all things."[51]

FIFTH NIGHT VISION

Zechariah 4:1 And the angel that talked with me came again, and waked me, as a man that is wakened out of his sleep, **2** And said unto me, What seest thou? And I said, I have looked, and behold a candlestick all of gold, with a bowl upon the top of it, and his seven lamps thereon, and seven pipes to the seven lamps, which are upon the top thereof: **3** And two olive trees by it, one upon the right side of the bowl, and the other upon the left side thereof.

Because all of the visions recorded so far occur on the same night, the vision in chapter 4 is usually referred to as the fifth "night vision." The same **angel** that Zechariah converses with throughout the night visions as his interpreting **angel... talked with** Zechariah here. Zechariah is not asleep, but in a special state that enables him to receive these visions, and apparently he is in a respite after the prior vision. It may well be that his sensation of what was occurring was not unlike a dream, and

51 *Ibid.*, 131–132.

here Zechariah says the break from his respite was **as a man that is wakened out of his sleep**. In other words, the interpreting **angel** gets Zechariah's attention suddenly as if he were being awakened.

Zechariah does not fully comprehend what he sees, but in response to the angel's question, **What seest thou?**, he describes for the **angel** (and for us) what he sees. The question is quite probably designed to focus Zechariah's observations, but also that he would be cognizant of his need for God's explanation. The same question will be asked in 5:1 by the interpreting **angel**. As Guzik points out, "What he saw was unusual but simple—a lampstand with lamps supplied with oil directly through pipes coming from two olive trees."[52] Zechariah responds to the **angel** that he sees a **candlestick all of gold**. Note that the Hebrew term translated **candlestick** is the familiar *menorah*. Zechariah no doubt would think immediately (as would most Jewish readers) of the "candlestick of pure gold" of Exodus 25:31-40 and 37:17-24. That menorah was specially fashioned to God's specifications for use in the Tabernacle, lighting its interior at all times (there were no windows). We should not be at all surprised by this imagery insofar as the **candlestick** was a key feature in the Temple before it was destroyed and the visions of the prior chapter and this one together encourage and ensure the completion of the new Temple.[53] As Hartman explains, the **candlestick** in the Temple "provided the only source of light in the holy place. Because no natural illumination ever entered the holy place, the light of the menorah was believed to represent the light of God. Within the inner chamber, the holy of holies, the Shekinah glory glowed above the mercy seat."[54] But this **candlestick** in Zechariah's vision is also different from the one that stood in the Temple.

[52] David Guzik, *Zechariah*, David Guzik's Commentaries on the Bible (Santa Barbara, CA: David Guzik, 2013), Zec 4:4–5.

[53] *Ibid.*, Zec 4:1–3.

[54] Fred H. Hartman, *Zechariah: Israel's Messenger of the Messiah's Triumph*, Zec 4.

Comparing the descriptions in Exodus to this vision shows there are several differences. Most notably, the **candlestick** in the Temple is powered by human means, that is, the priests continually replenish the oil to keep the light burning. But here, no human elements are involved, and instead, there is a continual source of oil. Zechariah also observes that the golden **candlestick** in his vision has a **bowl upon the top of it** to hold the oil that flows down by gravity to **seven lamps** through **seven pipes**. Merrill elaborates:

> The menorah of Zechariah's vision, although having much in common, also differs considerably with the menorah of Exodus. First, it appears to have a general vessel for storing the oil located somewhere above the center of the menorah. Called a גֻּלָּה (gullâ), it cannot be the ordinary cup for oil at the top of the central stem and branches, for that is always known as a gābîa as already noted. It seems rather to have been a reservoir from which pipes distributed oil to the cups on the lamps. The word appears elsewhere to describe a water pool (Josh. 15:19), a bowl (Eccles. 12:6), or the bowl-like shape of the tops of the Temple pillars (1 Kings 7:41). This leads to a second difference, namely, the pipes (מוּצָקוֹת, mûṣāqôt), which are never mentioned in connection with the menorah of the tabernacle/Temple. The reason for them here is obvious. The oil is not poured into the lamps by the Levites but comes from the olive trees via the reservoir and from thence into the cups. There is no human hand or effort whatsoever. The third difference is the presence of the olive trees, something unthinkable within the confines of the sanctuary. That the trees directly yield their oil

without benefit of plucking and crushing the
olives is also suggestive of the visionary nature
of this menorah, and hence its allowable
differences from the historical object.[55]

Unsurprisingly, this passage has generated debate both as to
what Zechariah sees, and what it symbolizes. The source of
confusion about what he sees is the phrase **seven pipes**. This
literally translates "seven and seven" and the question is
whether there are **seven** total **pipes**, or **seven** on each side of
the stem of the **candlestick** (thus fourteen total), or forty-nine
pipes, with **seven** to each of the **seven lamps**. Critically, while
wrestling with exactly what the **candlestick** looks like is an
interesting problem, it should not affect the interpretation of
what the vision means, as we shall see. But I will explore the
range of opinions a bit further here. Eugene Merrill argues
that there are fourteen total **pipes**:

> On balance it seems that the best
> understanding is that there is one menorah
> with an oil reservoir suspended above it. This
> provides oil to the seven lamps of the menorah
> through seven pipes on each side, or fourteen
> in all. The reservoir itself is connected to two
> olive trees, one on each side of it. How this
> latter aspect functions is clarified in the vision
> interpretation to follow (v. 12).[56]

On the other hand, many respected scholars take the view
there are forty-nine total **pipes**. Representative of this view is
the following:

> The precise meaning of the phrase rendered,
> **seven pipes each**, lit., "seven and seven," has
> been much contested. Hitzig and Henderson

---

[55] Eugene H. Merrill, *An Exegetical Commentary - Haggai, Zechariah, Malachi,*
132–133.
[56] *Ibid.*, 133–134.

propose an alteration of the text, omitting one of the *sevens*, in accordance with the LXX. and Vulgate. Pressel gains the same end by connecting the first *seven* with what precedes,— which is harsh, and forbidden by the interpunction. Köhler adds the two together, thus making the number of pipes fourteen, but if the prophet had meant that, he would have said so. It is better to take the text as it stands. Forty-nine tubes are very many to proceed from one oil-bowl, but as we know not the size of either the vessel or the pipes, no judgment can be expressed against the possibility of such a thing. That it was probable, seems to be clearly shown by the fact that the visionary candlestick is a designed enlargement of the real one made by Moses.[57]

Klein argues that "one cannot know whether the lampstand has 14 or 49 lights. The Hebrew text accommodates either possibility. Even though Merrill objects that 49 is virtually impossible because of the undue complexity of such a lampstand, North's rendering demonstrates the feasibility of the design."[58] In contrast, Feinberg believes the language unmistakably points to 49 pipes:

...and many others understand forty-nine in all. With this latter view we concur. There is no ambiguity in the original...for the expression *shibh'ah weshibh'ah* is to be taken distributively, seven pipes for each lamp. The usage is not without parallel as can be seen from II Samuel 21:20 and I Chronicles 20.6.

---

[57] John Peter Lange, Philip Schaff, and Talbot W. Chambers, *A Commentary on the Holy Scriptures: Zechariah* (Bellingham, WA: Logos Bible Software, 2008), 42.

[58] George L. Klein, *Zechariah*, 156.

> The multiplied channels are purposely
> introduced to bring out the enlarged and
> abundant supply of the oil.[59]

The view accepted here (but not dogmatically) is that the "seven and seven" language indicates seven **pipes** from the large **bowl** of oil to each side of the special menorah and therefore fourteen total **pipes**. This gives a literal understanding of "seven and seven." While in Hebrew that is not how one would typically express the number fourteen, we have to remember that here the prophet describes not only quantity but appearance, i.e., **seven** on each side and each side flanked with an olive tree. This design indicates not only an abundant supply of oil for each **lamp**, but that God supplies the unlimited resources that lights it. There is often significance to the use of the number seven in the Bible and that seems to be the case in this night vision. The number seven is typically associated with the outworking of God, as Feinberg explains:

> From Genesis to Revelation the number is to the fore. In Genesis there are the seven days of creation; the sevenfold vengeance called down upon the slayer of Cain; the seven of clean beasts and fowls received into the ark; the dove sent from the ark at intervals of seven days; Jacob serving seven years for Leah and then a similar period for Rachel, his first choice; the seven fat kine and seven lean, and seven good ears and seven thin of Pharaoh's dream; in Leviticus the sacrifices of seven victims often required by the Mosaic ritual; the sprinkling of the blood seven times; the sanctity of the seventh day, the seventh month, the seventh year, the seven weeks of years. The historical

[59] Charles L. Feinberg, *God Remembers: A Study of Zechariah*, 57.

books and prophetical books alike lay stress on the numeral. When we come to the Revelation the recurrence is still more prominent. There are seven churches, seven spirits, seven lampstands, stars, seals, horns, eyes, trumpets, thunders, seven angels, heads, crowns, plagues, bowls, mountains, kings, and beatitudes.[60]

However we envision the **candlestick** (7, 14 or 49 **pipes**), indisputably it is God-enabled to accomplish God's purposes. As already observed, this **candlestick** is different in appearance than the one kept in the Tabernacle, and later the Temple, in that those were filled by the priests from their resources, while this one is not filled by any human agent, and thus by implication draws from the limitless resources of God, which is the central point of the vision.

We are not explicitly told in these opening verses what the **candlestick** represents, and that too has generated considerable debate. Smith writes: "General agreement exists among the commentators that the lampstand signifies the people of God. Israel was precious to the Lord, as precious as gold. The design of Israel, like the lampstand, was to give light in the world. In this ministry Israel would experience supernatural vitality as is indicated in the endless supply of oil. The oil itself probably signifies the Holy Spirit or perhaps the grace of God."[61] The interpreter must keep in mind, however, that the Text itself tells Zechariah (and us) what is meant by the overall vision, but does not interpret each element in the vision. It is often in our nature to look for meaning in every element when that is not the central purpose for which God provided the vision in the first place. This can lead to fruitless debate, meanwhile missing what God has for us. With that caution in mind, the lampstand may represent, in the

---

[60] *Ibid.*, 62.

[61] James E. Smith, *The Minor Prophets*, Old Testament Survey Series (Joplin, MO: College Press, 1994), Zec 4:3–5.

immediate term, the faithful remnant of Judah that functions as a witness of God (a light in the world), and as will become clear in the rest of the chapter, the greater witness of the coming Messiah to the nations of the world is also in view.[62]

There are **two olive trees by** the lampstand. One tree is **upon the right side of the bowl** of oil and **the other upon the left side** of it. The **two olive trees** produce the oil that powers the candlestick. We have to look to verses 6 and 14 to better understand the vision. Verse 6 explains that the oil is the Spirit of God. And the **olive trees**, we are told in verse 14, are associated with the two anointed ones, which contextually points to Zerubbabel (the governor) and Joshua (the high priest), the leaders God selects for Judah as it returns to its task of being a witness or light to the world.

> **4** So I answered and spake to the angel that talked with me, saying, What are these, my lord? **5** Then the angel that talked with me answered and said unto me, Knowest thou not what these be? And I said, No, my lord. **6** Then he answered and spake unto me, saying, This is the word of the LORD unto Zerubbabel, saying, Not by might, nor by power, but by my spirit, saith the LORD of hosts. **7** Who art thou, O great mountain? before Zerubbabel thou shalt become a plain: and he shall bring forth the headstone thereof with shoutings, crying, Grace, grace unto it.

---

[62] In Scripture, we often see believers characterized as lights (Matthew 5:14, 16; Luke 12:35; Philippians 2:15), churches characterized as lampstands (Revelation 1:20), witnesses characterized as lampstands (Revelation 11:4), and Jesus characterized as the light of the world (John 1:4-5, 7-9; 3:10; 8:12; 12:35-36, 46). Israel was supposed to be a light to the Gentiles. (Isaiah 42:6) In Zechariah 3, the fourth night vision, we read about the cleansing of Joshua the High Priest for service. Now, the remnant of Judah is ready to again be a witness for God.

As we have seen before, Zechariah reports what he sees, but does not always understand it. God is not trying to hide the message, but reveals it in the way He does to better communicate truth to us. Zechariah asks **the angel that talked with** him for help in understanding the vision, **What are these, my lord?** It is debated whether Zechariah is asking about the candlestick, the olive trees, or whether "these" refers to everything he sees. Probably, Zechariah asks for understanding of the entire vision.

The **angel that talked with me** is an expression Zechariah frequently uses in the eight night visions in chapters 1 through 6. We are to understand that throughout these visions the **angel that talked with me** refers the same interpreting **angel** that helps the prophet understand the visions. Accordingly, the **angel** asks Zechariah, **Knowest thou not what these be?** Zechariah's response is **No, my lord**. The reason for the question is likely to emphasize that Zechariah (and by application, us) cannot understand the vision without God providing the explanation. We should also observe that because God provides an explanation, there is one right answer to the question.

Whereas chapter 3 focused on Joshua the high priest, chapter 4 focuses on **Zerubbabel** the governor. He was a nephew of Sheshbazzar, the leader of the original remnant that returned from the captivity, and also the grandson of Jeconiah, one of the kings of Judah.[63] The name **Zerubbabel** means "born in Babel," i.e., Babylon. He succeeded Shessbazzar as governor between 538 and 520 B.C.[64] We must remember that one purpose of Zechariah's prophecies is to encourage the people to rebuild the Temple. More broadly, he is to encourage them to be the people of God and enjoy a time of spiritual renewal. We should not be surprised that specific parts of Zechariah's ministry focus on the political and religious leaders God chose to lead His

---

[63] Israel P. Loken, *The Old Testament Prophetic Books: An Introduction*, 371-372.
[64] *Ibid.*, 371.

people during this time. Accordingly, God has a message for **Zerubbabel** that will be delivered through Zechariah.

The vision, Zechariah is told explicitly, is God's **word** for **Zerubbabel**. And the **word** God has for **Zerubbabel** is as follows: **Not by might, nor by power, but by my spirit, saith the LORD of hosts.** The word **might** "focuses on *collective* strength, the resources of a group or army," while **power** "focuses on individual strength."[65] If **Zerubbabel** is to successfully lead God's people, his success will not be based on corporate or individual strength, but his dependence and yielding to the **spirit** of God. As the explanation of the vision further unfolds, we will see that the oil represents the Holy Spirit, which empowers both **Zerubbabel** and Joshua for their ministry. And if we take the "candlestick" as the Jewish remnant then the same empowering of **Zerubbabel** works through the people for the Temple construction task ahead.[66] As believers in Christ in this time, we are promised the indwelling permanent presence of the Holy Spirit. (Romans 8:9, 16; Galatians 3:14, 4:6) And our successful walk as believers must be "in the Spirit." (Galatians 5:16)

Because of Zerubbabel's empowerment by the **spirit**, he is enabled to lead. The question is then asked, **Who art thou, O great mountain?** The imagery is that of Zerubbabel being able—by the **spirit** of God and not his own strength—to remove a **mountain** to accomplish his assigned tasks in the service of the Lord. For before **Zerubbabel,** the mountain will **become a plain.** As Merrill writes: "Mountain as metaphor for insuperable opposition or resistance is common in the OT, especially when it is overcome and reduced to a valley or plain (Isa. 40:4; 41:15; 42:15; 64:1, 3; Mic. 1:4; Nah. 1:5; Jer. 4:24; 51:25–26; Hab. 3:10; Zech. 14:4–5). Zerubbabel will be able to face this mountain, level it to a plain, and completely achieve

---

[65] David Guzik, *Zechariah*, David Guzik's Commentaries on the Bible, Zec 4:6–7.
[66] Roger Ellsworth, *Opening Up Zechariah*, Opening Up Commentary, 44.

the rebuilding committed to his charge."[67] Hartman well says that the **mountain** "represents all the obstacles and hindrances to completing the Temple in the time of Zechariah and Zerubbabel."[68]

That no **mountain** will stand in his way is confirmed because **Zerubbabel** is assured he **shall bring forth the headstone**. As Dennett explains, "The headstone is connected with the completion of the building; the foundation stone had long since been laid (see Ezra 3:10; 4:24; 5:1); and hence the promise refers to the conclusion of the work...."[69] When the project is coming to completion and the **headstone** is on display, God's people will cry **Grace, grace unto** the **headstone**, recognizing their full dependence on God for the success of the project. They recognize that God is the provider of the supplies and that they need God's blessing on the Temple construction project for it to succeed. The promise of **Zerubbabel** placing the capstone on the Temple is the promise of its completion under his leadership.

> **8** Moreover the word of the LORD came unto me, saying, **9** The hands of Zerubbabel have laid the foundation of this house; his hands shall also finish it; and thou shalt know that the LORD of hosts hath sent me unto you. **10** For who hath despised the day of small things? for they shall rejoice, and shall see the plummet in the hand of Zerubbabel with those seven; they are the eyes of the LORD, which run to and fro through the whole earth.

These three verses comprise an oracle building on the vision, and then in verse 11 the prophet makes further inquiry about the meaning of the vision. This oracle is frequently

[67] Eugene H. Merrill, *An Exegetical Commentary - Haggai, Zechariah, Malachi*, 143.
[68] Fred H. Hartman, *Zechariah: Israel's Messenger of the Messiah's Triumph*, Zec 4.
[69] Edward Dennett, *Zechariah the Prophet*, 42.

misunderstood as merely providing additional assurance to **Zerubbabel** that he will finish the task of rebuilding the Temple. But that would be unnecessarily duplicative because verses 6 and 7 already provide that assurance. The key to understanding the oracle lies in its relationship to Zechariah 3. The visions and oracles in Zechariah 3 and 4 comprise the middle of the chiasmus of the eight night visions and they are intertwined in subject matter and scope. Whereas the vision in Zechariah 3 relates to Joshua as a type for the coming Messiah (Jesus Christ), Zechariah 4 relates to **Zerubbabel** as a type for the coming Messiah. The combined symbolism provides a portrait of a coming Messiah who will be a priest-king, a point made explicit in Zechariah 6.

Recall that the fourth night vision focuses on Joshua the high priest, and the oracle following that vision says that Joshua and the priests under him are a sign or type of "my servant the BRANCH" (Zechariah 3:8) and the oracle looks forward to a day when God "will remove the iniquity of that land in one day" (Zechariah 3:9) after which there will be peace and prosperity (Zechariah 3:10). And critically, the oracle following the fourth night vision refers to the "stone" with "seven eyes" which God "will engrave the graving thereof." (Zechariah 3:9) In the present oracle, **the word of the LORD came unto** the prophet. At first glance, the message reaffirms what we already know, namely that **the hands of Zerubbabel have laid the foundation of this** Temple shortly after the return from exile in about 537/38 B.C. (see Ezra 3:8-11, 5:16). And **his hands shall also finish it**. And indeed that happens four years later in 515 B.C. But there is more.

Notice the phrase, **and thou shalt know that the LORD of hosts hath sent me unto you**. This phrase is used in 2:9 and 11 to speak specifically of the Messiah, the one **sent** by God. The same occurs again in 6:15. The point in this oracle is not that Zechariah's audience will acknowledge that God **sent** the prophet, but that they will acknowledge the Messiah as the

One **sent** by God. Verse 10 further confirms this. God asks the question, **Who despised the small beginnings?** Some people remember the Temple as originally constructed by Solomon (Haggai 2:1-5; cf. Ezra 3:12-13) and think the new construction pales in comparison. But they are to know, as are we in our time, that the true measure of the value of the ministry task is solely whether God is in it or not, and not the numbers. Those that might despise what God is doing in Zechariah's day also need to glimpse the significance of what their construction project foreshadowed, a future Millennial Temple.

The Text in the KJV is somewhat challenging, but when it says, **they shall rejoice, they** likely refers to **those seven...the eyes of the LORD**. The **eyes of the LORD** refers to the omniscient Spirit of God whose **eyes...run to and fro through the whole earth**. (see also Revelation 5:6) God uses **Zerubbabel** as a sign or type for the coming Messiah as He did of Joshua in the last chapter. The **eyes of the LORD** will witness the completion of a future Temple under the leadership of the coming Messiah and will **rejoice**. Compare this to the similar promise made to Joshua in 3:9: "For behold the stone that I have laid before Joshua; upon one stone shall be seven eyes: behold, I will engrave the graving thereof, saith the LORD of hosts, and I will remove the iniquity of that land in one day." As Feinberg correctly observes: "From the analogy of [2:9 and 11] it is evident that the prophetic finger is being pointed at the coming Messiah. Just as chapter 3 had an immediate application to Joshua, then went on to speak of the Messiah, the Branch, the Stone, so this chapter has an immediate reference to Zerubbabel and then beyond him to Christ...Just as the scion of the Davidic house was to accomplish the completion of the work on the restoration temple, so the One of whom Zerrubabel was a type, David's greater Son, would begin and consummate the work on the millennial temple (cf. 6:13). The building in the days of the return from captivity was but a foreshadowing of a far greater work in a future day."[70]

---

[70] Charles L. Feinberg, *God Remembers: A Study of Zechariah*, 61.

11 Then answered I, and said unto him, What
are these two olive trees upon the right side of
the candlestick and upon the left side thereof?
12 And I answered again, and said unto him,
What be these two olive branches which
through the two golden pipes empty the
golden oil out of themselves? 13 And he
answered me and said, Knowest thou not what
these be? And I said, No, my lord. 14 Then said
he, These are the two anointed ones, that
stand by the Lord of the whole earth.

Now, Zechariah returns to asking questions of the angel for an
explanation of the meaning of **the two olive trees upon the
right sight of the candlestick and upon the left side thereof**. It
is interesting that he does not ask for a further explanation of
the other aspects of the vision. The reason may simply be that
Zechariah believes he understands the symbol of the
candlestick. It is the **two olive trees** and the **oil** that he is
concerned about.

In verse 12, Zechariah focuses his question, and in so doing,
provides additional information about what he sees. He sees
**two olive branches which through the two golden pipes empty
the golden oil out**. The word **branches** is the Hebrew word for
"ears" like ears of grain and likely refers to **branches** of olives.
There are **two golden pipes**, presumably one pipe for each
olive tree, which connect from a branch of each tree and
empty the golden oil out of the branches and into the bowl of
oil. In other words, the **golden oil** that fuels the lamps comes
from the **two olive trees**. Without the intermediary of a
human agent obtaining the **oil** from the **trees** and filling the
bowl, the point is that of an unlimited supply of **oil**. The
resources of God are unlimited and always sufficient for us,
and that is why verse 6 is so powerful. Also, note that the color
of the oil is **golden**, probably indicating its great value.

As in verse 5, the angel asks Zechariah in verse 13 the question, **Knowest thou not what these be?** He specifically asks about the **branches**. Obviously, Zechariah does not know (**No, my lord**) what the **branches** represent and he needs revelation from God to understand. The response of God through the angel is, **These are the two anointed ones, that stand by the Lord of the whole earth.** The word **anointed** is not the usual word translated **anointed** and according to the NET translation notes means "sons of fresh oil." This makes sense because the **oil** is flowing directly from the **trees**. As Merrill explains, the concept of being **anointed** in the Old Testament was limited to certain persons: "Only two kinds of officials were anointed in OT Israel, the high priest and the king. The act of anointing set the individual apart for special service and also symbolized his enduement with the gifts necessary to his carrying out the work for which he had been chosen. As in the Zechariah vision, the oil of anointing was associated with the Spirit of God. It spoke of both his presence and His enablement."[71] From the context of chapters 3 and 4, the **two anointed ones** in Zechariah's day are plainly Joshua and Zerubbabel. These two people are pictured as **branches** from which golden oil flows and fuels the lamps. The **branches** are thus anointed with **golden oil**. As Guzik observes, Zerubbabel and Joshua "were not the entire trees, but **two olive branches** from the trees, probably one branch from each tree. The trees themselves may represent the kingly and priestly offices in Israel."[72]

What this means is that the **two** are **anointed** with God the Holy Spirit, empowered for the tasks of rebuilding the Temple and for leadership. That the **golden oil** represents the Holy Spirit is clear from the facts that (1) Joshua and Zerubbabel are the **branches** that supply the **golden oil** that fuels the lamps, and (2) in verse 6, we are told that the empowering of Joshua and Zerubbabel is by the Spirit of God. That the **oil** flows

[71] Eugene H. Merrill, *An Exegetical Commentary - Haggai, Zechariah, Malachi*, 140.
[72] David Guzik, *Zechariah*, Zec 4:11–14.

from the **trees** to the candlestick indicates that Joshua and Zerubbabel are channels for God the Holy Spirit to work through to serve and lead the nation of Judah. While there is nothing God cannot do without these two men, He chooses to work through their faithfulness and empowers their service.

We note also that they **stand by the Lord of the whole earth**. The term **Lord** is not the familiar Yahweh so frequently used by the prophet to refer to the "LORD of hosts," but *adon*, meaning sovereign or master. This is a Messianic reference expressing the coming Messiah's authority that we see exercised especially in the first and eighth night visions and then in Zechariah 14. (cf. Hebrews 1:2: "Hath in these last days spoken unto us by his Son, whom he hath appointed heir of all things..."). As will become even more evident in Zechariah 6, the **two anointed ones** working in unity to serve and lead the nation points forward to the priest-king Jesus, who will be **the Lord of the whole earth**. Reference will be made again to the **Lord of the whole earth** in Zechariah 6:5, who appears there to have the same role as the angel of the LORD in the first night vision and is none other than the preincarnate Christ. God exercises His sovereignty over the **whole earth** in these night visions through the promised Messiah, the coming priest-king. Hartman keenly observes: "In these portrayals we find instruction about the work of the Messiah, for this is exactly what is taught in Hebrews 9:24 about Jesus. He, as our High Priest, is at this very moment interceding in the presence of God on behalf of believers. This same Jesus is also Israel's coming King. These two offices converge in one person—the Messiah."[73]

Closing

One of the most common misconceptions among Christians is that we become Christians by faith but then mature in our walk by works. The Christian walk is viewed as a list of do's and do not's. Yet the apostle Paul in the New Testament

---

[73] Fred H. Hartman, *Zechariah: Israel's Messenger of the Messiah's Triumph*, Zec 4.

rejects that. He asks the Galatians who were succumbing to this heresy, "This only would I learn of you, Received ye the Spirit by the works of the law, or by the hearing of faith?" (Galatians 3:2) He then explains, "Are ye so foolish? Having begun in the Spirit, are ye now made perfect by the flesh?" (Galatians 3:3) We are justified by the grace of God through faith, and we are sanctified through faith as well. Those who think of the Christian walk as a to-do list may ask, if there is no to-do list, then how do we live? Paul says, "Walk in the Spirit, and ye shall not fulfil the lust of the flesh." (Galatians 5:16) What Zechariah sees in the fifth night vision is a beautiful picture on what Paul describes. As Christians, our growth in the Lord and service as disciples is not a list, but a life that is grace enabled by the Spirit of God. There is no other way. We should all commit to memory these words: "Not by might, nor by power, but by my spirit, saith the LORD of hosts."

Application Points

- **MAIN PRINCIPLE:** Zerubbabel the governor and Joshua the high priest are grace enabled by the Spirit of God for their leadership roles and Zerubbabel will lead the people to complete the construction of the Temple.

- Service to God is not based on our power and might, but the enablement provided by the Holy Spirit.

Discussion Questions

1. What are the implications for your Christian walk of God's words, "not by might, not by power, but by my spirit"?

2. In verse 7, as the cornerstone for the new Temple is finished, the people say, "grace, grace unto it." How can you apply this to your personal ministry or the ministry of your local church?

3. How have you experienced in your life the ministry principle that God does what we cannot do but expects us to do what we can do?

4. Why do you think the Holy Spirit is described as the seven eyes of the Lord, "which run to and fro through the whole earth"?

Chapter 7

Righteousness

Presidential slogans during election season are telling not just for what they say but what they never say. Some of them are not surprising, like Abraham Lincoln's 1864 slogan, "Don't swap horses in the middle of the stream." William McKinley's 1896 slogan was the maxim "good money never made times hard." In 1920, following our nation's involvement in World War I, William Harding used the slogan, "return to normalcy." Some slogans are silly, like Calvin Coolidge's 1924 slogan, "keep cool with Coolidge." Others are hopeful, like Dwight Eisenhower's 1956 slogan "peace and prosperity," and Richard Nixon's 1960 slogan "for the future." Jimmy Carter's 1976 slogan was "a leader, for a change." And Ronald Reagan's very famous slogan in 1984 was, "it's morning again in America." George Bush (Sr.) used in 1988 the somewhat unusual "kinder, gentler nation." And Bill Clinton used the slogan in 1992, "putting people first." In 2000, one of George W. Bush's memorable slogans was "leave no child behind." Barack Obama in 2008 used the simple, "hope" or "hope and change." Most recently, Donald Trump relied on the slogan, "make America great again."

When we read in the Bible about the leadership of the coming Messiah, we understand that there will be no campaigning, no election, and thus no need for pithy slogans. The Son of God, Jesus Christ, will be king of the world. Yet one word that will aptly describe His reign is a word unheard of in the various political slogans of the past presidential candidates. That word is "righteousness." No presidential candidate would ever run with the slogan, "righteousness," and if they did the American people would soundly reject it. But we read in Hebrews 1:8 of Jesus' reign during His Kingdom: "But unto the Son he saith, Thy throne, O God, is for ever and ever: a scepter of **righteousness** is the scepter of thy kingdom." The sixth and seventh night visions that comprise Zechariah 5 are all about the righteousness that will prevail during Christ's Millennial Kingdom. Righteousness will prevail because God's standards will be strictly enforced and wickedness will be banished to its source. The prosperity that the presidential candidates promised through economic and social legislation, the king of kings will actually deliver through a pervasive global righteousness. And this matters now, as our Lord said: "Blessed are they which do hunger and thirst after righteousness: for they shall be filled." (Matthew 5:6)

Scripture and Comments

In this chapter, Zechariah sets forth his sixth and seventh night visions (recall that there are eight total that he sees in a single evening). In these visions, God's standard of righteousness, represented by two of the Ten Commandments, is enforced against those that would defy it, and wickedness is removed from Israel. Certainly Zechariah's audience could see an immediate application. That God "returned to Jerusalem with mercies" and promises His "house shall be built in it" (Zechariah 1:16) concerns both physical and spiritual restoration. But in Zechariah's day, wickedness is not eliminated from Israel. Rather, it will be the coming Messiah, of whom the high priest Joshua is a type, that "will remove the iniquity of that land in one day." (Zechariah 3:9) These two visions, as with the other six visions, are forward looking to Messiah and the Messianic Age.

SIXTH NIGHT VISION

> **Zechariah 5:1** Then I turned, and lifted up mine eyes, and looked, and behold a flying roll.
> **2** And he said unto me, What seest thou? And I answered, I see a flying roll; the length thereof is twenty cubits, and the breadth thereof ten cubits.

Within the chiastic structure of the eight night visions, the sixth vision strongly relates to the third vision (2:1-5) where Jerusalem is measured for its future blessings. Eugene Merrill calls them "a matching pair."[74] The oracle that follows the third vision explains that Messiah is coming and "will dwell in the midst" of Jerusalem (2:10), and that at that time "many nations shall be joined to the LORD, and shall be [Messiah's] people" (2:11). It should not be surprising to us that when Messiah physically dwells among his people and reigns from the Holy City that God's righteous standards will be enforced. And that is exactly what the sixth night vision shows us.

Typical of the beginning of the prior night visions, Zechariah **lifted up** his **eyes and looked** as the vision unfolds before him (Zechariah 1:18, 2:1, 5:1, 5:5, 6:1). He sees a **flying roll** or scroll. Roger Ellsworth describes the scene in ominous terms: "This scroll is also described as 'flying', like a giant bird of prey ready

---

[74] Eugene H. Merrill, *An Exegetical Commentary - Haggai, Zechariah, Malachi*, 147.

to swoop down on the people."[75] But as we will see, his description is fitting. The Hebrew *megillah* is literally a **roll** because the writings were done on sheets of papyrus or animal skins and attached in long rolls. Modern Jewish synagogues still read from handwritten Torah scrolls today. We are to understand that the scroll completely unrolled and open is moving through the air like a billboard for all to see.

We next read, **and he said unto** Zechariah. The pronoun **he** is a carryover from the prior chapter and refers to the interpreting angel. The angel asks Zechariah, **What seest thou?** Zechariah responds to the angel, **I see a flying roll** or scroll. He also reports the dimensions of the open scroll, **the length thereof is twenty cubits, and the breadth thereof ten cubits.** There is debate about the length of a cubit, but many scholars take it to be about 18 inches or 1.5 feet. If this is correct, the scroll measures about 30 feet long and 15 feet wide. Obviously, this is much larger than an ordinary scroll. A typical scroll "seldom exceeded 8–12 inches, and the length would rarely be more than 25–30 feet."[76] Moreover, its width is out of proportion to its length. The size emphasizes that the message is readily seen; God's standards are not hidden. These dimensions match those of the Holy Place in the Tabernacle (Exodus 26:15-25) and the Porch of Solomon's Temple (1 Kings 6:3), and on this basis some find a common symbolism. The text itself does not make these connections so we should be very cautious about such conclusions.

> **3** Then said he unto me, This is the curse that goeth forth over the face of the whole earth: for every one that stealeth shall be cut off as on this side according to it; and every one that sweareth shall be cut off as on that side according to it. **4** I will bring it forth, saith the LORD of hosts, and it shall enter into the

[75] Roger Ellsworth, *Opening Up Zechariah*, 48.
[76] Eugene H. Merrill, *An Exegetical Commentary - Haggai, Zechariah, Malachi*, 148.

house of the thief, and into the house of him that sweareth falsely by my name: and it shall remain in the midst of his house, and shall consume it with the timber thereof and the stones thereof.

As with some of the prior visions, the angel explains the meaning of the vision. Specifically, **he said unto** Zechariah, **This is the curse that goeth forth over the face of the whole earth.** The word **curse** refers to the covenant penalties for violation of the Mosaic Covenant between God and Israel. (see, e.g., Deuteronomy 29:12, 14, 20-21) The term is Strong No. 423 in Strong's Hebrew dictionary, which defines it as "curse, cursing, execration, oath, swearing." The word is often translated as an oath, **curse**, or swearing. (see Deuteronomy 11:26-28) Of course, scrolls are for writing on, which means the specific **curse** refers to the penalty for violation of what is written on the large scroll. That it goes over the **whole earth** indicates that what is happening will be global in scope and not limited to Israel. This further confirms the connection to the third vision (and its accompanying oracle), which speaks of Messiah's global reign.

In this context, the **curse** or oath is God's enforcement of His standards written on both sides of the scroll against a people that characteristically defy it. Indeed, these are the standards of the Law, which apply to Israel in Zechariah's time. The scroll only lists two of the Ten Commandments, but they are representative of all the Ten Commandments of Exodus 20: (1) the command against stealing (**for every one that stealeth shall be cut off as on this side according to it**); and (2) the command against swearing falsely (**and every one that sweareth shall be cut off as on that side according to it**). The first is representative of God's standard that governs His people's relationship to other people, and the second is representative of the standard applicable to their relationship to Him. As Guzik comments: "The two sins, one from each side of the tablets of the Ten Commandments, represent all of Israel's sin. God will curse the people who commit these sins and their house."[77] The text here says the evildoer will be **cut off** or banished or purged from the community. But when this occurs in the Millennium, to be **cut off** has a finality to it, as the next verse confirms.

God will not only set the standard, but enforce it worldwide to completion. The LORD of hosts...**will bring it forth** and pursue the evildoer, so that His standard shall **enter into the house of the thief, and into the house of him that sweareth falsely by** God's **name**. No one will be able to avoid the enforcement of God's standard. God's Word will **remain in the midst of** the **house** of the evildoer until its purpose is fulfilled and consume **it with the timber thereof and the stones thereof**. The vision pictures the scroll entering a house and consuming it like a fire, taking both the timbers and the stones. But the **house** is almost certainly a metaphor for the person, and the consuming fire is God's wrath upon them. As Loken comments, "The scroll is sent by Yahweh to enter the house of all who break the law. The scroll will 'spend the night' (i.e., remain until its intended mission is accomplished) at that house and destroy it. The metaphor used here is probably a reference to an individual's life. In other words, those who violate the Lord's commands will be struck down by God."[78] God's standard cannot be rejected, for those that do so will surely be consumed. The **thief** and the person that **sweareth falsely by** God's **name** have nowhere to run because God is a consuming fire. (Deuteronomy 4:24)

This standard is a refining standard, and Zechariah's audience is a refined remnant (from their 70 years of captivity under Babylonian domination) who must remain refined. And so no doubt Zechariah's audience could see an immediate application

[77] David Guzik, *Zechariah*, Zec 5:3–4.
[78] Israel P. Loken, *The Old Testament Prophetic Books: An Introduction*, 372-373.

of this vision. But what this vision pictures is a cleansing of the earth from sin. And the question becomes, when will this happen? As previously pointed out in these notes, the entire set of night visions is organized in a chiasm. The third and sixth visions correspond. The third vision sees a prosperous Jerusalem in the Messianic Age when the scattered Jewish people have returned home, their enemies are defeated, Jesus Christ rules and reigns from the Holy City, and "many nations shall be joined to the LORD in that day, and shall be my people." (Zechariah 2:11) The message in the sixth vision is that a cleansing according to God's standards of righteousness will occur, presumably just before the Messianic Age. This cleansing is addressed further in Zechariah 13 and occurs "in that day" or in the day of the LORD. The result will be a refined remnant of Jewish and Gentile peoples who will inhabit the Kingdom. This is necessary because the Messianic Kingdom will be characterized by holiness. (Zechariah 14:20-21)

We should question how it is that everyone will not be consumed by the curse. Those caught by the **curse** are identified only with their sins. But as Zechariah will expound later in the book, "in that day there shall be a fountain opened to the house of David and to the inhabitants of Jerusalem for sin and for uncleanness." (Zechariah 13:1) That fountain is opened to the world when the Son of God in the first century dies on a Roman cross. In the day of the Lord, the fountain will be experientially realized in a time of revival among the Jewish people. As Baron rightly says, "There is only one way by which we can escape the curse of a broken law, and that is, instead of being 'cleansed away' *with* our sins by God's wrath into perdition, to be cleansed *from* our sins in that fountain which God has opened in the pierced side of Messiah for sin and uncleanness, and which makes the *vilest* 'whiter than snow.'"[79]

---

[79] David Baron, *Zechariah: A Commentary On His Visions And Prophecies*, 150-151.

SEVENTH NIGHT VISION

5 Then the angel that talked with me went forth, and said unto me, Lift up now thine eyes, and see what is this that goeth forth. **6** And I said, What is it? And he said, This is an ephah that goeth forth. He said moreover, This is their resemblance through all the earth. **7** And, behold, there was lifted up a talent of lead: and this is a woman that sitteth in the midst of the ephah. **8** And he said, This is wickedness. And he cast it into the midst of the ephah; and he cast the weight of lead upon the mouth thereof.

Once again, we are well to keep in mind the chiastic structure of the eight night visions. This seventh vision strongly relates to the second vision (1:18-21), the vision of the four horns and four carpenters or artisans. We read there that "the horns...have scattered Judah" and "these [carpenters] come to fray them, to cast out the horns of the Gentiles, which lifted up their horn over the land of Judah to scatter it." (Zechariah 1:21) But expelling physical enemies is not enough to implement a Kingdom characterized by righteousness. The spiritual enemies must also be expelled.

Zechariah again references the **angel that talked with me** (see note on 5:2), a reference to the interpreting **angel** that accompanies and assists Zechariah throughout the visions. This begins the seventh of the eight night visions. Zechariah is told **to lift up now thine eyes** to **see what is this that goeth forth**. Zechariah's immediate response is **What is it?** As before, Zechariah seeks understanding that only comes through God's revelation. What he sees, as reported by the **angel**, is **an ephah that goeth forth**. An **ephah** is a measurement, usually of grain but it can measure liquids or solids. An **ephah** is, according to the NET translation notes, "about a bushel (five gallons or just under twenty liters)." Here the term **ephah** is used as metonymy for the measuring container, in essence, a basket or bucket used to measure out an **ephah**. It was the largest dry measure used by the Jews, indicative of the volume of what it must contain in this vision.[80]

This is no ordinary **ephah**, however, for it **goeth forth**. Like the scroll that flies, this **ephah** is in motion. The **angel** further says, in explanation of the **ephah**, that it is **their resemblance through all the earth**. The term translated **resemblance** is normally translated in terms of eyes or sight. The **ephah** contains what God sees as He looks at the world. We will see that this is the iniquity of the world, which connects this vision to the flying scroll vision earlier in the chapter. The **ephah** has on it a **talent of lead**. The Hebrew term translated **talent** can indicate a measurement of weight (about 70 pounds), as well as a plain or flat surface or even a loaf of bread. Here, it indicates a lid covering the **ephah**. The cover is made of lead, which is heavy and implies that what is in the **ephah** should be contained there and not released. When the cover is lifted, Zechariah sees **a woman that sitteth in the midst of the ephah**.

We need not guess at what the **woman** in the **ephah** represents. For the **angel** tells Zechariah that she is **wickedness** or iniquity. The angel **cast** her **into the midst of the ephah**, suggesting she would escape if not trapped, and then **he cast the weight of lead upon the mouth thereof**, that is, he slams the lid shut on her. Merrill is correct in his observation here: "That the woman is dangerous is most apparent, for no sooner has the interpreting messenger pronounced her name than he slams the heavy cover down upon the ephah to be certain that she cannot escape."[81] This is a picture of the putting away of iniquity, which intertwines with the vision of the flying scroll where the scroll symbolizes God's moral standard enforced.

[80] F. Duane Lindsey, "Zechariah," in *The Bible Knowledge Commentary: An Exposition of the Scriptures*, 1556.

[81] Eugene H. Merrill, *An Exegetical Commentary - Haggai, Zechariah, Malachi*, 156.

9 Then lifted I up mine eyes, and looked, and, behold, there came out two women, and the wind was in their wings; for they had wings like the wings of a stork: and they lifted up the ephah between the earth and the heaven. 10 Then said I to the angel that talked with me, Whither do these bear the ephah? 11 And he said unto me, To build it an house in the land of Shinar: and it shall be established, and set there upon her own base.

Zechariah now sees **two women** with **wings** that fly to the ephah and carry it away. As Lindsey comments, "Not only must the wicked in Israel be punished (the vision of the flying scroll, vv. 1–4) but also wickedness itself must be removed from the land."[82] Their wings are **like the wings of a stork**, which under the Law was an unclean bird (Leviticus 11:13-20), a fitting image for those that would carry away wickedness, but it may simply be that they have stork-like wings because those wings are powerful and able to carry this heavy weight far away. Whereas in the past God exiled his people because of their **wickedness**, in this future day God will purify the people and exile their **wickedness**.

There is nothing indicating that these **two women** are angels, although that is sometimes assumed. If they are angels, they would be the only angels in the Bible that are indisputably feminine in appearance and the only ones described as having stork-like **wings**. Probably, people have given too much significance to the **two women** when the focus of the vision is the **ephah**, the **talent**, and the woman within that personifies **wickedness**. The word **wickedness** is feminine in Hebrew, and so it is not surprising that it is personified by a female. The **ephah** is **lifted up... between the earth and the heaven**, that is, into the sky, and flown into exile.

---

[82] F. Duane Lindsey, "Zechariah," in *The Bible Knowledge Commentary: An Exposition of the Scriptures*, 1557.

Zechariah responds to what he sees with an important question to **the angel that talked with me**, his interpreting angel. The question is **wither do these bear the ephah?** He wants to know the destination for the **wickedness** in the **ephah**. The **angel** responds that they will **build it an house in the land of Shinar: and it shall be established, and set there upon her own** base. **Shinar** is another term for the ancient region of Babylonia. (see Genesis 11:2, Daniel 1:2) As Merrill elaborates: "Shinar is an ancient name for Sumer and Akkad, the district in which the earliest of cities such as Babel, Erech, Accad, and Calneh were located (Gen. 10:10). Babel, of course, is the same as Babylon, 'the gate of the gods' (Akk. bābu+ ilāni, or bābilāni). Erech is the Sumerian city Uruk (modern Warka), near the Persian Gulf. Accad (or Akkad) is Agade, the capital of the Old Akkadian empire of Sargon. Calneh (if not Calah) cannot be identified with certainty, for it can hardly be the same as the city by that name just north of Aleppo in Syria."[83]

The **wickedness** is not only being taken to **Shinar**, but it will **be established** there. The **woman** in the **ephah** will dwell in a **house** or temple built in **Shinar**. We must remember that the much repeated sin of Israel is idolatry. And indeed, only during the future Millennium will idolatry finally be removed from the land forever. (Zechariah 13:2) Thus, it is not surprising that when **wickedness** is exiled to Babylonia, it will have a temple to dwell in, and will be perched upon a pedestal or **base** as most idols are. She will be given a place of honor in the eyes of the people there where she can be worshiped. Lindsey summarizes this well:

> Israel's corporate sin, associated with idolatry, will be removed from her land. The phrases in Zechariah 5:11—**to build a house for it**, and **be set there in its place** (i.e., on an idol pedestal)— suggest that the ephah of wickedness will be erected in a temple as an idol. Such idols of

[83] Eugene H. Merrill, *An Exegetical Commentary - Haggai, Zechariah, Malachi*, 157.

Babylon were powerlessness personified, as
indicated in Isaiah's many idol satires (Isa. 44:9–
20; 46:1–2; etc.). Returning the wickedness of
idolatry to its place of origin in Babylon
apparently will set the stage for final judgment
on Babylon (Rev. 17–18). Its removal from Israel
will prepare the way for Christ's second coming
and millennial kingdom (Rev. 19–20).[84]

This vision, like so many of the passages in Zechariah, has
application in his present day but primarily looks to the future.
Babylon is a real place, but throughout Scripture is symbolic of
everything opposed to God. This began with the tower of
Babel (i.e. Tower of Babylon) back in Genesis 11:9, and
continues through the Bible until the consummation of all
things. As Merrill recounts: "It was at Babylon, in the land of
Shinar, that the rebel human race erected a great ziggurat, the
purpose of which was to frustrate God's mandate to 'be
fruitful, multiply, and fill the earth' (Gen. 1:28; 9:1). The men of
Babylon had said, 'Let us make a name for ourselves, lest we be
scattered abroad upon the surface of the whole earth' (Gen.
11:4). From that time Babylon became synonymous with
arrogant human independence, the very fountainhead of
antitheocratic social, political, and religious ideology."[85] In
Revelation 17 and 18, we again see the images of a woman
representing sinfulness and the city of Babylon united within
the same vision. Zechariah's vision looks forward to the future
just prior to the implementation of the Messianic Kingdom, in
which sin is removed and wickedness exiled to Babylon for
destruction so that holiness will characterize Messiah's
Kingdom. God's people in Zechariah's day are to be motivated
to a spiritual renewal that will accompany the rebuilding of the
Temple where they will worship a holy God.

---

[84] F. Duane Lindsey, "Zechariah," in *The Bible Knowledge Commentary: An Exposition of the Scriptures*, 1557.

[85] Eugene H. Merrill, *An Exegetical Commentary - Haggai, Zechariah, Malachi*, 157.

Closing

It is easy to read something profound in the Bible and fly right by it without taking the time to meditate on the implications of what we have read. The two visions in Zechariah 5 are that type of profound truth where we might miss the implications. Even as I write these words, the world is aflame with violence. This has been the case since the "Bible days." But the misplaced optimism of humanist philosophies like Darwinism have fallen in on our heads, as the last 150 years of wars, holocausts and terrorism proves. To the violence we must add political corruption, religious persecution, the "word police" culture that abhors free speech and individuality, and the "no boundaries" sexuality that proliferated a slave trade and at this moment is making the inevitable move toward spinning pedophilia as an acceptable lifestyle choice rather than a violent exploitation of children. If humanity has evolved in any sense, it is only in our insatiable appetite for unrighteousness while calling it righteousness as if labels change substance.

In contrast, Jesus is soon going to take over the world and implement a Holy Kingdom. He is not going to run for election or ask permission. Nor is He going to trade in the currency of labels and elevate form over substance. Holy righteousness will flourish and all the rebellious expressions of unrighteousness that plague our world now will be eradicated. God's Word will be the standard and not moral relativism. The violence, riots, school shootings, racism, abortions, slave trade, sexualization of children, corruption, poverty, wars, all of it, will be gone. Many people do not want this because they do not want to submit to the king. As the parable goes, "We will not have this man to reign over us." (Luke 19:14) But the people of God should look forward with anticipation to the reign of the righteous king and do our best to be a voice and a living testimony for that righteousness now.

Application Points

- **MAIN PRINCIPLE:** In the Messianic Kingdom, righteousness will flourish and wickedness will be exiled.

- We must see sin from God's perspective and be motivated to do right. This is only possible by the enabling power of the Holy Spirit. (Zechariah 4:6)

Discussion Questions

1. What are some ways in which the culture where you live is unrighteous?

2. If the flying scroll were to tarry in your life right now consuming all unrighteousness, what parts of your thinking, speech, and actions (habits) would be consumed?

3. List some of the biggest changes you would expect to see when Jesus reigns in His Kingdom.

4. Why would anyone resist Jesus' Kingdom?

5. When you think of wickedness being stuffed into the basket and exiled to Babylon, in practical terms how is life thereafter different?

6. How should God's promise of a future Messianic Kingdom characterized by righteousness impact what you do today? (what you read, listen to, think about, the entertainment you enjoy, priorities)

Chapter 8

The Priest-King Messiah

Early in the history of the Bible, it introduces a man of faith, who would also be called a friend of God. God takes a man named Abram, later named Abraham, and instructs him to leave his homeland in Ur of the Chaldees to go to another "land that I will shew thee." (Genesis 12:1) God makes grand promises to this man Abraham, to provide him land and "make of thee a great nation...and make thy name great." (Genesis 12:2) Abraham, in turn, will "be a blessing" to the world because "in thee shall all families of the earth be blessed." (Genesis 12:2-3) As God's progressive revelation unfolds, we learn that the centerpiece of all these promises is Jesus Christ. And though not stated in Genesis, Abraham knew this. As Jesus says, "Your father Abraham rejoiced to see my day: and he saw it, and was glad." (John 8:56) We should not be at all surprised that Jesus Christ is the primary subject matter of the forward looking book of Zechariah.

One other promise to Abraham was that God "will bless them that bless thee, and curse him that curseth thee." (Genesis 12:3) The history of Israel is largely a story of adversity from foreign nations, and that remains true today. We need to know that Jesus Christ is also at the center of God's promise to Abraham to deal with the enemies of Israel. As the long evening of night visions comes to a close with the eighth and final vision, we find Jesus Christ, variously referred to in Zechariah as the angel of the LORD, servant, and Branch, presented as the Lord of the whole earth. And when He returns, an event future from the time in which we live, the Lord of the whole earth will dispense with Israel's enemies and take His place as the priest-king of the world.

Scripture and Comments

We now reach the final night vision. As Duane Lindsey writes, "This eighth vision concludes the messages which Zechariah saw in one night and which outline the future history of the nation Israel."[86] As I pointed out in the notes to the first vision, there is a chiastic structure to the eight night visions, and few expositors dispute that the first and eighth visions are closely related. Indeed, Eugene Merrill concludes: "If ever a case could be made for matching complementary visions throughout the unfolding of the night visions structure in Zechariah, it can be made here. This last of the eight shares so much in common with the first that the two, at least, must be viewed as book ends enveloping the whole series."[87] The commonalities include imagery of different colored horses, the role of the interpreting angel, Zechariah's identical requests for an interpretation (1:9 and 6:4), the emphasis on "four" and walking "to and fro through the earth" to express God's sovereignty, the idea of peace or rest (on the earth in the first vision and for God in the

---

86 F. Duane Lindsey, "Zechariah," in *The Bible Knowledge Commentary: An Exposition of the Scriptures*, 1557.

87 Eugene H. Merrill, *An Exegetical Commentary - Haggai, Zechariah, Malachi*, 161.

eighth), and the global scope of the visions. Of course, there are differences. Most notably the eighth vision involves chariots and the first did not. But as we will see, the present vision builds upon and reacts to the first. Whereas the first involves horses and riders (apparent angelic beings) sent to do reconnaissance throughout the earth, now God's forces are sent to execute judgment. Austel rightly observes: "In the first vision the nations live in undisturbed quietness and God is disturbed and angry with them. In this vision the nations are judged and the Spirit of God is satisfied and at rest because his purpose has been accomplished."[88] The two visions unquestionably form bookends in the series of eight visions.

Despite all the similarities between the first and eighth visions, the latter is more heavily debated, so much so that one commentator claims that "[t]he last of Zechariah's eight visions is also the most difficult to understand."[89] But I think the overall message of the eighth vision is clear even if some details may be debated. As always, the best approach is to look for the keys within the text of Zechariah that answer the questions raised by what the prophet sees.

EIGHTH NIGHT VISION

Zechariah 6:1 And I turned, and lifted up mine eyes, and looked, and, behold, there came four chariots out from between two mountains; and the mountains *were* mountains of brass.

As with many of the other night visions, this one begins as the prophet **turned, and lifted up** his **eyes, and looked.** Explaining what he sees in this last glorious vision of that long evening, Zechariah says, **behold, there came four chariots out from**

---

[88] Hermann J. Austel, "Zechariah," in *Evangelical Commentary on the Bible*, vol. 3, Baker Reference Library (Grand Rapids, MI: Baker Book House, 1995), 693–694.

[89] Roger Ellsworth, *Opening Up Zechariah*, 52.

between two mountains; and the mountains were of brass.
There are **four chariots**, which parallels the four horses of the
first vision. That there are **four chariots** emphasizes the global
extent of God's power and sovereignty as His agents reach all
four directions of the earth to carry out His purposes. (see
Zechariah 1:18, 20; 2:6) But it is significant that there are no
chariots in the first vision. This indicates a change of purpose
as **chariots** were in the ancient world a standard "war machine,
not just a mode of transportation (cf. Ex. 14:25; Josh. 11:6; Judg.
4:15; 1 Sam. 8:11; 1 Kings 12:18; 22:35)."[90] Also, other passages
view God utilizing **chariots** for His purposes. (e.g., Isaiah
66:15-16; Psalm 68:17) The purpose of these **chariots** will
become clear as the vision continues.

Zechariah sees **two mountains** and the **four chariots** come **out
from between** the **two mountains**, which implies they are
pulled by horses. That point is confirmed in the next verse.
The prophet adds that the **two mountains** are **of brass**. The
word **brass** (an alloy of copper and zinc) should be translated
bronze (an alloy of copper and tin). According to historians and
archaeologists, bronze was used as early as 3500 B.C. by the
Sumerians in the Tigris-Euphrates Valley, and spread from
there to Persia and later Egypt and China by 2000 B.C. I agree
with Lindsey that bronze "seems to symbolize righteous divine
judgment against sin (cf. Rev. 1:15; 2:18)."[91] In the Revelation,
Jesus' feet are described as refined bronze as He is prepared to
bring divine judgment. This alloy is also heavily associated with
the construction of the tabernacle, which may suggest holiness
or righteousness. (e.g., Exodus 25:3, 26:11, 26:37, 27:2) Certainly,
two mountains of bronze also present an immovable strength.

Most commentators view the **two mountains** as real mountains
in Jerusalem because the prophet is there as he ministers and
because in the subsequent verses the **chariots** move from the

---

[90] Eugene H. Merrill, *An Exegetical Commentary - Haggai, Zechariah, Malachi,* 162.
[91] F. Duane Lindsey, "Zechariah," in *The Bible Knowledge Commentary: An Exposition of the Scriptures,* 1557.

mountains to the north and south to earthly destinations. Specifically, most take the **mountains** to be Mount Zion and the Mount of Olives. The Kidron Valley runs between these two mountains. But another, and in my view, more satisfactory solution is that these are the two mountains formed from the Mount of Olives in Zechariah 14:4.[92] In Zechariah 14, a "very great valley" is formed by the splitting of the Mount of Olives, and the people "flee to the valley of the mountains" for protection. (Zechariah 14:5) It is to be noted that Jesus provides His famous Olivet Discourse from this same mountain, in which He teaches that during the tribulation (part of the day of the LORD) the Jewish people must "flee into the mountains." (Matthew 24:16) These **mountains** will provide the Jewish remnant an escape from enemy invaders. It is also likely that they will be pursued and the pursuers destroyed in this same valley. (e.g., Joel 3:2, 12) As Loken explains: "The Mount of Olives will split in two, making a large valley through which the faithful remnant will flee. The Lord will then enter into judgment with the nations at the entrance to that valley, named by Joel as the 'Valley of Jehoshaphat' (Joel 3:2), i.e., the 'Valley Where Yahweh Judges.'"[93]

> **2** In the first chariot *were* red horses; and in the second chariot black horses; **3** And in the third chariot white horses; and in the fourth chariot grisled and bay horses.

Continuing to describe the four chariots he sees in this final vision, Zechariah describes that **in the first chariot were red horses**, meaning **the first chariot** is pulled by **red horses**. Similarly, **the second chariot** is pulled by **black horses, the third chariot** by **white horses**, and **the fourth chariot** by **grisled and bay horses**. The word **grisled** indicates dappled or spotted. The word **bay** means "strong" and is taken by the KJV translators as strong in color; in that sense, **bay** means a strong reddish-

---

[92] Israel P. Loken, *The Old Testament Prophetic Books: An Introduction*, 373.
[93] *Ibid.*, 382.

brown horse with black at certain places like the mane and tail. Some newer translations take the word "strong" as a descriptor of all of the horses, which as shown below is probably correct. The translation would then read, "and in the fourth chariot grisled horses, all of them strong" horses or steeds.

Note that in Zechariah's first vision, there were two **red horses**, one speckled and one **white**, which does not exactly match the colors here. Many expositors assign meanings to the colors in both visions and these seem for the most part contrived. There is no more basis here in chapter six, for example, to say that the **white horses** represent righteousness than to say they represent victory. Proper Bible hermeneutics must build such meanings first from the text at hand and then potentially from other clear Bible texts. And while there is some support for the symbolism of the colors of the horses in Revelation 6 evident in that text, there is none here. This does not mean, however, that there is no significance to the colors. Rather, my point is that the significance is not in the individual colors. The emphasis throughout the vision is on God's global sovereignty, as Ellsworth observes:

> Zechariah sees four chariots. The number four represents the points of the compass. These four chariots are also called the 'four winds [or spirits] of heaven' (v. 5). What part of the earth is exempt from the wind? It is also significant that the Lord is called 'the Lord of all the earth' (v. 5). Furthermore, we are told that the horses 'walked to and fro throughout the earth' (v. 7).

> All these elements remind us that no part of this world and no person in it falls beyond the scope of God's providence. Many think they are beyond the reach of God, but no one is![94]

---

[94] Roger Ellsworth, *Opening Up Zechariah*, 53.

There are four chariots that are the "four spirits of the heavens" (6:5) and, to the point here, there are **horses** of four colors. In my view, then, it is not the individual colors but the fact there are four colors that reinforces the global emphasis of the vision. (see Isaiah 11:12; Revelation 7:1)

> **4** Then I answered and said unto the angel that talked with me, What *are* these, my lord? **5** And the angel answered and said unto me, These *are* the four spirits of the heavens, which go forth from standing before the Lord of all the earth. **6** The black horses which *are* therein go forth into the north country; and the white go forth after them; and the grisled go forth toward the south country.

As he did in the first vision (1:9), the prophet **answered and said unto the angel that talked with me**, that is, the familiar interpreting **angel** (see Zechariah 1:9, 13; 2:3; 4:1, 4, 5; 5:5, 10; 6:4). His questions is, **What are these, my lord?** The **angel** responds that **these are the four spirits of the heavens, which go forth from standing before the Lord of all the earth**. While Zechariah repeatedly refers to "LORD" (Yahweh), here he uses **Lord** (adon), which emphasizes sovereignty and control. The same expression occurs in Zechariah 4:14 ("These are the two anointed ones, that stand by the Lord of the whole earth."), a verse that presents Joshua and Zerubbabel as a type for the coming priest-king. The **Lord of all the earth** in this vision parallels the role of the "angel of the LORD" (1:11) in the first night vision, and as I noted there, he is none other than the pre-incarnate Christ, the promised Messiah. In both visions, he sends out the angelic forces across the planet. We should not be surprised that it is our Lord Jesus Christ in view in this eighth vision, as in the first vision, as the moving agent of God's sovereignty over the planet. Jesus is, after all, "heir of all things." (Hebrews 1:2) He is the coming king of the world (Zechariah 14:9, "king over all the earth") that will finish Israel's enemies in the climactic end-times battle that is prominent in Zechariah 14.

Note also that what Zechariah sees represents **the four spirits of the heavens**. The word **spirits** is in Zechariah 2:6 translated as the "four **winds** of the heaven." Commentators disagree whether these refer to angels or are merely an expression of God's force of action. Certainly in other places the term **spirits** is used explicitly of angels. (see Psalm 104:4; Hebrews 1:14) While in this vision no chariot drivers are expressly mentioned, the first vision references riders and the riders provide a verbal report to the angel of the Lord. (Zechariah 1:11) This supports the view that angelic beings are in view in the first vision, and because of the close relationship of the first and eighth visions it seems likely that the same is true here.

Note also **the four spirits** are **standing** at attention awaiting their instructions, which implies there are chariot drivers that are angelic beings. Moreover, the explanations in both visions are similar. (cf. Zechariah 1:10 ("These are they whom the LORD hath sent to walk to and fro through the earth.")) What is apparent is that the horses are "visual representations of God's angels, who are the agents he uses to carry out his plans and purposes."[95] Again the emphasis on **four** expresses God's authority in all four directions, that is, a global authority. As Lindsey writes, "The **four chariots** with different-colored **horses** speak of the universality of divine judgment which will go in all directions throughout the earth."[96]

The interpreting angel continues his response to the prophet's request for an understanding of the vision, stating that **the black horses which are therein go forth into the north country; and the white** horses **go forth after them.** Similarly, **the grisled** horses **go forth toward the south country.** The generic references to the **north country** and **south country** are global in scope because Gentile invaders must invade from the **north** or **south**. At the time of Zechariah's vision, the immediate

---

[95] *Ibid.*, 55.
[96] F. Duane Lindsey, "Zechariah," in *The Bible Knowledge Commentary: An Exposition of the Scriptures*, 1557.

references were to Babylon in the **north** and Egypt in the **south**. But at that time, the Babylonians were superseded by the Persians, who did not present the same threat to Israel as their predecessors in power. And the Egyptians were also not a threat at that time. Notice that Zechariah is not told that the red horses go **north** or **south**. Also notice that two groups of **horses** go north, and only one to the **south**. This is probably because the Gentile enemy under judgment at the time was the Babylonian empire, which finds further confirmation in verse 8.

> 7 And the bay went forth, and sought to go that they might walk to and fro through the earth: and he said, Get you hence, walk to and fro through the earth. So they walked to and fro through the earth.

Next, we read that **the bay** horses **went forth**. As observed in the notes to verse 3 above, **bay** means strong. In verse 3, the KJV translates "grisled and bay horses" but verse 6 states that "the grisled go forth toward the south country." This confirms that the word **bay** (strong) is intended to describe all of the horses and not just the grisled horses. Thus, verse 7 applies to all the horses. The strong horses or steeds (with their chariots) **went forth, and sought** or asked **that they might walk to and fro through the earth**. The request is made to "the Lord of all the earth" (6:5), and his response is, **Get you hence, walk to and fro through the earth**. This parallels the first vision where, of the horses, "the man that stood among the myrtle trees" (1:10), who is the angel of the LORD (1:11), explained, "these are they whom the LORD hath sent to walk to and fro through the earth" (1:10). The concept of walking **to and fro through the earth** is an expression of God's global dominion. In Job 1:7, Satan uses similar language to express his belief in his own dominion over the earth (a belief God challenges): "And the LORD said unto Satan, Whence comest thou? Then Satan answered the LORD, and said, From going to and fro in the earth, and from walking up and down in it." Similarly, in

Genesis 13:17, God tells Abraham to walk the promised land that God had given him; Abraham's walking over it would establish his ownership and dominion over it. Thus, here, the angels visualized as horse-drawn chariots, are agents of God's sovereignty over the world. As the prophet concludes, **so they walked to and fro through the earth**.

> **8** Then cried he upon me, and spake unto me, saying, Behold, these that go toward the north country have quieted my spirit in the north country.

Note that in verse 7, the Lord of all the earth answers the request of the angelic beings. When Zechariah says, **then cried he upon me**, the prophet is not talking about the interpreting angel, but the One with authority that permits the horse-drawn chariots to walk to and fro over the planet. It is the Lord of all the earth who speaks to Zechariah, **saying, Behold, these that go toward the north country have quieted my spirit** or brought me peace **in the north country**. Because the Babylonians fell to the Persians, the report comforts the angel of the LORD. But this did not all happen at once, as Mark Boda explains:

> This depiction of the punishment of Babylon echoes the historical reality at the outset of Darius's reign. The expectation of the exilic community was that Babylon ultimately would be punished for their cruel treatment of the Jewish community at the demise of their kingdom in the early sixth century B.C. However, the reality was that Babylon was left relatively unscathed by Cyrus's rise to power in 539. Although he deposed the Babylonian emperor Nabonidus and his family and incorporated the former Babylonian kingdom into his own empire, the political structure of Babylon was left largely unscathed by this political change. However, after Babylon's

repeated revolts against the Persians in the transition between Cambyses and Darius, the new emperor Darius would treat the Babylonians severely and finally bring to fulfillment those earlier prophetic hopes.[97]

By implication, if there is victory over the **north country**, the seat of all that is wicked and opposed to Judah, there is victory over all enemies. Whereas in the first night vision it is the Gentile powers that are at rest, it is now God who is at rest. The victory over Babylon already occurred, but remember that in the seventh night vision, the woman Wickedness is sent back to Babylon (Shinar). Thus, while the Babylonian Empire that prospered under King Nebuchadnezzar had fallen, the Babylon that is God's constant enemy has not finally fallen. In the first night vision, the Gentile nations were "at ease" because of their oppression of God's people, and in Zechariah's day that changed temporarily, but this vision looks also to a future complete destruction of God's enemies, and in particular, a victory over wickedness or sin. Merrill articulates the wider scope of the final night vision: "There can be little doubt that Zechariah's vision pertains to his own times, but its eschatological, apocalyptic character means it cannot be limited to that era. The picture here, as throughout the apocalyptic literature, is one of final and universal dominion by YHWH over His creation. How that will take place is a major part of the message of the oracles of Zechariah in chapters 7–14."[98]

THE CROWNING

Prophets were often instructed by God to carry out an act with symbolic meaning, and that is what happens in Zechariah 6.

---

[97] Mark J. Boda, *The Book of Zechariah*, ed. R. K. Harrison and Robert L. Hubbard Jr., The New International Commentary on the Old Testament (Grand Rapids, MI; Cambridge, U.K.: William B. Eerdmans Publishing Company, 2016), 358.

[98] Eugene H. Merrill, *An Exegetical Commentary - Haggai, Zechariah, Malachi*, 168.

As with most of the book of Zechariah, this act looks forward. And specifically, it looks forward to the coming priest-king Messiah. As I previously commented, God does not tell us the future without a practical purpose in the present. He beckons us to look forward and live now. The prophet's audience needs encouragement as they are tasked with rebuilding the Temple, which will be a key part of God's physical and spiritual restoration of Israel. As Ellsworth writes, "The inspiration they needed to complete the temple would be found by seeing the greatness of the coming Saviour."[99]

> **9** And the word of the LORD came unto me, saying, **10** Take of *them of* the captivity, *even* of Heldai, of Tobijah, and of Jedaiah, which are come from Babylon, and come thou the same day, and go into the house of Josiah the son of Zephaniah; **11** Then take silver and gold, and make crowns, and set *them* upon the head of Joshua the son of Josedech, the high priest.

The night visions are complete, but we have a closing message in the form of a symbolic act that builds on the eight night visions as a unit. Zechariah receives **the word of the LORD** and is instructed to **take them of the captivity** or exiles **which are come** back to Israel **from Babylon**. Specifically, God instructs the prophet to **take...of Heldai, of Tobijah, and of Jedaiah**. These individuals are not mentioned elsewhere and so we know nothing more about them than what is presented here. The prophet is instructed to get these three men and **come thou the same day, and go into the house of** a fourth man, **Josiah the son of Zephaniah**. He also is unknown outside of this passage. The task is to **take silver and gold, and make crowns, and set them upon the head of Joshua the son of Josedech, the high priest**. The implication is that **Heldai, Tobijah, and Jedaiah** contribute the **silver and gold**, and **Josiah**

---

[99] Roger Ellsworth, *Opening Up Zechariah*, 58–59.

possibly is skilled in fashioning the **crowns**. The word **crowns** is plural but most take it to refer to a single crown, while some argue there are two crowns, one for **Joshua** and one for Zerubbabel. However, the text gives no indication of crowning Zerubbabel. Also, this term is never used of a priestly crown or mitre and thus likely refers to only a single crown.

The symbolism of a priest-king looks forward to Jesus, who is our High Priest and king (Hebrews 9:11; Revelation 19:16). This passage, along with Psalm 110, provides the strongest Old Testament evidence that Messiah will fulfill the roles of priest and king. Because only a man from the tribe of Judah can be king, and only a man from the tribe of Levi could be a priest under the Mosaic Covenant, what Psalm 110:4 states and the New Testament affirms is that Jesus is a high priest after the order of Melchizedek, and not a Levitical high priest. (see Hebrews 5:1-10, 6:20-7:28) No doubt this symbolic crowning is an encouragement to the people. Ellsworth rightly concludes that "[t]his coronation was designed by God to fan the flames of faith in the hearts of his people."[100]

> **12** And speak unto him, saying, Thus speaketh the LORD of hosts, saying, Behold the man whose name *is* The BRANCH; and he shall grow up out of his place, and he shall build the temple of the LORD.

Zechariah is given the words to speak **unto him**, meaning **unto** Joshua the high priest. The words make it clear that Joshua stands in as a type for the priest-king Messiah. Zechariah is to tell him, **thus speaketh the LORD of hosts, saying, Behold the man whose name is The BRANCH**. The language pulls directly from the night visions as **the man** is introduced in the first vision as the angel of the Lord (1:8-11), and **the BRANCH** is introduced in association with Joshua in the fourth vision (3:8). Just as Joshua will prosper in his ministry and build the

---

[100] *Ibid.*, 59.

earthly Temple (3:7), the One for whom Joshua is a type will prosper in his ministry (**he shall grow up out of his place**) and **he shall build the temple of the** LORD. The term **BRANCH** is unquestionably Messianic as seen in Zechariah 3:8 and elsewhere. (see also Isaiah 4:2, 11:1; Jeremiah 23:5, 33:15)

That **he shall grow up out of his place** indicates he will become a great leader, and provides commentary on the significance of the term **BRANCH**. The Hebrew term (*tzemach*) is elsewhere translated "grew" (Genesis 19:25), "springing" (Psalm 65:10), and "bud" (Isaiah 61:11). The point is that from a humble beginning Messiah will **grow** and spring into his priest-king role, which we see affirmed elsewhere:

> **Jeremiah 23:5** Behold, the days come, saith the LORD, that I will raise unto David a righteous Branch, and a King shall reign and prosper, and shall execute judgment and justice in the earth.

> **Jeremiah 33:15** In those days, and at that time, will I cause the Branch of righteousness to grow up unto David; and he shall execute judgment and righteousness in the land.

Because we know the **Temple** under construction at the time of the night visions is completed under Joshua's leadership, the **Temple** to be built by **the BRANCH** is necessarily a different and future **Temple**. Because Jesus did not **build** a **Temple** during His first advent, He must do so after His second coming. This **Temple** will be constructed during Jesus' millennial reign and is addressed in Ezekiel 40-42. I note here that some spiritualize away this passage and say the **Temple** in view is Jesus' body. (John 2:19) But Jesus did not **build** His body. (Hebrews 10:5) The word **build** is *banah* and is usually translated "made" (Genesis 2:22: God "made he a woman") or build / builded (Genesis 4:17: Cain "builded a city"; Genesis 10:11: "Asshur...builded Nineveh") or for having a child (Genesis 30:3). Set against Joshua's leadership of the people to complete the construction of the **Temple**, the future Messianic **Temple** must also be literal, and as the next verse confirms, it must house Jesus' throne.

> **13** Even he shall build the temple of the LORD; and he shall bear the glory, and shall sit and rule upon his throne; and he shall be a priest upon his throne: and the counsel of peace shall be between them both.

Again the prophet says to Joshua, the Branch (the Messiah, Jesus) **shall build the temple of the LORD**. This is a future millennial **temple** to be constructed during Jesus' second advent. Charles Simeon explains how the present **temple** is a shadow of the one to come: "The material temple was now rebuilding under the auspices of Zerubbabel and Joshua. In reference to that, the prophet speaks of another temple (of which that which was now erecting was but a type or shadow,) which should in due time be raised by the Messiah himself; and he repeats his declaration both to denote the great importance of it, and the certainty of its accomplishment."[101]

Moreover, **he shall bear the glory** of God. (see Isaiah 4:2; John 1:14). Also, he **shall sit and rule upon his throne; and he shall be a priest upon his throne**. That Messiah will **sit and rule upon his throne** denotes his role as king. The language, **he shall** also **be a priest upon his throne,** confirms the **throne** is located within the **temple.** Merrill well observes: "Apart from Psalm 110 there is no OT passage that comes as close as this one in Zechariah to uniting the royal and priestly offices. With this in mind, the 'wholesome counsel between the two of them' takes on a greatly enhanced meaning. Joshua and Zerubbabel are messianic forerunners whose persons and functions prototypically portray that One to come who died as servant, intercedes as priest, and will return as king, even Christ

---

[101] Charles Simeon, *Horae Homileticae: Hosea to Malachi*, vol. 10 (London: Holdsworth and Ball, 1832), 475.

Jesus."[102] Jesus will be a priest after the order of Melchizedec (Psalm 110:4; Hebrews 6:20) and a Davidic king. Only the Branch could carry out both roles, and it is in that sense that **the counsel of peace shall be between them both**. This is in contrast to Israel's prior experience where the priestly and royal lines were separate.

The **temple** is completed during Zechariah's ministry, and renovated by Herod (a project that continued even during Jesus' earthly ministry), contained no **throne** because it was not intended for a priest-king in the order of Melchizedec. In contrast, as stated here and in Ezekiel 43:7, the millennial **temple** will contain the **throne** for the priest-king, from which he will fulfill both priestly and kingly functions for the people of God.

> **14** And the crowns shall be to Helem, and to Tobijah, and to Jedaiah, and to Hen the son of Zephaniah, for a memorial in the temple of the LORD.

After Joshua completes the symbolic act of wearing the **crowns**, the **crowns shall be to Helem, and to Tobijah, and to Jedaiah, and to Hen the son of Zephaniah, for a memorial in the temple of the LORD**. The name **Hen** means "gracious one" and is another name for Josiah **son of Zephaniah** (cf. 6:10). Once the **temple of the LORD** is completed, these men will see to it that it is placed there **for a memorial**. A **memorial** is an object that serves the purpose of calling something to memory. In this case, it calls to memory the promise of the coming Branch, his priest-king role and construction of a future **temple** for which the current is only a shadow or sketch. People will remember that God called out four specific men to construct the crown and place it in the **temple** as a **memorial** of God's promises. It is fitting that this memorial should be placed in the Temple, awaiting the only One for whom it was made. Note that Jesus is pictured as wearing a crown in the Revelation (see Revelation 14:14, 19:12).

102 Eugene H. Merrill, *An Exegetical Commentary - Haggai, Zechariah, Malachi*, 177.

15 And they *that are* far off shall come and build in the temple of the LORD, and ye shall know that the LORD of hosts hath sent me unto you. And *this* shall come to pass, if ye will diligently obey the voice of the LORD your God.

Continuing to speak of the Millennial **temple**, we are told that **they that are far off shall come and build in the temple of the LORD.** In other words, not only will the Jewish people be involved in the construction of the future **temple** under the leadership of Messiah, but Gentiles from throughout the world will also. We have already seen reference to the fact that in Messiah's second advent "many nations shall be joined to the Lord in that day, and shall be my people, and [Messiah] will dwell in the midst of" Jerusalem. (Zechariah 2:11; see also 8:23, 9:7) In fact, in Zechariah 2:11, the prophet writes of Messiah when he dwells in Jerusalem, "thou shalt know that the LORD of hosts hath sent me unto thee." As I argued in the notes there, the point is not that the people alive at that future time will know that Zechariah was sent by God, but that the Jewish people will know that Messiah is the **sent** one of God. This is critical because by and large at Jesus' first advent they reject His claim. In contrast, at his second advent a refined remnant will accept Jesus as Messiah, the one **sent** from God. So also here as the same subject matter is addressed, the prophet writes, **and ye shall know that the LORD of hosts hath sent me unto you**, again indicating a time when **ye** (the Jewish people) will **know** (accept and not reject) **that the LORD of hosts** (God the Father) **sent me** (Messiah) **unto you**. Other prophetic passages confirm Messiah's reign from the Millennial **temple** over God's people, not just in Israel but the whole world:

> **Micah 4:1** But in the last days it shall come to pass, *that* the mountain of the house of the LORD shall be established in the top of the mountains, and it shall be exalted above the hills; and people shall flow unto it. **2** And many

nations shall come, and say, Come, and let us
go up to the mountain of the LORD, and to the
house of the God of Jacob; and he will teach us
of his ways, and we will walk in his paths: for
the law shall go forth of Zion, and the word of
the LORD from Jerusalem.

Jeremiah 23:5 Behold, the days come, saith the
LORD, that I will raise unto David a righteous
Branch, and a King shall reign and prosper, and
shall execute judgment and justice in the earth.

While all of what the prophet says will certainly come to pass,
the timing depends on Israel. He writes, **this shall come to
pass, if ye will diligently obey the voice of the LORD your God.**
The prologue before the visions (1:1-6) instructs the Jewish
remnant not to follow the rebellious ways of their ancestors.
But history shows that during Jesus' earthly ministry they did
exactly that. It is when their unbelief in Messiah becomes
belief that these glorious promises about the future will
happen. The events that will bring about this change of heart
are explained later in the book, but in short, it will require
God permitting Gentile invaders to overtake Israel before
they will turn to God and call upon Jesus for deliverance.

Closing

It is entirely fitting that night visions end climactically with an
oracle about the coronation of the king. As I have emphasized
throughout these notes, the book of Zechariah is all about the
Messiah and the coming Messianic age. But how easy it is for
modern Christians to see only the suffering servant and miss
the heavy emphasis on the future triumphant priest-king. One
of the most outrageous errors of so much of the modern
"church" is the acceptance of a literal fulfillment of prophecies
concerning the punishment of Israel and the first advent of
Messiah but denying the future blessings on Israel and the
second coming of the king. The future has tremendous

implications now. Jesus will reign over the planet from Jerusalem in a Kingdom of truth and righteousness. It is incumbent upon us to live now like the people of the coming king. The ministry of Zechariah is all about looking forward and living now in light of God's promised future blessings. If we are going to live in a Kingdom of truth and righteousness in the very presence of Jesus Christ, we should give no place now to the world. We are on a train bound for glory and at many places along the way we could get off at some worldly station for temporary gratification. But how much better will it be to stay on the train, focused on the destination, longing to see the priest-king face-to-face.

Application Points

- **MAIN PRINCIPLE:** God will presently protect the Jewish remnant while they complete the Temple and in a future time God will deliver Israel from her enemies. The present Temple construction and high priest are a type for the coming priest-king Messiah, the Branch, who will construct a Temple containing his throne from which he will rule the world.

Discussion Questions

1. What indications are in the text of Zechariah that show the eighth night vision to speak both to present circumstances and future circumstances?

2. What is meant by the four different colors of horses?

3. What does it mean for someone to "walk to and fro through the earth"? (6:7)

4. What does the Messianic term "BRANCH" suggest to you about the ministry of the coming Messiah? How did or how will Jesus fulfill the implications of the term "BRANCH"?

5. What are some key differences between the Temple constructed during Zechariah's ministry and the coming Messianic Temple?

6. Jesus is a priest after the order of Melchizedek. Who is Melchizedek and how does he provide a type for Jesus? (consider Genesis 14)

7. Why was it important for the eight night visions to occur in a single evening?

Chapter 9

Religion

Religion is far more effective in keeping people from God than atheism ever will be. It may well be that religion is one of Satan's greatest achievements. Specifically, it is that type of religion whose sole means of knowing or pleasing a deity or deities is a set of ritualistic tasks. In the name of such religions, people have sacrificed children, engaged in orgies, walked hot coals or carried out some other means of self-injury on a theory of penance, contributed fortunes, engaged in monastic lifestyles, bowed before idols carved of stone or wood, worshiped ancestors and much more. It is in our flesh nature to shape a god to our likeness (Romans 1:23), a god that is beset with human frailties like us and therefore affirms us without requiring change, and then to worship our creation through religious rituals. Unfortunately, proper spiritual practices can also be perverted into this type of crass religion. Our heart motivations matter. We know that good things like prayer (Matthew 6:5) and giving (Matthew 23:23) can become perverted. Such perverted practices deceive people into a false sense of spirituality when in fact they are not drawing near to God at all. Christians are not immune to this. Our giving, praying, Bible study, singing, keeping of the Lord's Supper, and even church attendance, can become a matter of going through the motions and checking off our list. Our heart attitude can transform our enjoyment of a relationship with God into empty religion. During the captivity in Babylon, many of the Jewish people continued their religious practices, and what Zechariah will say is that those practices were for themselves and not for God at all. It was empty religion, but God is calling the Jewish remnant to a genuine spiritual renewal and not more religion.

Scripture and Comments

As we have seen, chapters 1 through 6 form a single unit of thought within the book of Zechariah. These chapters contain an introductory oracle (1:1-6) where the prophet challenges the remnant not to repeat the disobedience of their forefathers. The introduction is followed by eight visions Zechariah receives in a single evening that look to their present situation and a future glory for Israel tied to the coming Messiah, while also encouraging obedience in their daily lives as the children of God (1:7-6:8). And as stated before, the critical concern of the moment is completing the Temple, a project God promises in these visions to bring to completion. The first and last visions utilize similar imagery involving colored horses to express God's sovereignty over the entire world, and together form an inclusio for the entire sequence of eight visions. These are followed in 6:9-15 with the crowning of Joshua, an explicit type for the crowning of The Branch, Jesus Christ, the only one qualified to serve as priest and king and to bring about the glorious future for Israel that God promises in the night visions, the rest of Zechariah, and so many other places in Scripture.

Chapters 7 and 8 form a hinge unit between the night visions and the eschatologically focused chapters 9 through 14. These two chapters address proper heart motivations in worship and true righteousness and relate these to the blessings to be experienced in the future Messianic Kingdom. This reminds Zechariah's audience, and us, that the details about history future should encourage us to reorient our lives now and bring about practical change in how we think and live.

> **Zechariah 7:1** And it came to pass in the fourth year of king Darius, *that* the word of the LORD came unto Zechariah in the fourth *day* of the ninth month, *even* in Chisleu;

Zechariah provides us a time marker for this prophecy. We are told that it is **the fourth year of** the reign **of King Darius** (known in history as King Darius the Great or Darius Hystaspes, see further notes in chapter 1). It is the **fourth day of the ninth month** on the Jewish Calendar, but **Chisleu** or kislev is the Babylonian name for that month. This is approximately December 7, 518 B.C. on our calendar.[103] The eight night visions occur approximately 22 months earlier on February 15, 519 B.C. In the intervening period, the construction of the Temple steadily proceeded, and indeed, the project would be completed in another two years. As Ezra 6:15 records: "And this house was finished on the third day of the month Adar, which was in the sixth year of the reign of Darius the king." More important than the date, this is the **word of the LORD** that Zechariah receives. The language parallels the language in Zechariah 1:1 when he receives his first word from God.

> **2** When they had sent unto the house of God Sherezer and Regemmelech, and their men, to pray before the LORD, **3** *And* to speak unto the priests which *were* in the house of the LORD of hosts, and to the prophets, saying, Should I

---

[103] Mark J. Boda, *The Book of Zechariah*, 424.

weep in the fifth month, separating myself, as I
have done these so many years?

As the KJV translates verse 2, we are not told who **they** are, but
apparently there is a larger group who send representatives to ask
a religious question. The language could be translated
differently and it hinges on the Hebrew term *bayith-el*
translated **house of God**. And while **house of God** accurately
translates what *bayith-el* means, these two Hebrew words are
never used elsewhere in the Bible to refer to the Temple.[104]
Indeed, Zechariah refers to the "temple of the LORD" four
times in chapter 6:12-15 as the *heykal Yahweh* or temple of
Yahweh, and refers again to the Temple in verse 8:9 as the
heykal. The phrase "house of God" by this time period is
frequently *beth elohim* (see e.g., 2 Chronicles 36:19; Ezra 1:4,
2:68, 3:8-9, 4:24, 5:2, 5:13-17; Nehemiah 6:10, 8:16, 11:11; Daniel
1:2, 5:3). And in the next verse, 7:3, Zechariah unquestionably
refers to the **house of the LORD of hosts** using the Hebrew
bayith Yahweh. Thus, it is improbable that Zechariah would
use the shortened *bayith-el* to refer to the Temple. This
instead is intended as a proper noun referring to the city of
Bethel, so that the subject of the verse is "they of Bethel" or
the "people of Bethel" who send a delegation to Jerusalem.
This view makes the best sense of the language, is consistent
with Zechariah's references to the Temple before and after
this verse, and makes sense of the historical context.

It is helpful to recall that Bethel is a city with a rich history
that was already a city by the time of Abraham and is
referenced in the book of Genesis. The ark of the covenant was
kept there for a time during the judges. (Judges 20:27) But after
Solomon, when the nation was divided into southern (Judah)
and northern (Israel) kingdoms, Bethel became a seat of
idolatry. The Holman Illustrated Bible Dictionary summarizes:
"Whereas Bethel had been a place of orthodox worship from

104 H. D. M. Spence-Jones, ed., *Zechariah*, 67.

Abraham to the judges, Jeroboam I made it a religious center of his innovative, apostate religion of the Northern Kingdom. He erected a golden calf both here and in Dan with non-Levitic priests and an illegitimate feast to compete with the celebrations and religion of Jerusalem, 10.5 miles to the south in Judah (1 Kings 12:29–33)."[105] God's prophet Amos referred to this idolatry and pronounced judgment on it. (Amos 3:14, 4:4, 5;5-5) But the captivity in Babylon and the return of relatively small numbers of people resulted in a refined remnant returning by faith to the Holy Land. In particular, people came with Zerubbabel (Ezra 2:2) around 536 B.C. including 223 men to Bethel and Ai (Ezra 2:28).

The significance of Zechariah 7:2-3 is that Bethel sent a delegation to Jerusalem **to pray before the LORD and to speak unto the priests which were in the house of the LORD of hosts, and to the prophets.** The city that previously was a center of idolatry in defiance to God's requirement of worship at the Temple in Jerusalem is once again looking to the **priests** and **prophets** in the Temple (still under construction) in Jerusalem for direction in proper worship. This change of heart no doubt is representative of the entire nation at this point. It is unfortunate that it took severe judgment and 70 years of captivity to accomplish this cleansing, but it is also a promising indication of a people ready to again live as the people of God. This episode confirms the relative success of the ministries of Haggai and Zechariah in inspiring the people Godward. Leupold's comments are insightful here:

> On the whole, there is something epochal about this episode, something that would scarcely escape the eye of the prophet. Bethel had been a center of the calf worship that had been instituted by Jeroboam. It had had its own sanctuary and its own priests. As long as

[105] Daniel C. Fredericks, "Bethel," ed. Chad Brand et al., *Holman Illustrated Bible Dictionary* (Nashville, TN: Holman Bible Publishers, 2003), 191.

this rival sanctuary continued in opposition to the divinely appointed Zion, Bethel was a symbol of schism and idolatry and of a divided nation. Though many warnings had been spoken that testified to the divine displeasure at this sinful worship, yet they had fallen on deaf ears until the severe corrections of the Assyrian Exile had done their work. Israel was now cured of seeking God after its own devices, at least, cured in so far as to send to *Jerusalem* and its priests for divine guidance. From this point of view Zechariah must have regarded the event as a very good omen. Besides, the fact that these representatives are intent upon securing the Lord's good will ("stroke the countenance") augured well. Both of these were hopeful signs.[106]

The representatives from Bethel include **Sherezer and Regemmelech, and their men.** The name **Sherezer** is of uncertain meaning. **Regemmelech** is likely a Babylonian name indicating the chief spokesman of the king but could also simply indicate a Babylonian title. Taking it as a name, some infer that **Regemmelech** is a Babylonian proselyte, but it is more likely that he and probably **Sherezer** were born in Babylon during the captivity and **Regemmelech** was given a Babylonian name. Possibly, he was given that name because he was an important person who served the king, just as Daniel and his three friends were given Babylonian names. In any event, **Sherezer** and **Regemmelech** were specially selected on behalf of Bethel for this important mission **to speak** to **the priests** and **the prophets.** The **prophets** include Haggai and Zechariah. That Bethel could send the delegation to Jerusalem to speak to the **priests** and **prophets** reflects that the Temple reconstruction is well

---

106 H. C. Leupold, *Exposition of Zechariah* (Grand Rapids, MI: Baker Book House, 1956), 130.

underway and again seen as the center of Jewish religious practice. The **priests** and **prophets** were "regarded as organs of divine communications. See Hag. 2:11, Mal. 2:7."[107]

The question the men present is **should I weep in the fifth month, separating myself, as I have done these so many years?** The fifth month does not correspond to any Biblical Jewish feast. Rather, a practice evolved during the Babylonian captivity in which there were certain days of mourning and fasting. Specifically, this fast commemorated the burning of Jerusalem in 586 B.C. (Jeremiah 52:12-13), which included the destruction of the first Temple (2 Kings 25:9). This fast day is held on the ninth day of Ab (July / August), which corresponds to the **fifth month** of the old Hebrew lunar calendar.[108] As we shall see in what follows, "[t]he question is put in the name of the population of Bethel, but they represented what was a general feeling, and hence the Lord's answer is addressed to the people at large."[109]

Since this text raises the issue of fasting, a brief note is in order. Fasting is an Old Testament and New Testament practice that most often is done in the following contexts: (1) seeking God's will in prayer (Judges 20:20-28); (2) petitioning God in a time of distress (2 Samuel 12:15-16; Nehemiah 1:2-4); (3) mourning (1 Samuel 31:11-13; Esther 4:1-3); (4) confession of sin and repentance (1 Samuel 7:1-6; Joel 2:9-13); and (5) commissioning / sending a person for a task (Esther 4:15-17; Acts 13:1-3, 14:20-23). We should note that fasting is nearly always associated with sincere, deliberate prayer. Fasting outwardly demonstrates a heart that looks to God to sustain and not merely the physical things of the world. The Scripture

[107] John Peter Lange, Philip Schaff, and Talbot W. Chambers, *A Commentary on the Holy Scriptures: Zechariah*, 57.
[108] Richard D. Patterson and Andrew E. Hill, *Cornerstone Biblical Commentary, Vol 10: Minor Prophets, Hosea–Malachi*, 560.
[109] John Peter Lange, Philip Schaff, and Talbot W. Chambers, *A Commentary on the Holy Scriptures: Zechariah*, 57.

warns against fake fasts, mere empty ritualistic fasts, and self-exalting fasts (see Matthew 6:16-20; Luke 18:12-14). In the New Testament, Jesus nullifies ritualistic fasting. Christians should fast because of Jesus' absence and in anticipation of His return. (Luke 5:33-39) When Jesus returns, the fasting will be changed to feasting (Revelation 19:1-9), a point that will be picked up in Zechariah 8 as well.

Returning to the text, these men ask whether they should continue their fasting practice. Zechariah's night visions occur almost two years before this event, and so we can assume that by this time the "good words and comfortable words" (1:13) God gave to Zechariah were public knowledge. Given God's good and comfortable words and the progress on the Temple, what reason would they have to mourn in the fifth month? Not all rituals are bad, but sometimes the ritual becomes an end in itself so that people go through the motions for the sake of tradition or some other motive other than love of the Lord.

> **4** Then came the word of the LORD of hosts unto me, saying, **5** Speak unto all the people of the land, and to the priests, saying, When ye fasted and mourned in the fifth and seventh *month*, even those seventy years, did ye at all fast unto me, *even* to me? **6** And when ye did eat, and when ye did drink, did not ye eat *for yourselves*, and drink *for yourselves*?

Zechariah responds to the Bethel delegation and to the nation as **the word of the LORD of hosts came unto** him with the directive that he **speak unto all the people of the land, and to the priests** who act on their behalf. God does not directly answer the question asked. Here in Zechariah 7, God speaks to the issue that must be addressed, and then provides further response in the next chapter. God says through the prophet, **when ye fasted and mourned in the fifth and seventh month, even those seventy years, did ye at all fast unto me, even to me? And when ye did eat, and when ye did drink, did not ye**

eat for yourselves, and drink for yourselves? First, notice that God's response not only addresses the fast of the **fifth** month, but also of the **seventh**. The **seventh month** fast (the month of Tishri, in September / October) lamented the assassination of Gedaliah, the governor of Judah (2 Kings 25:22-26).[110]

Second, God answers the delegation's question with questions, the rhetorical nature of which demands a negative response. In other words, during the 70 **years** of captivity, these fasts were not done in devotion to God or to acknowledge the past transgressions that resulted in the captivity. God does not mince words, but cuts right to the heart of the matter. When certain people fasted during the seventy years of Babylonian captivity, they went through the motions, but it was not for God. They fasted unto themselves—they carried on with empty religion. God's rebuke is similar to what we read in Isaiah 1:10-17, where God calls out the nation's empty rituals, sacrifices and prayers, and tells them to do right:

> **Isaiah 1:16** Wash you, make you clean; put away the evil of your doings from before mine eyes; cease to do evil; **17** Learn to do well; seek judgment, relieve the oppressed, judge the fatherless, plead for the widow.

And in Isaiah 58, the prophet specifically addresses fasting as an empty ritual:

> **Isaiah 58:3** Wherefore have we fasted, *say they*, and thou seest not? *wherefore* have we afflicted our soul, and thou takest no knowledge? Behold, in the day of your fast ye find pleasure, and exact all your labours. **4** Behold, ye fast for strife and debate, and to smite with the fist of wickedness: ye shall not fast as *ye do this* day,

---

[110] Richard D. Patterson and Andrew E. Hill, *Cornerstone Biblical Commentary, Vol 10: Minor Prophets, Hosea–Malachi*, 560.

to make your voice to be heard on high. **5** Is it such a fast that I have chosen? a day for a man to afflict his soul? *is it* to bow down his head as a bulrush, and to spread sackcloth and ashes *under him?* wilt thou call this a fast, and an acceptable day to the LORD? **6** *Is* not this the fast that I have chosen? to loose the bands of wickedness, to undo the heavy burdens, and to let the oppressed go free, and that ye break every yoke? **7** *Is it* not to deal thy bread to the hungry, and that thou bring the poor that are cast out to thy house? when thou seest the naked, that thou cover him; and that thou hide not thyself from thine own flesh?

Isaiah says they fasted without understanding, and did so for their pleasure and not righteously. But true fasting issues from a heart of righteousness that produces righteous behavior. There is no eternal benefit in empty rituals, as Jesus warns in Matthew 6:5 and 23:14:

> **Matthew 6:5** And when thou prayest, thou shalt not be as the hypocrites are: for they love to pray standing in the synagogues and in the corners of the streets, that they may be seen of men. Verily I say unto you, They have their reward.

> **Matthew 23:14** Woe unto you, scribes and Pharisees, hypocrites! for ye devour widows' houses, and for a pretence make long prayer: therefore ye shall receive the greater damnation.

To be clear, God's answer to the delegation is not "don't fast." But He says that their motivation in worship matters. As Ellsworth comments, "Think of it! They had been observing

these fasts for more than seventy years, and they had done
nothing but displease the Lord!"[111]

> 7 *Should ye* not *hear* the words which the
> LORD hath cried by the former prophets, when
> Jerusalem was inhabited and in prosperity, and
> the cities thereof round about her, when *men*
> inhabited the south and the plain?

Building on the rhetorical questions of verse 6, God presents
through Zechariah a question about learning from the
mistakes of the past. This verse is reminiscent of the
introductory oracle (1:1-6) that functions as a prologue for the
book. Everything the **former prophets** said was God's Word,
and as such, came to pass regardless of how it was received by
the people. God's standards have not changed simply because
there is now a remnant returned to Israel. And thus the
question, **should ye not hear** or listen to and obey **the words
which the LORD hath cried** through the **former prophets**. In
the verses that follow, God addresses a present audience by
reminding them of their past. While Zechariah does not
identify by name the **former prophets**, which certainly
included men such as Amos, Habakkuk, Jeremiah and Micah,
the point is to remind them of the nation's rebellious behavior
before the destruction of Jerusalem and before the Babylonian
captivity **when Jerusalem was** still **inhabited and in prosperity,**
together with **the cities thereof round about her, when men
inhabited the south and the plain.** They should remember the
cause and effect that led to divine discipline previously and
seek to live truly righteous lives grounded in proper motives. If
they live right, then they are free to fast or not. Keil and
Delitzsch summarize the thought well:

> The thought of vv. 6 and 7 is the following: It is
> a matter of indifference to God whether the
> people fast or not. The true fasting, which is

[111] Roger Ellsworth, *Opening Up Zechariah*, 66.

well pleasing to God, consists not in a pharisaical abstinence from eating and drinking, but in the fact that men observe the word of God and live thereby, as the prophets before the captivity had already preached to the people. This overthrew the notion that men could acquire the favour of God by fasting....[112]

At this point, the message transitions to the type of righteousness God desires instead of empty rituals. But Zechariah will return to the fasting issue in chapter 8.

8 And the word of the LORD came unto Zechariah, saying, **9** Thus speaketh the LORD of hosts, saying, Execute true judgment, and shew mercy and compassions every man to his brother: **10** And oppress not the widow, nor the fatherless, the stranger, nor the poor; and let none of you imagine evil against his brother in your heart.

James writes in his epistle, "Pure religion and undefiled before God and the Father is this, To visit the fatherless and widows in their affliction, and to keep himself unspotted from the world." (James 1:27) You cannot fast on Monday and refuse mercy and compassion to your brother on Tuesday and claim to be godly. Nor can you claim to be godly simply because you attend church on Sunday if you are oppressive and uncompassionate on Monday. The two claims are inconsistent. Prior to the Babylonian captivity, the people had not ceased from their religious practices, but most of them lacked genuine godly living to match their outward rituals. The former prophets warned against it. Now, Zechariah receives **the word of the LORD** about what God desires instead of empty rituals. He first reminds the nation that these are not

---

[112] Carl Friedrich Keil and Franz Delitzsch, *Commentary on the Old Testament,* 560.

Zechariah's words but God's, saying, **thus speaketh the LORD of hosts.** The often-repeated title for God, LORD **of hosts,** reminds them of God's sovereignty over the affairs of men and nations. The instruction of God is not complex and requires no seminary degree to grasp. God says, **execute true judgment.** This means to be fair and honest, and while this no doubt speaks of justice in the courtroom so that the poor are not oppressed, it also speaks of dealing with people fairly and with integrity in general. God also says, **shew mercy and compassions every man to his brother.** It is difficult here not to think of James' words in the New Testament:

> **James 2:15** If a brother or sister be naked, and destitute of daily food, **16** And one of you say unto them, Depart in peace, be *ye* warmed and filled; notwithstanding ye give them not those things which are needful to the body; what *doth it* profit?

What James says in the New Testament, and what Zechariah says, is live out your faith and show love to others. The word **mercy** is the frequently used Hebrew word *chesed* that means lovingkindness in its various dimensions, including **mercy,** and frequently speaks of God's love for His people. This is especially needful for those who are most vulnerable, and so Zechariah amplifies the command to love, saying, **oppress not the widow, nor the fatherless** or orphan, **the stranger** or foreigner, **nor the poor.**

We do well to note that some in our time have construed the New Testament through the lens of a so-called social gospel. Instead of a primary focus on God's redemptive plan for lost sinners through Jesus Christ, the New Testament is more or less political fodder for various agendas. At the same time, however, far too many theologically conservative evangelicals have grown cold toward the vulnerable and less fortunate. They overlook the admonitions we find in the New Testament like those of James quoted above about true religion and how a maturing Christian should help to meet the needs of the poor and vulnerable within their sphere of influence and their means. And indeed, we see this emphasis in Zechariah and many of the writing prophets. For the believer who seeks to be honest with the text, the gospel of Jesus Christ and loving people go together. We cannot replace evangelism with efforts for social justice and soup lines. But neither can we present the gospel well before a world in need of Jesus and not be a consistent and reasoned voice for justice and display compassion for hurting and vulnerable people.

Zechariah adds the admonition to **let none of you imagine evil against his brother in your heart**. In other words, do not plot evil against other people. We find repeated exhortations in the Bible to humility. (e.g., James 4:6, 10) Indeed, "God resisteth the proud, and giveth grace to the humble. Humble yourselves therefore under the mighty hand of God, that he may exalt you in due time." (1 Peter 5:5-6) But some would not have God exalt them in due time. Their hearts are not humbled, but consumed by selfish ambition. That ambition drives them to manipulate others and take advantage of or trample over others to promote themselves. And that is what Zechariah is speaking to on the heels of his instructions about not oppressing people. Bad people (bad Christians) will oppress people out of a heart of selfish ambition. Zechariah warns against such behavior, which is the polar opposite of the **mercy and compassions** God's people are called to exhibit. Put in these terms, it is apparent that the ritual of fasting is a bankrupt practice in the absence of **mercy and compassions**.

> **11** But they refused to hearken, and pulled away the shoulder, and stopped their ears, that they should not hear. **12** Yea, they made their hearts *as* an adamant stone, lest they should hear the law, and the words which the LORD of hosts hath sent in his spirit by the former prophets: therefore came a great wrath from the LORD of hosts.

Zechariah earlier referenced the **former prophets** and here describes the nation's prior characteristic response to their messages from God. They **refused to hearken** or pay attention to the **former prophets** and **stopped their ears, that they should not hear**. The words of the **prophets** fell on deaf ears as it were. As we saw in Zechariah 1:4, God beckoned them to "turn ye now from your evil ways, and from your evil doings: but they did not hear, nor hearken unto me." Not only did they not listen, but **they made their hearts as an adamant stone, lest they should hear the law, and the words which the LORD of hosts hath sent in his spirit by the former prophets**. They became hard-hearted. It is not just that they would not heed the prophetic message brought to them by the **spirit** of God, but their heart attitude was altogether rebellious. To **hear the law** means to receive it with a welcoming ear and responsive attitude. But their mindset was the opposite of what God's people should have. They were deaf to God's pleas by the **prophets** and not only rejected the message but would not even consider it. The Bible teaches about actions and consequences. Their disdain for God's word caused **a great wrath from the LORD of hosts**, which no doubt refers to the invasion of Judah by Nebuchadnezzar, the destruction of Jerusalem and the first Temple, and 70 years of captivity in Babylon.

The heart attitude of that prior generation of Israel should sound familiar to many today. Most of us live in a culture that considers itself enlightened and religious but rejects God's Word out-of-hand. We have the Word of God in our grasp (the Holy Bible) but largely reject it. We live in an age of deception and these that reject God's Word will eventually learn that "the wrath of God is revealed from heaven against all ungodliness and unrighteousness of men, who hold the truth in unrighteousness." (Romans 1:18) But how much worse is it when those that claim the name of Jesus show no interest in engaging God's Word as a routine life practice and living out God's Word in their daily lives. How foolish we are if we believe God will deal with us or the nation where we live differently than He did with Israel when it did the same things.

> **13** Therefore it is come to pass, *that* as he cried, and they would not hear; so they cried, and I would not hear, saith the LORD of hosts: **14** But I scattered them with a whirlwind among all the nations whom they knew not. Thus the land was desolate after them, that no man passed through nor returned: for they laid the pleasant land desolate.

God sent prophets to present His Word to the people and by that means God **cried** out to them, but **they would not hear**, meaning they would not respond obediently. The "wrath" referenced in verse 12 is explained to be the result of their refusal to **hear** God. Specifically, God **scattered them with a whirlwind** of judgment **among all the nations whom they knew not**. We know from history that Nebuchadnezzar was God's tool to scatter the people. Nebuchadnezzar assaulted Jerusalem in 605 B.C., later in 597 B.C., and then destroyed the city in 586/587 B.C. The people **cried** out to God (for deliverance), but just as they previously refused His pleas, He **would** not hear theirs. The land that flowed with milk and honey and could be described as **the pleasant land** was **laid...desolate** and made a "ghost town" that **no man passed through nor returned**.

We must bear in mind that the Jewish nation covenanted with God in what is referred to as the Mosaic Covenant. God spells out the blessings for faithful obedience and cursings or penalties for rebellion in Deuteronomy 28. The divine discipline grows harsher in response to continued rebellion, and culminates in God removing them from the land to "a nation which neither thou nor thy fathers have known...and thou shalt become an astonishment, a proverb, and a byword, among all the nations whither the LORD shall lead thee." (Deuteronomy 28:36-37) The **former prophets** warned the people what God would do, and in response to their continued rebellion, God allowed Nebuchadnezzar to lay waste to the land and scatter the people. But the point of Zechariah is that all is not lost. God is faithful to His promises and will bless the nation again. As Zechariah's name suggests, God remembers.

We do well to consider our own situation as a nation. It is ludicrous to believe that God dealt with Israel in the way He did but will not deal likewise with other nations, including the United States (or wherever you find yourself a sojourner). God takes seriously this matter of mercy and compassion, and He is especially jealous for the most vulnerable who are easily the victims of abuse and injustice. Christians who profess to love the Lord and His Word should be a voice of clarity and take a leadership role on matters of social justice. If they do not, others will do so and their agenda will not display the love of Christ and spread the gospel.

Closing

The Christian religion in the good sense of that word is the greatest threat to darkness. Empty religious rituals will not change us. But the kind of religion God calls us to is on a spiritual plane, imbued with a Biblical view of God and His plan for the ages, and enabled by His Spirit so that we may live out a life now that reflects our high calling. When God is at the center of our religious practices, we change, and that affects how we respond to others. A natural consequence of drawing near to God is mercy and compassion toward other people and a special concern for the most vulnerable people. For many in this world, the lives of other people are an inconvenience to be manipulated or removed in order to forward a personal or political agenda. But for the people of God, every life is one God cares about, and the Son died for. As we look forward to a Kingdom characterized by righteousness (see Zechariah 5), we take a stand now for what is right, by our words and actions. These bear witness to the substance of our religious and in this way we reflect God's glory to a world that needs to see it.

Application Points

- **MAIN PRINCIPLE:** Our religious practices must be God-centered and not empty, self-serving rituals.

- True religion will exhibit itself in how we show mercy and compassion for others, especially for those most vulnerable to abuse and injustice.

- We must not close our hearts to God's Word, even when it requires us to change or give up something God does not want in our lives.

Discussion Questions

1. The delegation from Bethel came to Jerusalem with sincere questions about fasting, seemingly unaware that God rejected their fasting. What would this look like in a modern church context?

2. What role do our heart attitudes and motivations have in the legitimacy of our worship?

3. Should Christians be politically active?

4. If you believe there is a systemic injustice in the government where you live, do Christians have an obligation to speak out or do anything about it? How does the obligation to submit to civil government (e.g., Romans 13) affect your answer.

5. Why do you think the people of Judah refused to obey God's commands about showing mercy and compassion, not oppressing the vulnerable, and not imagining evil against their brothers?

6. What does it look like in practical terms when an individual is hard-hearted (see Zechariah 7:12)?

7. Is there reason to expect that God would drop the hammer on Judah for their disobedience to His word but would give a free pass to other nations (like the United States)?

Chapter 10

Kingdom Blessings

It is part of our human experience that when we anticipate a significant future event it changes how we plan, think and live in anticipation of that event. When a couple is expecting a baby, they prepare a nursery, purchase car seats and clothes and various other necessaries, all based on a future event they believe will happen. When we plan a vacation and get it on the calendar, book the flights and hotels, we look forward to it with great anticipation. In the interim before the vacation, we make plans about what to pack, what to do each day of the trip, and we tell others about it. In the second *Back to the Future* movie, the antagonist (Biff Tannen) obtains a magazine showing the outcome of all major sporting events for the next several decades. Naturally, he gambles on all of them and becomes wealthy and powerful since he knows ahead of time who all the winners are. We also know who the winners are.

The prophetic content of the Bible is practical and not mere head knowledge because what we believe about the future will affect what we think and do now. The significance of the future event is proportional to how it affects us now. To the remnant in Jerusalem, a city in need of repair and the new Temple still incomplete, what greater assurance could they have than hearing God promise a glorious future for the city wherein God will personally dwell. And for Christians today, our place in God's plan for the future is also assured. If we believe God's promised future blessings, that should change us. And if we understand the nature of Jesus' Kingdom, one of our responses should be a devotion to righteousness.

Scripture and Comments

Chapters 7 and 8 form a hinge between the night visions and the eschatologically focused chapters 9 through 14. Chapter 7 begins with a delegation from Bethel with religious questions about fasting for the priests and prophets. Those questions are not directly answered in chapter 7, and this chapter will present the second half of God's response. This chapter may best be described as a complete reversal of the circumstances for the nation described in the prior chapter. These two chapters together address proper heart motivations in worship, practical righteousness, and the blessings to be experienced in the future Messianic Kingdom. In this way, the practical principles of the first six chapters are linked to the remaining chapters that look primarily to the future work of Jesus Christ. Lindsey aptly captures the organization of chapters 7 and 8 and how they relate back to the prior material:

> As chapter 7 resembles the call to repentance in 1:2–6, so chapter 8 reflects the promised blessings pictured throughout the night visions (1:7–6:8). Thus the third and fourth messages view the restoration from Exile in Zechariah's day as a precursor of future blessing and

prosperity in the Millennial Age. They also place emphasis on that future time when righteousness, justice, and peace will fill the earth.[113]

The material in chapter 8 is organized around "a decalogue of promises each of which begins with the words 'thus says Yahweh of hosts.'"[114] The emphasis throughout is on the sovereign God who is able to bring these promises to pass for His people.

> **Zechariah 8:1** Again the word of the LORD of hosts came *to me*, saying, **2** Thus saith the LORD of hosts; I was jealous for Zion with great jealousy, and I was jealous for her with great fury.

In this chapter, the focus is on a restored Israel. Much of what God says will be fulfilled in part by His people in Zechariah's day, but completely fulfilled in the future. As Merrill comments: "The eschatological springs from the historical and cannot be separated from it. This is one reason that the two frequently seem to merge and why a 'dual fulfillment' is not only possible but necessary."[115] But it is critical that God did not only, or even primarily, speak to their time. God gives Zechariah a message for the people about a glorious future in order to encourage them to see themselves in God's unfolding plan. This "looking forward" perspective will allow them to move in faith as their thinking and actions are reoriented around the promises of God.

Zechariah first says, **again the word of the LORD of hosts came to me**. These words introduce the prophecy that appears in verses 1 through 17, and the same phrase introduces the prophecy in verses 18 through 23. Unlike the eight night

---

[113] F. Duane Lindsey, "Zechariah," in *The Bible Knowledge Commentary: An Exposition of the Scriptures*, 1560.

[114] James E. Smith, *The Minor Prophets*, Zec 7:13–14.

[115] Eugene H. Merrill, *An Exegetical Commentary - Haggai, Zechariah, Malachi*, 195.

visions of chapters one through six, we do not find Zechariah looking up and observing what God has for him or in some other way receiving a vision. Instead, Zechariah receives **the word of the LORD of hosts**, just as he does with the messages in chapter seven. We are not told exactly how God gives the word to Zechariah, only the fact of it. Zechariah emphasizes throughout this chapter that it is God's message. Indeed, it is the message of the sovereign **LORD of hosts**, who **saith, I was jealous for Zion with great jealousy, and I was jealous for her with great fury**. Critically, both instances of **was** should be the present tense ("am"), consistent with the translation in 1:14: "I am jealous for Jerusalem and for Zion with a great jealousy." We should note that 1:14-17 is very similar to these opening verses in chapter 8 and is present tense, e.g., compare "I am returned to Jerusalem with mercies: my house shall be built in it" (1:16) with "I am returned unto Zion, and will dwell in the midst of Jerusalem" (8:3). God speaks to His people through Zechariah about what He is presently doing and will do **for Zion** because of his **great jealousy**.

Zion is a mountain in Jerusalem, but is used here to represent Jerusalem and its people. This is a figure of speech where a part is used for the whole, and the reference to this mountain as representative of Jerusalem is very common in the Old Testament (see, e.g., 2 Kings 19:31, Psalm 51:18). The word **jealousy** is usually understood in our day as a negative emotion, but it can be positive or negative depending on the context, as Smith explains:

> Jealousy is an ambivalent term. It is a strong emotion expressed in an intolerance of rivals. It can be good or evil, depending on the legitimacy of the rival. God had chosen Israel and made a covenant with her. He bound her to himself in an exclusive relationship of God and people. "You shall have no other gods before me" (Exod 20:3). Zion and/or Jerusalem

was the chosen earthly dwelling place of Yahweh (Ps 132), and Zion became in the biblical materials a symbol for the kingdom of God (Isa 65:17–18). After reviewing the place of Zion in many OT passages, Norman Porteous says, "We have been watching the process in the Old Testament by which Jerusalem, the chosen city of God, not just the chosen city of David, gradually gave its name as a symbol of the transcendent action of God in creating a people for himself in the world, that is, in bringing in his kingdom" (*Living the Mystery*, 109). Yahweh is often presented as a jealous God in the OT. Yahweh's jealousy caused him to bring great hardships on Israel when she broke her covenant with him (Deut 29:20–28; Ezek 5:13; 16:38, 42; 23:25). But here and in 1:14, God's jealousy is for Jerusalem and against the nations that had grossly abused her.[116]

Accordingly, the point in this first promise is that God will bless them and protect them **with great fury** from their enemies. God's **jealousy** for His people speaks of His love in action for their protection and wellbeing (physically and spiritually). We see this in the New Testament when Paul speaks of his having "godly jealousy" for the people he ministered to in the Corinthian church, "For I am jealous over you with godly jealousy: for I have espoused you to one husband, that I may present you as a chaste virgin to Christ" (2 Corinthians 11:2). We could certainly say that parents have (or should have) jealousy for their children in this same sense, aggressively looking out for their physical and spiritual wellbeing. And by application, in God's love for us, He jealously looks out for our wellbeing and has no tolerance for rivals.

[116] Ralph L. Smith, *Micah–Malachi*, 231.

> **3** Thus saith the LORD; I am returned unto Zion, and will dwell in the midst of Jerusalem: and Jerusalem shall be called a city of truth; and the mountain of the LORD of hosts the holy mountain.

With this second promise, God assures His people, **I am returned unto Zion, and will dwell in the midst of Jerusalem**. As already noted, reference to **Zion** is used for **Jerusalem**, and that is clear from the parallelism here. God **had returned unto Zion** with blessing for His people, but there is yet more. God promises His Holy presence in **the midst** of His people. Surely there is no greater blessing and protection than to have God Himself dwelling in Jerusalem. When we read this promise about God's return to **Jerusalem**, we must keep in mind that according to the prophet Ezekiel, God previously abandoned the temple and Jerusalem and permitted the Babylonians to destroy both:

> **Ezekiel 10:18** Then the glory of the LORD departed from off the threshold of the house, and stood over the cherubims. **19** And the cherubims lifted up their wings, and mounted up from the earth in my sight: when they went out, the wheels also *were* beside them, and *every one* stood at the door of the east gate of the LORD'S house; and the glory of the God of Israel *was* over them above.

> **Ezekiel 11:22** Then did the cherubims lift up their wings, and the wheels beside them; and the glory of the God of Israel *was* over them above. **23** And the glory of the LORD went up from the midst of the city, and stood upon the mountain which *is* on the east side of the city.

These promises raise basic questions about how and when God **will dwell in the midst of Jerusalem**. Some expositors err at this verse by spiritualizing away the force of what is written.

But Zechariah says that God "will be the glory in the midst of" Jerusalem (2:5) and "will dwell in the midst of thee" (2:10, 11). And the promise of the present verse parallels the promise of 8:8 that "I will bring them [my people], and they shall dwell in the midst of Jerusalem." Just as God's people delivered "from the east country, and from the west country" (8:7) will literally "dwell in the midst of Jerusalem" (8:8) at that future time, so also will God literally dwell in Jerusalem with His people. What becomes indisputably evident later in the book is that the moving agent for God dwelling (being physically manifest) in Jerusalem will be the coming Messiah.

We previously noted the parallel to chapter 1, and in particular we read in 1:16: "I am returned to Jerusalem with mercies: my house shall be built in it, saith the LORD of hosts, and a line shall be stretched forth upon Jerusalem." We have the further reference here to **the mountain of the LORD of hosts the holy mountain**, which is a reference to the Temple mount (cf. Haggai 1:8), suggesting the presence also of the Temple in Jerusalem. But the promises here and in the balance of the chapter of God's literal presence in **Jerusalem**, the regathering of His people from the nations to the land, and the nations coming "to seek the LORD of hosts in Jerusalem, and to pray before the LORD" (8:22), all point forward to the conditions immediately before and in the Messianic Kingdom. Isaiah also referred to the place of God's Temple during the Messianic Kingdom as His **mountain**:

> **Isaiah 2:2** And it shall come to pass in the last days, *that* the mountain of the LORD'S house shall be established in the top of the mountains, and shall be exalted above the hills; and all nations shall flow unto it. **3** And many people shall go and say, Come ye, and let us go up to the mountain of the LORD, to the house of the God of Jacob; and he will teach us of his ways, and we will walk in his paths: for out of Zion shall go forth the law, and the word of the LORD from Jerusalem.

Ezekiel likewise confirmed not only a future Temple constructed during the Messianic Kingdom, but God's return to it, in contrast to His abandoning the Temple that Solomon built. (Ezekiel 43:1-5) Thus, God is **returned unto Zion** with blessing, but the words, **will dwell in the midst of Jerusalem,** look ahead for their literal fulfillment. As Dennett explains, there is a gap of centuries between the promises:

> He would not yet dwell in Zion—not indeed until many weary years should have passed, not until the establishment of Messiah's kingdom. But, as we have before seen in Haggai, and in the former parts of this book, the work which the children of the captivity were at this moment doing, contained in itself the promise and the guarantee, of the fulfilment of all that God had spoken concerning the future glory of Jerusalem. A long interval of centuries, therefore, must be interposed between the words, "*I am returned unto Zion*" and I "*will dwell in the midst of Jerusalem,*" though the two are linked together as a cause and effect in the divine mind.[117]

With God's presence, the city will be radically transformed, no longer the place of sin that brought God's wrath (the Babylonian captivity), but a **city of truth**. The Hebrew word here, *emet,* carries the idea of faithfulness. Because of God's presence, **Jerusalem** will enjoy a reputation of faithfulness to God. It is also a place of holiness, for **the holy mountain** is there. It is not merely that the city is different in the future, but its inhabitants are radically different people than their forefathers. We should recall that the visions in Zechariah 4 show the Messianic Age will be characterized by righteousness. Zechariah builds further on this theme in 14:20-21, observing

---

[117] Edward Dennett, *Zechariah the Prophet,* 86.

that "the bells of the horses" and "every pot in Jerusalem and Judah shall be holiness unto the LORD of hosts." Holiness will characterize even the smallest detail of daily life. As Dennett states, "Wherever God condescends to dwell, whether in the tabernacle, temple, or in the church, truth and holiness must be maintained."[118]

This promise has never been fulfilled at any time in Israel's history. But looking at these promises through the lens of the New Testament, we recognize that while there is some level of revival in Zechariah's day, this was but a foretaste of what lies ahead when Jesus Christ returns to rule and reign from **Jerusalem**. But at the same time, it is critical when we read about events still future even from our standpoint that we understand God's words are meant to stir His people, then and now, to action in the moment. In Zechariah's day, they are motivated to complete the Temple. The glory of the coming Kingdom should likewise change our perspective and stir us to action, especially evangelism and discipleship.

> **4** Thus saith the LORD of hosts; There shall yet old men and old women dwell in the streets of Jerusalem, and every man with his staff in his hand for very age. **5** And the streets of the city shall be full of boys and girls playing in the streets thereof.

This verse presents the third promise from the **LORD of hosts**, and continues the description of the conditions that will prevail when God "dwell[s] in the midst of Jerusalem" (8:3). In contrast to the pervasive death, destruction and defeat of their recent history, Israel's future will be characterized by security, joy and longevity. This era of prosperity will see **old men and old women dwell[ing] in the streets of Jerusalem**. To emphasize their age, Zechariah adds, **every man with his staff in his hand for very age**. In times of war, the most vulnerable are the first

---

118 *Ibid.*, 86–87.

to perish, and when there is the cloud of potential attack and destruction, the people do not assemble in the **streets**. But the picture here is of a reversal of circumstances so that people reach old age and dwell securely, which means the entirety of the remnant at that future time will enjoy peace and security.

At the other end of the spectrum are the young. Mirroring verse 4, Zechariah says **the streets of the city shall be full of boys and girls playing in the streets thereof**. This pictures not only security, but prosperity in a way that is not measured in dollars and cents. Families are returned to Jerusalem and thriving, untarnished by poverty, violence, and war, as evidenced by an abundance of children. And they are happy and safe. "That holy city would be a happy city, even for the little ones."[119] Sadly, this is not a present reality in many parts of the world, and even in many parts of the United States. What the politicians promised but failed to deliver, God will accomplish when the Messianic Kingdom is established. This will be a golden era never before experienced.

> 6 Thus saith the LORD of hosts; If it be marvellous in the eyes of the remnant of this people in these days, should it also be marvellous in mine eyes? saith the LORD of hosts.

This verse presents the fourth promise from the **LORD of hosts**, but does so in the form of a rhetorical question that "warns against allowing human reason to decide what God is likely to do."[120] Zechariah addresses **the remnant of this people in these days**. We should first note the use of the term **remnant** (also Zechariah 8:11-12), a term that refers to those that survived the Babylonian exile. God anticipates their doubts about these promised future blessings. When God says, **if it be**

[119] James E. Smith, *The Minor Prophets*, Zec 8:4–5.
[120] Joyce G. Baldwin, *Haggai, Zechariah and Malachi: An Introduction and Commentary*, vol. 28, Tyndale Old Testament Commentaries (Downers Grove, IL: InterVarsity Press, 1972), 160.

marvelous in the eyes of the remnant of this people in these days, should it also be marvellous in mine eyes, He is asking a rhetorical question. The required answer is no. But the question speaks with assurance to those tempted to walk by sight and not by faith (2 Corinthians 5:7), or to borrow from a familiar example from the time of the Exodus (Numbers 13-14), to those who would stop at the river of impossibilities instead of crossing the Jordan with their spiritual eyes firmly focused on the promises of God waiting on the other side. Faith looks beyond circumstances and even beyond reason when what God says is clear. Regardless of whether these promises might seem incredible or **marvellous** in their eyes, they are not impossible or **marvellous** for God. Indeed, such promised future blessings about the conditions of the Kingdom are the natural result of God dwelling in their midst. The force of God's rhetorical question is to double down on His promises, assuring the **remnant** these things shall come to pass. We do well to remember Jesus' words in Luke 18:27, "The things which are impossible with men are possible with God." The heart of the matter is faith, for "without faith it is impossible to please [God]." (Hebrews 11:6) And critically, believing what God says about the future should change us now.

> 7 Thus saith the LORD of hosts; Behold, I will save my people from the east country, and from the west country; 8 And I will bring them, and they shall dwell in the midst of Jerusalem: and they shall be my people, and I will be their God, in truth and in righteousness.

This presents the fifth promise from the LORD **of hosts**, namely the regathering of God's dispersed people to **Jerusalem**. These two verses explain how God will bring about the blessings of the preceding verses.[121] Zechariah records God's promise that He **will save [His] people from the east country and from the west country**. As Merrill explains: "The

---

terms for the directions here are much more cosmic in scope than the usual ones, referring respectively to the rising and setting of the sun. This suggests that the immigrants will come not only from the immediately surrounding areas but from the very ends of the earth. This is also the import of limiting the scope to the two directions, for the sun relates to the earth only in terms of east and west, not north and south."[122] In short, God assures the small remnant a complete restoration will come about as God brings the Jewish people scattered abroad back home. Note that Zechariah indicates a future blessing with **I will save** and **I will bring** and **they shall dwell** and **they shall be**. While a limited return of exiles from Babylon already occurred, this future regathering is global in scope. It will coincide with the time when God himself "will dwell in the midst of Jerusalem: and Jerusalem shall be called a city of truth." (8:3) At that time, God **will bring them, and they shall** also **dwell in the midst of Jerusalem: and they shall be my people, and I will be their God, in truth and in righteousness**.

This is not merely a physical gathering, but a time of spiritual revival, for **they shall be** His **people...in truth and righteousness**. Zechariah will return to this theme of spiritual revival in 12:10-14. These promises look forward to the enlarged Jerusalem promised in Zechariah 2, when God shall call the scattered people home (2:6-7), "will dwell in the midst of thee" (2:10), and will be joined by many nations (2:11). This, of course, will occur when Messiah establishes His Kingdom, for only then will "many nations...be joined to the LORD in that day, and shall be [His] people." (2:11) We read Jesus' promise of His return and regathering of His people in the Olivet Discourse:

> **Matthew 24:29** Immediately after the tribulation of those days shall the sun be darkened, and the moon shall not give her light, and the stars shall fall from heaven, and the

---

[122] Eugene H. Merrill, *An Exegetical Commentary - Haggai, Zechariah, Malachi*, 196.

> powers of the heavens shall be shaken: **30** And
> then shall appear the sign of the Son of man in
> heaven: and then shall all the tribes of the earth
> mourn, and they shall see the Son of man
> coming in the clouds of heaven with power and
> great glory. **31** And he shall send his angels with
> a great sound of a trumpet, and they shall
> gather together his elect from the four winds,
> from one end of heaven to the other.

The spiritual revival that is promised is key to the assurance of the other blessings. "It is of great moment to observe that all the happiness and prosperity above described will flow from their established relationship with God. They shall be His people, and He will be their God in truth—in the truth of what He is as revealed in His covenant relationship with Israel—and in righteousness, this characterizing the government under which they will be placed."[123]

> **9** Thus saith the LORD of hosts; Let your
> hands be strong, ye that hear in these days
> these words by the mouth of the prophets,
> which *were* in the day *that* the foundation of
> the house of the LORD of hosts was laid, that
> the temple might be built.

The short message contained in 8:9-13 is about encouragement, and contains the bookends, **let your hands be strong**. (cf. 8:8, 13) Now the **LORD of hosts** addresses those that **hear in these days these words by the mouth of the prophets, which were in the day that the foundation of the house of the Lord of hosts was laid**. In other words, the message addresses the people in Zechariah's present day (**in these days**) who were also alive and heard **the prophets** when **the foundation of the** Temple **was laid**. They are being called upon to look back in their minds and remember when the

---

123 Edward Dennett, *Zechariah the Prophet*, 89.

prophets spoke to them in the past and encouraged them in their rebuilding effort. The present state of progress on the Temple reconstruction provides ample confirmation of the truth of the **words...of the prophets** then spoken to them. The referenced **prophets** are not named but may include Haggai and others. Now it is time to once again move forward in assurance of what God promises. They must **let their hands be strong**. In other places in the Old Testament (e.g., Judges 7:11, 1 Samuel 23:16, 2 Samuel 16:21), this expression means to take courage. And here it is time to take courage in God's faithfulness. All of the promised blessings earlier in the chapter will come to pass, but in response to an obedient people. As Merrill explains: "Now it is important for the remnant people there to shoulder the responsibilities requisite to the fulfillment of the promise. Their deliverance and return may depend wholly on God's grace (vv. 7–8), but prosperity in the land, both now and in the eschaton, is directly related to obedience and hard work."[124]

We too have many promised future blessings of God as well as assigned tasks in the interim. How easy it is to be overwhelmed by circumstances or even overwhelmed by good things like being at church every time the doors are opened, getting the kids to school and extracurricular activities, and taking care of our work responsibilities. To us as well, we need to not lose sight of the main thing—being God's ambassadors in a world that needs to hear about Jesus. And to us, Zechariah would say, **let your hands be strong**. This is not finding strength in our resources, but courage in God's resources. For otherwise, we could never **be strong**.

> **10** For before these days there was no hire for man, nor any hire for beast; neither *was there any* peace to him that went out or came in because of the affliction: for I set all men every one against his neighbour. **11** But now I *will* not

[124] Eugene H. Merrill, *An Exegetical Commentary - Haggai, Zechariah, Malachi*, 197.

be unto the residue of this people as in the former days, saith the LORD of hosts. **12** For the seed *shall be* prosperous; the vine shall give her fruit, and the ground shall give her increase, and the heavens shall give their dew; and I will cause the remnant of this people to possess all these *things.*

In this sixth promise, God takes them back **before these days,** that is, before the Temple construction was well under way. Often we need to look back before we can get the right focus looking forward. And to this end, God reminded them of **these days** when **there was no hire for man, nor any hire for beast; neither was there any peace to him that went out or came in because of the affliction: for I set all men every one against his neighbor.** Before God brought the remnant back to Jerusalem, during the captivity, Judah was a desolate place. It was characterized by what we would call an economic depression. There were no jobs, and this resulted in **affliction** and violence of such a degree that people would stay off the streets. This is a far cry from the future prosperity God's promises in 8:4-5 that looks to a time of **peace** when the streets are filled with people old and young. God brought about those dire conditions, and indeed, God **set all men every one against his neighbor.** We should realize that as Christians we are fools if we believe we can find political solutions to spiritual problems. Imagine how the politicians would have promised a way out of the conditions that prevailed. But if God created these conditions in response to the rebellion of His people, it is only God that can turn despair into blessing in response to the renewed faithfulness of His people.

At the time of Zechariah's message, the people moved in faith in rebuilding the Temple. Baldwin comments, "On this ground alone God is dealing with them altogether differently. How utterly basic is repentance!"[125] In response, we have the

---

[125] Joyce G. Baldwin, *Haggai, Zechariah and Malachi: An Introduction and Commentary,* 162.

promised sixth blessing of the LORD **of hosts**, that in contrast to before, **now I will not be unto this residue** or remnant **of this people as in the former days**. Instead of economic depression and rampant violence, **now...the seed shall be prosperous; the vine shall give her fruit, and the ground shall give her increase, and the heavens shall give their dew**. Zechariah speaks in agricultural terms about abundant rain and crops, but the message is simple—God promises prosperity to His people. Israel's economic prosperity—and ours today—is in God's hands. This does not mean, of course, that we should not take an interest in politics and vote on people based on Biblical principles to do what we can to foster prosperity. But in the end, the politicians can do nothing if God's hand of blessing is not upon us. God says, **I will cause the remnant of this people to possess all these** blessings. This message parallels Haggai's message in Haggai 1:10-11 and 2:19, and brings to fulfillment the warnings and blessings of Leviticus 26:3-10 and Deuteronomy 28:11-12.

> **13** And it shall come to pass, *that* as ye were a curse among the heathen, O house of Judah, and house of Israel; so will I save you, and ye shall be a blessing: fear not, *but* let your hands be strong.

Although it had been centuries since Israel was a united kingdom, God now makes clear that the blessings He promises are for all of His people, not just Judah. The Northern Kingdom (the **house of Israel**) was defeated and scattered by the Assyrians, and later the Southern Kingdom (the **house of Judah**) was defeated and scattered by the Babylonians. In their scattering, they **were a curse among the heathen**, meaning the Gentile nations. But what does it mean that they **were a curse among** them? They were looked upon by the nations where they were scattered as **a curse** or a **byword**. Deuteronomy 28:37 specifically warned of the recompense for sustained disobedience to the Mosaic Covenant: "And thou shalt become an astonishment, a proverb, and a byword, among all nations whither the LORD shall lead thee." Indeed, the prophet Jeremiah repeatedly warned the people of Judah that this would come to pass if they persisted in their rebelliousness:

> **Jeremiah 24:9** And I will deliver them to be removed into all the kingdoms of the earth for *their* hurt, *to be* a reproach and a proverb, a taunt and a curse, in all places whither I shall drive them.

> **Jeremiah 25:18** *To wit,* Jerusalem, and the cities of Judah, and the kings thereof, and the princes thereof, to make them a desolation, an astonishment, an hissing, and a curse; as *it is* this day;

> **Jeremiah 44:8** In that ye provoke me unto wrath with the works of your hands, burning incense unto other gods in the land of Egypt, whither ye be gone to dwell, that ye might cut yourselves off, and that ye might be a curse and a reproach among all the nations of the earth?...**12** And I will take the remnant of Judah, that have set their faces to go into the land of Egypt to sojourn there, and they shall all be consumed, *and* fall in the land of Egypt; they shall *even* be consumed by the sword *and* by the famine: they shall die, from the least even unto the greatest, by the sword and by the famine: and they shall be an execration, *and* an astonishment, and a curse, and a reproach.

But now God will reverse all of that. They will no longer be a cursed or judged people scattered among the Gentiles, but a blessed people in their land. God assures His people a future restoration as a unified nation. He **will save** or deliver them, meaning He will restore them to the land. And instead of being a **curse among the** nations, they **shall be a blessing** to the world, which will recognize the reversal of fortune God brings about. In light of this promised future blessing, God ends this short message where it started, with the admonition to **fear not, but let your hands be strong**. "Take courage in light of my promises," God says. In the immediate context, they should continue pressing forward with the construction of the Temple, but they should also continue pressing forward in spiritual revitalization.

> **14** For thus saith the LORD of hosts; As I thought to punish you, when your fathers provoked me to wrath, saith the LORD of hosts, and I repented not: **15** So again have I thought in these days to do well unto Jerusalem and to the house of Judah: fear ye not.

In this seventh promise, the **LORD of hosts** promises His divine favor. God reminds them that he previously **thought to punish** His people by bringing in the Babylonians to take them into captivity **when** their **fathers provoked** Him **to wrath**, and at that time God **repented not**, meaning He did not have second thoughts, change course or relent. But now, **in these days**, God has **thought...to do well unto Jerusalem and to the house of Judah**. God determines to pour out blessings on them and once again He will not have second thoughts. The word used here for **thought** is the Hebrew *zamamti* and, except for this verse, it is exclusively used of God's determination to bring judgment on His people. Only here is it used to show an equal determination to bring blessing. Because the fulfillment of this promise is certain, God could encourage them through Zechariah, **fear ye not**. Fear should be replaced with faith. Fear shrinks back, but faith presses forward in the earnest expectation that God will do what He promises.

> **16** These *are* the things that ye shall do; Speak ye every man the truth to his neighbour;

execute the judgment of truth and peace in your gates: **17** And let none of you imagine evil in your hearts against his neighbour; and love no false oath: for all these *are things* that I hate, saith the LORD.

We err if we read about God's promised future blessings and do not see the practical edge of these truths for our lives today. When Habakkuk said "the just shall live by faith" (Habakkuk 2:4), he meant that they would live on the basis of a conviction in the veracity of God's Word. The author of Hebrews described faith for the Christian life as "the substance of things hoped for, the evidence of things not seen." Those "things hoped for" and "things not seen" are the fulfillment of God's promised future blessings. A person living by faith is convinced of God's promises and his or her life is reoriented around those promises. Faith makes the promises tangible ("substance") and transformative ("evidence"). In these verses, Zechariah calls for a response to God's promises that hearkens back to the similar exhortations to righteousness in Zechariah 7:9-10 made to the generation that went into exile. This generation has the opportunity to obey and be blessed where an earlier generation failed.

Zechariah specifies **the things that ye shall do**. We need to put this exhortation against the earlier promises in this chapter of God's future blessings that included regathering the people, dwelling in their midst, and providing peace and prosperity. It would be absurd for a people to believe such promises and not change. And practical righteousness is a proper response to the promises. They should **speak ye every man the truth to his neighbour**. Remember, "Jerusalem shall be called a city of truth" (8:3). The faith response to this promised future blessing is that they **speak...the truth** now. Similarly, they should **execute the judgment of truth and peace in your gates**. As conflicts are resolved at the city **gates**, they should be done so on the basis of truthful testimony, for they should **love no false**

oath. God does not mince words here. He detests dishonesty and injustice, **for all these are things that I hate**. When God dwells in their midst, the city will be characterized by truth, and so God's people should live that way in the present. **None of** them should **imagine evil in** their **hearts against** their **neighbour**. The absence of peace characterized the desolation after the Babylonians destroyed Jerusalem (8:10), but since God promises the blessings of peace and prosperity in the future, His people should purpose to live in harmony now.

One final comment about these verses is in order. God says He hates dishonesty and ill-treatment of our neighbors. Being the people of God entails hating what God hates and loving what He loves.

> **18** And the word of the LORD of hosts came unto me, saying, **19** Thus saith the LORD of hosts; The fast of the fourth *month*, and the fast of the fifth, and the fast of the seventh, and the fast of the tenth, shall be to the house of Judah joy and gladness, and cheerful feasts; therefore love the truth and peace.

The remaining verses in Zechariah 8 prove that chapters 7 and 8 are a cohesive unit. Chapter 7 opens with a question from the envoy from Bethel about fasting. God answers there with a question about their motives when they fasted during the captivity. But here, God resumes his response to the fasting inquiry. The organization of these two chapters—with bookends about fasting—makes good sense because the intervening materials emphasize God's promised blessings for His people. Those blessings must factor into the analysis of the fasting issue since fasting is more often associated with mourning and sorrow than blessings. This bookend of God's response not only explains that the prior fasts in sorrow will be turned to fasts of joy, but also that this joy will be associated with such blessings on the nation that instead of one city (Bethel) sending a delegation to Jerusalem the nations of the world will do so.[126] As Keil and Delitzsch comment: "These fast-days the Lord will turn into days of joy and cheerful feast-days—namely, by bestowing upon them such a fulness of salvation, that Judah will forget to commemorate the former mournful events, and will only have occasion to rejoice in the blessings of grace bestowed upon it by God; though only when the condition mentioned in vv. 16 and 17 has been fulfilled."[127]

Zechariah again reminds us that what he says is **the word of the LORD of hosts** that **came unto** him. The LORD of hosts specifically addresses **the fast of the fourth month, and the fast of the fifth, and the fast of the seventh, and the fast of the tenth.** The Bethel delegation only inquires about **the fast of the fifth month** (7:4) and God's initial response addresses the fasts of the **fifth** and **seventh** months (7:5). But now God addresses four separate fasts. The **fast of the fourth month** commemorates the day when the Babylonian army broke through the walls of Jerusalem. (2 Kings 25:3-4; Jeremiah 39:2) The **fast of the tenth month** commemorates the beginning of the siege on Jerusalem. (2 Kings 25:1-2; Jeremiah 39:1) The **fast of the fifth month** commemorates the burning of Jerusalem in 586 B.C. (Jeremiah 52:12-13) The **fast of the seventh month** commemorates the death of Gedaliah, the Jewish governor. (2 Kings 25:23-26; Jeremiah 41:1-3)

Whereas during the captivity the fasts were times of sorrow and mourning over their captivity, the destruction of their homeland and their removal from it, in the coming Kingdom the fast days will be **to the house of Judah joy and gladness, and cheerful feasts.** Three different words or phrases are used to describe the change of circumstances. The first is the Hebrew *sason,* which means exultation or rejoicing. The term translated **gladness** is *simhah* and means mirth and usually

---

[126] Eugene H. Merrill, *An Exegetical Commentary - Haggai, Zechariah, Malachi*, 202.

[127] Carl Friedrich Keil and Franz Delitzsch, *Commentary on the Old Testament*, 566.

refers to fellowship. The third term, translated **cheerful feasts**, is *moadim* and only occurs here in the entire Bible. It means good or pleasant assemblies. Whereas Jerusalem's past brings painful memories, the future will be a cause for celebration, just as God also promised through the prophet Jeremiah. (see Jeremiah 31:10-14) As the subsequent verses will show, the time of **joy and gladness** is in the coming Messianic Age when the LORD dwells among His people and they are prospered in every way. But based on those promised future blessings and God's assurance that He is presently returned to Israel with blessing, in their present circumstances there is reason for **gladness** at what God is doing and will do.

In light of (**therefore**) their reversal of fortune and promised blessings, God's appeal to them is to **love the truth and peace**. Here again, as in 8:16-17, God's promised future blessings should elicit a response of righteousness. The time of future peace and prosperity when God dwells with His people will be characterized by "truth" and holiness (8:3) and for that reason God's people should presently fashion their lives in light of this reality. It would be absurd if God's people should live the opposite of **truth and peace** while allegedly looking forward with great anticipation to the Messianic Kingdom that will be an unprecedented time of **truth and peace**. We must also take notice that God says through Zechariah that they should not merely do **truth and peace**, but **love** those qualities. This is inward reality.

> **20** Thus saith the LORD of hosts; *It shall* yet *come to pass*, that there shall come people, and the inhabitants of many cities: **21** And the inhabitants of one *city* shall go to another, saying, Let us go speedily to pray before the LORD, and to seek the LORD of hosts: I will go also. **22** Yea, many people and strong nations shall come to seek the LORD of hosts in Jerusalem, and to pray before the LORD.

23 Thus saith the LORD of hosts; In those days *it shall come to pass,* that ten men shall take hold out of all languages of the nations, even shall take hold of the skirt of him that is a Jew, saying, We will go with you: for we have heard *that* God *is* with you.

Once again, we read the familiar **thus saith the LORD of hosts.** We must put what follows in the context of what Zechariah already said, and especially his reference in 8:13 that "ye were a curse among the heathen, O house of Judah, and house of Israel." The reversal of fortune outlined in this chapter includes unified Israel's place among the nations of the world. Rather than a curse among the heathen, the Jewish people will be a blessing to the **nations.** In place of the rampant antisemitism we witness today—sadly, even in the United States and too often among professing Christians—there will be an acknowledgement of God's bountiful blessings among them.

Accordingly, God says through the prophet, **It shall come to pass, that there shall come people, and the inhabitants of many cities: and the inhabitants of one city shall go to another, saying, Let us go speedily to pray before the LORD, and to seek the LORD of hosts: I will go also.** In contrast to a single small delegation from Bethel coming to Jerusalem to seek answers from God's priests and prophets, in this future time, **the inhabitants of many cities** will make the pilgrimage to Jerusalem. But they do not seek the wisdom of priests and prophets because the LORD will "dwell in the midst of Jerusalem." (8:3) These **people** from **many cities** come **to pray before the LORD.** And not only that, they come **speedily,** meaning with great urgency because of their deep desire **to seek the LORD of hosts.** Moreover, **the inhabitants of one city shall go to another** city to encourage others to join them on their journey, promising to **go also** with them. This pictures a national revival in Israel resulting in a believing Jewish remnant that seek **the LORD** who is in Jerusalem, whom Zechariah later confirms is the promised Messiah.

Indeed, Zechariah will speak to both advents of Messiah, his rejection at the first advent, his death, and his return. We know from God's progressive revelation in the New Testament that Jesus is the Christ (Messiah) and Son of God, who is largely rejected by the Jewish people during His earthly ministry in the first century. But Zechariah looks beyond that to a future time when all of that is reversed. Jesus anticipates this even just days before His crucifixion when He says, "For I say unto you, Ye shall not see me henceforth, till ye shall say, Blessed *is* he that cometh in the name of the Lord." (Matthew 23:39) The generation during the first advent wanted Barabbas but a future generation will welcome Jesus as the Messiah, and that is what Zechariah sees. God is not through with Israel because of their rebellion in the first century. As Paul wrote in Romans, "because of unbelief they were broken off" (Romans 11:10) but also "if they abide not still in unbelief, shall be graffed in: for God is able to graff them in again" (Romans 11:23). That is exactly the future Zechariah sees here, and Paul also. (Romans 11:25-32)

Moreover, **many people and strong nations shall come to seek the LORD of hosts in Jerusalem, and to pray before the LORD.** Again, there is a literal emphasis and Zechariah shows us the revival is not localized to Israel, but is global in scope. All of the false religions of the **nations** are discarded and replaced with worship of **the LORD**. People from the **nations** of the world are not coming to worship in Jerusalem for anything less than the reality that **the LORD** dwells there. They **seek the LORD of hosts in Jerusalem** because He is physically and visibly there. They do not make the pilgrimage **to pray** to **the LORD** but to **pray before** Him, meaning in His very presence. Too many modern expositors, unwilling to accept God's plainspoken promise at face value, spiritualize away the force of this passage. But what more could God say that is not here to unequivocally promise His actual presence in the Holy City and His receiving believers from all **the nations** to worship Him there. Jerusalem will be at the center of a great worldwide revival. (Isaiah 2:1-5, 60:1-3; Micah 4:1-5) This is the Tower of Babel episode reversed as **the nations** come together in unity, peace and prosperity in the very presence of God. The Temple there is no longer just the place of worship for the Jewish people, but for all people. God also speaks of this moment in Isaiah 56:7: "Even them will I bring to my holy mountain, and make them joyful in my house of prayer: their burnt offerings and their sacrifices *shall be* accepted upon mine altar; for mine house shall be called an house of prayer for all people."

Building this theme further, the prophet again says, **thus saith the LORD of hosts; In those days it shall come to pass, that ten men shall take hold out of all languages of the nations, even shall take hold of the skirt of him that is a Jew.** The picture is ten Gentiles **taking hold of the skirt** of a single Jew to join him because of their recognition **that God is with** him. The Gentiles **have heard** how that **God is with** the Jewish people, showing that their reputation is global in scope. The nation Israel finally is a light to the world. "Instead of being despised and ridiculed by neighboring nations, the people of God would find themselves the envy of the world."[128] So excited are the peoples of the world to share in the blessings on the Jewish people that they **take hold of the skirt of** the Jew. The Hebrew term for **take hold of** "is used of Moses snatching the serpents by the tail (Exod. 4:4), and of David taking the lion by the beard (1 Sam. 17:35). They could not afford to let go!"[129]

This unprecedented time in Israel's history will happen **in those days**. This is in contrast to "in the day" (8:9) that looked back and "in these days" (8:15) that looked to the present. Zechariah's reference to **those days** looks forward to the literal and earthly fulfillment of all the great promises of this chapter during the Messianic Kingdom when Jesus reigns on David's throne in Jerusalem. (Luke 1:32; Hebrews 1:8) This is "that day" when

128 James E. Smith, *The Minor Prophets*, Zec 8:20–22.
129 Joyce G. Baldwin, *Haggai, Zechariah and Malachi: An Introduction and Commentary*, 167.

"many nations shall be joined to the Lord" (2:11), and "that day" when "every man" will be at peace with "his neighbour under the vine and under the fig tree" (3:10). This is the "last days" of Isaiah 2:2. This is the day of the LORD of Joel 2:10-11 and so many other prophetic utterances in the Old Testament. This is the future day that hearkens us to righteousness now.

Closing

Zechariah 8 closes with a glimpse of Israel's future when it fulfills its designated role of being a light to the world. Gentiles ("men...out of all languages of the nations") will implore a Jewish person to take them to Jerusalem to go before the Lord. This picture of the future seems impossible today, both because of the poor relations between Israel and most of the nations of the world, and because Israel is largely secularized and the Jewish people generally reject Messiah Jesus. God does not struggle with seemingly hopeless cases, and that is a good thing. If God can bring about this extraordinary transformation in Israel and turn of events in their relationship with the Gentile nations, what can He do in your life? How easy it is to size up the circumstances, realize they are beyond our control, and give up. God is not limited by circumstances and nothing is beyond His control. Zechariah reminds us that we as Christians have a glorious future, but he also reminds us of God's power and His care for His people in this moment. May we remember to let our hands be strong.

Application Points

• **MAIN PRINCIPLE:** Because of God's jealousy for Israel, He will in the future bless the nation and the entire world in a time of physical and spiritual prosperity and the Messiah will literally dwell in a revitalized Jerusalem and the peoples of the world will go to Jerusalem to pray before him.

- The Jewish remnant in Zechariah's day should let their hands be strong (take courage) based on God's promised blessings to them in their time and God's promised future blessings.

- Our response to God's promised future blessings in the Messianic Age, which will be characterized by peace, righteousness, and truth, should be a practical righteousness.

Discussion Questions

1. God says He will dwell in Jerusalem and it will "be called a city of truth." What value should we place on our personal integrity now, knowing that in the Kingdom integrity will be the norm?

2. God says in the Kingdom Jerusalem will be a place of complete peace and prosperity (8:4-5). How should Israel's promised glorious future impact our political opinions concerning foreign policy as it concerns Israel?

3. Read 8:6. Can you share an example where you thought some situation was beyond hope and God did something extraordinary and turned it all around?

4. God told the Jewish remnant in Zechariah's day to let their hands be strong, in other words, to take courage. What are some ways in the difficult times in which we live that Christians need to take courage in God's promises?

5. Read 8:10. Who ultimately controls the health of the economy in our nation? What are some non-economic factors that will impact our economic prosperity?

6. What is the purpose of fasting, if any, for Christians today?

Chapter 11

Behold the King

One of the practices too often lacking in Bible study today is focusing on a book or letter in the Bible as a completed unit of thought that must be engaged in its entirety in order to make sense of the pieces. This type of Bible study, which this book strives to carry out, is challenging and time intensive because the student of God's Word must begin with reading the entire book through several times before engaging in the deeper study of individual subunits of thought or individual verses within the book. This process looks to understand the author's original intended message for his audience by grappling with the context and structure of the entire writing, the big picture argument of the writing, and then how the subunits of thought fit together and further the author's intended message. This approach looks first to answer the questions one passage in the book or epistle may raise by looking for clarification in other parts of the same book or epistle before turning to another book of the Bible. At the same time, we do not ignore that

God does make progressive revelation. That is, God did not say everything He had to say to us in Genesis. We have 65 other books of the Bible written over several centuries, and there are things God reveals in part in one place and time and then supplements later. Such is the case here.

Zechariah paints a portrait of Messiah, but not all at once. In our study, we move through a passage or chapter at a time, but as we do so, we need to have already reviewed the entire book of Zechariah through multiple times so that we are aware of the many "connection points" binding the book together in a single unit. These connection points are the themes and persons who come up in multiple places in the book such as the interpreting angel in the night visions. The single most critical connection point is Messiah. As we strive to understand what Zechariah is saying in one place, we should also consider how he builds on the same theme in another. No one would look to understand a famous painting by isolating only 5% of the painting in the lower left corner (but that is how most preaching and Bible study is done!). Nor would they isolate that lower left corner and then try to understand it first by looking at other paintings by other artists even if those paintings have some similarities. In the first instance, we would look at the entire painting as a completed and cohesive work. If we do that here, we will find a fulsome portrait of the coming Messiah, the one God refers to as the Branch, a priest king who will rule and reign from Jerusalem in a glorious future for Israel and the world. But Zechariah does not say all of this at once, hence the necessity of reviewing the whole of his writings first. But seeing all of this, the next step is to question what other or subsequent revelation of God informs our understanding of Zechariah. Regarding Zechariah 9, we find that all four gospels record the event in Jesus' earthly ministry at the beginning of the Passion Week popularly referred to as the Triumphal Entry. Both Matthew and John in their respective Gospels specifically state that the Triumphal Entry fulfills Zechariah 9:9, and this gives us a critical tie down point based on God's progressive revelation. That is, Zechariah's portrait of Messiah is indisputably a portrait of Jesus Christ, the Son of God.

Scripture and Comments

This chapter begins the third division in the book (9-14), the first two being the night visions (1-6) and the messages centered on the fasting question from the Bethel delegation (7-8). This final portion of the book contains two burdens or weighty messages: "The first deals with the coming of the Messiah and his rejection (9:1–11:17); the second (12:1–14:21) presents the future in terms of a day (the phrase 'in that day' appears seventeen times in the last three chapters)."[130] The exegetical challenge of chapter 9 especially centers on 9:1-8. Many conservative scholars understand from this passage that Zechariah foretold the coming conquest of Alexander the Great, the king of Greece who unquestionably followed a victorious path that mirrors some aspects of 9:1-8. Others caution against seeking any historical fulfillment of 9:1-8 because the passage speaks only of what the Lord will do and most of the passage was not fulfilled in any sense during the time of Alexander. Other expositors argue that Alexander at least fulfilled part of 9:1-8. Along these grounds, Dennett comments, "the march of Alexander through these regions was, if not *the* fulfilment, yet *a* fulfilment of Zechariah's predictions."[131]

As the notes below will elaborate, the overall tenor of the passage is indisputably eschatological and global in scope, calling the attention of the entire world on God's actions and culminating in the presentation of Messiah to reign from Jerusalem. Nothing in the words used in the passage suggest a "double fulfillment" whereby Alexander will fulfill limited aspects of the prophecy in the near term followed by a complete eschatological fulfillment. But it is undeniable that

---

[130] Roger Ellsworth, *Opening Up Zechariah*, 85.
[131] Edward Dennett, *Zechariah the Prophet*, 101–103.

part of the passage was fulfilled during the First Advent with the Triumphal Entry of our Lord Jesus Christ into Jerusalem at the beginning of the Passion Week. I conclude that the passage has immediate application for God's people, promising them security as the Temple is completed, but as with most of the book, Zechariah 9 orients their thinking to events future as Messiah comes during the first and second advents. And while there is no "double fulfillment," part of the passage is fulfilled at the Triumphal Entry and the balance of the prophecy remains to be fulfilled when the Lord returns. In this regard, I note that Zechariah 14 provides additional detail about Jesus' triumph over Israel's enemies and places these events in the future day of the Lord associated with Jesus' return, which confirms the proposed interpretation in the notes below.

> **Zechariah 9:1** The burden of the word of the LORD in the land of Hadrach, and Damascus *shall be* the rest thereof: when the eyes of man, as of all the tribes of Israel, *shall be* toward the LORD.

In contrast to earlier chapters where Zechariah sees the night visions (1-6) or receives a word from the Lord (7-8), chapters 9 through 11 comprise a **burden of the word of the LORD** and chapters 12 through 14 comprise a second **burden of the word of the LORD**. The concept of **burden** is heaviness. The heavy **burden** of chapter 9 portends destruction of Israel's neighbors, as does Zechariah 14. Yet it also promises God's protection of Israel. Geographically, this verse and those that follow paint a detailed picture of a relentless march of conquest and destruction on the way to Jerusalem, beginning **in the land of Hadrach, and Damascus shall be the rest thereof**. The path of this march is the path an invader would take on its way to Jerusalem, not unlike prior invaders. Yet there is no indication in the text of any human element involved. The emphasis throughout is on what the LORD will do while the world watches. Because of that, we need not insist that God will engage in a physical conflict like hand-to-hand combat with the enemies' troops. What God will do is set in terms of the familiar pattern of invaders. But looking to Zechariah 14, when God gathers the nations to the Holy Land to destroy them in the battle we refer to as Armageddon, He will use a "plague" that rapidly consumes their flesh. (Zechariah 14:12; see also Revelation 19:15) Exactly how God will overthrow Israel's immediate neighbors in a rapid geographic pattern that begins in the north and moves toward Jerusalem is not stated, but He will do it, culminating in the second advent of Messiah and the events of Zechariah 14.

The first stop in the march of destruction is **Hadrach and Damascus**. Hadrach refers to Hatarikka, an Aramean city-state near the cities of **Damascus** and Hamath, the latter being a significant fortress city on the Orontes River and a major trade route. "Hamath was considered the northern boundary of Israel according to Numbers 13:21 and Joshua 13:5."[132] **Damascus** "was the capital city of the Aramean state that flourished in Syria during the tenth to eighth centuries B.C. The rival Aramean kingdom was sometimes an ally and at other times an enemy to the divided kingdoms of Israel and Judah. The city lay adjacent to the Abana River and was located on the caravan route connecting Mesopotamia to the Mediterranean coast. The border of Damascus was regarded as the northern boundary of the ideal Hebrew state (Ezek. 47:16–18)."[133]

As indicated above, there is debate about whether the conqueror in view is Alexander the Great. We can easily see why, in hindsight, the passage may be seen as partially (albeit minimally) fulfilled by Alexander. For it was Alexander that defeated the Persians (the reigning empire in Zechariah's day) in October 333 B.C. at Issus. He then marched toward Egypt

---

[132] Andrew E. Hill, *Haggai, Zechariah and Malachi: An Introduction and Commentary*, ed. David G. Firth, vol. 28, Tyndale Old Testament Commentaries (Nottingham, England: Inter-Varsity Press, 2012), 205.
[133] *Ibid.*, 205.

and conquered Syria, Phoenicia and Philistia along the way, and these are all historic enemies of Israel. And yet, Alexander did not attack Israel. Indeed, Lindsey comments: "Most conservative commentators regard 9:1–8 as a prophecy of the conquests of Alexander the Great throughout the area of Palestine after the battle of Issus in 333 B.C."[134] Those taking this view typically rely on the idea that "[a]n earthly conqueror may perform the work, but the ultimate agency is the Lord, who beholds and controls all things."[135] Yet we must ask whether the text indicates God or a human military leader that overthrows Israel's enemies:

> One of the first questions one should decide in interpreting 9:1–8 is: Does this material refer to an invasion of Palestine by an earthly king such as Alexander the Great, Nebuchadnezzar or one of Assyria's kings? Our answer is no. Hanson is surely correct in saying, "No specific historical conquest by a specific historical conqueror is being described, nor is there anywhere in these verses so much as a hint that a foreign king is being used by Yahweh as his instrument" (*Apocalyptic*, 316). It is Yahweh who is about to come and do these things.[136]

The language **when the eyes of man, as of all the tribes of Israel, shall be toward the LORD**, is critical to our interpretation of the passage. It points to a future time when **all the tribes of Israel** are reunited to witness these events. But also, the events are witnessed by **the eyes of man**, which captures the idea of all people witnessing these tremendous events. The NET translation reads, "the eyes of all humanity, especially the tribes

[134] F. Duane Lindsey, "Zechariah," in *The Bible Knowledge Commentary: An Exposition of the Scriptures*, 1562.

[135] John Peter Lange, Philip Schaff, and Talbot W. Chambers, *A Commentary on the Holy Scriptures: Zechariah*, 67.

[136] Ralph L. Smith, *Micah–Malachi*, 252.

of Israel, are toward the LORD." In addition to the emphasis on a global witness to these future events, we cannot disconnect this **burden** from the preceding messages in the book, and in particular the climax of chapters 7 and 8 that pictures future global events and all of humanity coming to seek the Lord in Jerusalem. (Zechariah 8:20-23) And to this we must add that the march in view culminates in verse 8 with God "encamp[ing] about mine house...and no oppressor shall pass through them any more: for now have I seen with mine eyes." This mirrors God's promise in 2:5 to "be unto her a wall of fire round about, and...the glory in the midst of" Jerusalem. Many see fulfillment of verse 8 when Alexander did not conquer Israel, and as some have pointed out, Alexander is reported to have had a dream that induced him to spare Israel.[137]

The difficulty with interpreting the passage to speak of Alexander is that he indisputably did not fulfill most of what is recorded in 9:1-8. And the purpose of his military exploits was power. In contrast, the victories in 9:1-8 result in the removal of idolatry from the Philistines and a remnant of the Philistines turning to God. Even if Alexander really did spare Israel because of a dream, the language "I will encamp about mine house" describes a permanent culminating presence in Jerusalem as God (through the agent of the coming Messiah) dwells in Jerusalem, as prior verses in Zechariah promise. Those who view this passage as being fulfilled by Alexander must also limit the scope of verse 8 to allow for the fact that the Temple was destroyed in 70 A.D. even though verse 8 plainly says, "no oppressor shall pass through them any more." But nothing in the passage admits of such limitations, and indeed, those limitations remove the very comfort these passages are intended to provide.

On balance, to make sense of the entire passage and its relationship to the rest of the book, the triumphant march in view that will be witnessed by the world is the march of God,

---

[137] Roger Ellsworth, *Opening Up Zechariah*, 88.

likely indicating a rapid geographic pattern and sequence of judgments, vanquishing Israel's enemies and then manifesting Messiah in Jerusalem permanently, providing total security. This sequence of judgments will culminate in the battle of Armageddon that is the subject of Zechariah 14, confirming these events happen during the day of the Lord (e.g., Zechariah 14:1: "Behold, the day of the LORD cometh...."). As Merrill explains: "What is in view is that the triumphant procession of YHWH has captured the attention of the whole world. To refer to God's people as the 'tribes of Israel' in this postexilic period points to the eschatological milieu of the passage, a time when the scattered tribes will be reassembled."[138] Indeed, God says in verse 8, "for now have I seen with my eyes." God sees the future and guarantees the result. As Merrill further describes:

> The march that commenced in the North will overwhelm successively Hadrach, Damascus, Hamath, Tyre, and Sidon, and four of the Philistine cities. It will end at Jerusalem with YHWH, triumphant in His procession, standing guard over His house and His people. In the tradition of holy war He has come against the foe, defeated him in battle, and established Himself as ruler in His royal palace. This is precisely the pattern seen elsewhere in such holy war passages as Ex. 15:1–18, many of the Psalms (e.g., 2, 9, 24, 29, 46, 47, 48, 65, 68, 76, 77:17–21 [EB 77:16–20], 89b, 97, 98, 104, 106:9–13, 110), Isaiah (11:1–9, 42:10–16, 43:16–21, 51:9–11, 52:7–12), and Habakkuk 3:1–19.[139]

Thus, the events of 9:1-8 likely take place near the end of the Tribulation before Jesus returns. This is consistent with

---

[138] Eugene H. Merrill, *An Exegetical Commentary - Haggai, Zechariah, Malachi*, 214.

[139] *Ibid.*, 217.

judgments described at that time in the book of Revelation, including the sixth trumpet judgment of Revelation 9:14-20 where "the four angels were loosed, which were prepared for an hour, and a day, and a month, and a year, for to slay the third part of men." (Revelation 9:15) That passage states "the number of the army of horsemen were two hundred thousand thousand...I saw the horses in the vision, and them that sat on them, having breastplates of fire...and the heads of the horses were as the heads of lions; and out of their mouths issued fire and smoke and brimstone. By these three was the third part of men killed...."

But if the primary focus of 9:1-8 is future in its orientation, then what of the people of God in Zechariah's day? They too have assurance of God's hand of protection in their time. Their effort to complete the Temple is part of God's larger plan that will culminate in a reunified nation where God personally rules from Jerusalem. As we have repeatedly seen, God through Zechariah seeks to encourage and exhort His people by telling them of the coming Messiah and Messianic Age. Those who think prophecy is not practical or needful deny God's wisdom in this matter. When we accept (have faith in) God's promised future blessings, our behavior, perspective and priorities change now.

> **2** And Hamath also shall border thereby; Tyrus, and Zidon, though it be very wise. **3** And Tyrus did build herself a strong hold, and heaped up silver as the dust, and fine gold as the mire of the streets. **4** Behold, the Lord will cast her out, and he will smite her power in the sea; and she shall be devoured with fire.

Here, as in the prior verse, there is no suggestion of a human conqueror. Key cities are selected to indicate the more general overthrow of the nations or regions where they are located. Zechariah states that **Hamath also shall border thereby**, meaning that it adjoins Damascus. **Hamath** was a region now called Hama, located some 130 miles north of Damascus on the Orontes River. **Hamath** was an Aramean city-state. **Tyrus and Zidon** (or Tyre and Sidon) were coastal cities in Phoenicia (now Lebanon). These two cities are called **very wise**, and yet they are included in the judgment to come. Their wisdom may refer to their commercial acumen as well as their military strategy, but it will not save them. Just as the judgment of Damascus is indicative of the judgment on Syria, so also the judgment on Tyre and Sidon is indicative of the judgment on Phoenicia.

We know from the historical evidence that Tyre considered herself invincible. Tyre was divided into two cities, a mainland city and an island city a half-mile off the coast surrounded by a 150-foot high wall. Tyre was subdued (not destroyed) in 722 B.C. after a 5-year siege by the Assyrians. The Babylonian king Nebuchadnezzar later conquered the mainland city after a 13-year siege (585 – 573 B.C.), but he never took the island city, to which the mainland residents retreated with their wealth. He withdrew in 572 B.C. (Ezekiel 29:18). Zechariah knows about the island fortress when he writes that **Tyrus did build herself a strong hold**. And he knows of her wealth, writing that she **heaped up silver as the dust and fine gold as the mire** or mud **of the streets**. But all of her resources could not protect her because God said, **Behold, the LORD will cast her out, and he will smite her power in the sea; and she shall be devoured with fire**. This is an obvious reference not only to the overthrow of Tyre, but specifically of the utter destruction of the famous island fortification. We know that Tyre survived even Alexander's attack, but never again flourished as it had before its defeat by Nebuchadnezzar.

We know from history that Alexander attacked the island city for seven months in 332 B.C. He used the stones from the destroyed mainland city to build a bridge across the water to the island city (even today, this is a peninsula). This was what Ezekiel had in mind when he wrote, "And they shall destroy the walls of Tyrus, and break down her towers: I will also scrape her dust from her, and make her like the top of a rock" (Ezekiel 26:4). Alexander caused a bridge 2,600 feet long and some 600 to 900 feet wide to be built across the water, and by it, his soldiers conquered the island, executing eight to ten thousand of its inhabitants, selling 30,000 into slavery, and burning the city. But the question remains, did God intend through Zechariah to foretell of Alexander's conquest? Was his march toward Jerusalem the victorious march Zechariah foresaw? Some argue, and not unreasonably, that Alexander fulfilled the passage in part and that a complete fulfillment is future. The difficulty in assigning fulfillment, even in part, to Alexander, is that this march will have key purposes of removing idolatry and refining the Gentiles so that those that remain are believers, which are foreign to Alexander's military mission. And as already noted, Tyre survived Alexander's assault, and in fact, it recovered quickly. In the New Testament, we read that Jesus traveled "into the coasts of Tyre and Sidon" (Matthew 15:21) and that a great multitude" from "about Tyre and Sidon...came unto him" (Mark 3:8). Paul also went there. (Acts 21:3, 7) This is at odds with the permanent destruction of the city in verse 4.

While the concept of a partial fulfillment is possible, the text more strongly supports a single unified future and permanent fulfillment by the LORD. Moreover, we need not insist on finding an historical fulfillment by any human agent, nor look for one to come. Again, the focus throughout the passage is the result of God's actions and not any human agent. The march of any conqueror in the ancient world, Alexander or otherwise, would follow the familiar pattern described, coming from the north and working toward Jerusalem. But what God describes through Zechariah is different than any historic conquerors. Instead, God systematically removes Israel's enemies and appears in Jerusalem, not to conquer but to protect.

> **5** Ashkelon shall see *it*, and fear; Gaza also *shall see it*, and be very sorrowful, and Ekron; for

her expectation shall be ashamed; and the king
shall perish from Gaza, and Ashkelon shall not
be inhabited.

The path of destruction continues with the judgment on
Philistia, and the cities named in this verse are all Philistine
cities. Zechariah states that **Ashkelon shall see** what the Lord
does to Tyre **and fear** for its future. In fact, **Ashkelon shall not
be inhabited**, a likely reference to the people fleeing the
coastal city. We also read that **Gaza** shall **also see** the
overthrow of Tyre **and be very sorrowful**. **Gaza** was a city
fortress atop a 60-foot mound that the Persians used in their
attacks on Egypt. History records that the city fought for two
months in defiance of Alexander before it was overtaken. He
then slaughtered 10,000 of its inhabitants and sold the rest
into slavery. Its king (Batis) was tied to a chariot and dragged
to death in the city streets, which many see as the fulfillment
of the phrase, **and the king shall perish from Gaza**. But I
would note that in the ancient world, a king that
unsuccessfully resisted an invader would always be killed and
so it is not necessary to take Alexander's actions as fulfilling
this verse. What God describes through Zechariah is a familiar
military pattern like that of Alexander, but with a divine
purpose and result contrary to Alexander's conquest.

Zechariah also explains that **Ekron, for her expectation shall
be ashamed**. **Ekron** was another Philistine city, located west of
the coastal city of Ashdod. The reason she **shall be ashamed** is
because of her mistaken **expectation** that Tyre would survive
the attack. The fall of mighty Tyre portends the fall of these
other less defensible cities.

> 6 And a bastard shall dwell in Ashdod, and I
> will cut off the pride of the Philistines. 7 And I
> will take away his blood out of his mouth, and
> his abominations from between his teeth: but
> he that remaineth, even he, *shall be* for our
> God, and he shall be as a governor in Judah,
> and Ekron as a Jebusite.

Ashdod is yet another Philistine city that will fall. God says through Zechariah that **a bastard shall dwell** there **and I will cut off the pride of the Philistines**. The reference to **a bastard** means a mongrel or intermixed people will **dwell in Ashdod** after its defeat. Their **pride** will be taken away as they lose their identity as a distinct people group through the intermingling of the peoples. We should note that other writing prophets also foretold the destruction of the Philistines. Amos specified that Gaza would be overthrown (Amos 1:7), **Ashdod** would be depopulated (1:8), Ekron judged and the "remnant of the Philistines shall perish" (1:8), and Tyre punished (1:9). Similarly, Zephaniah wrote of the coming judgment of Ashkelon, Ekron and Gaza (Zephaniah 2:4). It is notable that this destruction is in the context of global destruction during the future "day of the Lord." (Zephaniah 2:1-3)

Again, without reference to any human agent, God says, **I will take away his** (i.e., Philistia) **blood out of his mouth, and his abominations from between his teeth**. The **abominations** refers to their religious practices, as that same Hebrew term (*siqqus*) is used in Deuteronomy 29:17, 1 Kings 11:5, 6, Jeremiah 7:30, 13:27, and Ezekiel 5:11, just to list a few examples. Philistines ate their idolatrous sacrifices to their gods with blood (compare the sacrifices in Leviticus 7:26, 17:10, 12). God will judge their idolatry and bring their religious practices to an end. By these actions, God refines a Gentile remnant (**he that remaineth**) that will be **for our God** and **be as a governor in Judah, and Ekron as a Jebusite**. Instead of being aliens they will be a part of the covenant community, even taking leadership roles like **a governor**. The **Jebusites** are the ancient inhabitants of the city of Jerusalem who were absorbed into the community after King David took the city. The point here is that a refined remnant of Gentiles will be part of the family of God and be blessed like the refined remnant of Israel. This blessing is directed at **Ekron** but no doubt, consistent with the rest of the book (see Zechariah 2:22, 8:22-23, 14:16), has general application to the Gentiles.

We cannot place fulfillment of this eschatological blessing of Jews and Gentiles together during the time of Alexander or any other time in history. This demands that the fulfillment of 9:1-8 occurs in the future from Zechariah's time. As already indicated, the events of 9:1-8 occur during the Tribulation just prior to the return of Christ. Whereas the judgments of 9:1-8 focus on Israel's enemies within the surrounding nations, the balance of the chapter addresses God's spiritual and physical rescue of Israel proper in connection with the two advents of Messiah. In regard to the second advent, Zechariah 14 details the battle of Armageddon by which the Gentile armies invading Israel are defeated, after which "every one that is left of all the nations which came against Jerusalem shall even go up from year to year to worship the king." (Zechariah 14:16) This shows two key connections between Zechariah 9 and 14, the reference to the coming king and that the judgments result in a refined remnant of Gentiles who worship the king.

> **8** And I will encamp about mine house because of the army, because of him that passeth by, and because of him that returneth: and no oppressor shall pass through them any more: for now have I seen with mine eyes.

Having come in from the north and removed Israel's enemies, God says in the first person, **I will encamp about mine house** or Temple **because of the army**. In other words, God will protect the Temple, and by extension, the city of Jerusalem, from any Gentile **army**. Because Israel was a natural land bridge between Asia and Africa, conquerors would pass through going north or south. Thus, Zechariah continues God's words, **because of him that passeth by** or through the nation, and **because of him that returneth** through the nation, God **will encamp about** His **house** or Temple. God will make sure it never happens again— **no oppressor shall pass through them any more**. This is consistent with the parallel promise of Zechariah 14:11 that people will dwell in Jerusalem safely "and there shall be no more utter destruction." And again, Zechariah 14 places these events in the future day of the LORD.

Attempts to attach 9:1-7 to the actions of Alexander are difficult. It is true that Alexander did not attempt to conquer Israel. In fact, the Jewish historian Josephus recorded that Alexander went to Jerusalem, was presented with Daniel's prophecy, believed it referred to him and left them in peace: "And when he had said this to Parmenion, and had given the high-priest his right hand, the priests ran along by him, and he came into the city. And when he went up into the temple, he offered sacrifice to God, according to the high-priest's direction, and magnificently treated both the high-priest and the priests. And when the *Book of Daniel* was showed him wherein Daniel declared that one of the Greeks should destroy the empire of the Persians, he supposed that himself was the person intended. And as he was then glad, he dismissed the multitude for the present." But others would come through and desecrate (Antiochus IV) and later destroy (the Romans) the Temple. The verse at hand foresees a time when the passing through of conquerors is over forever because of God's personal presence in Jerusalem, because He decreed it (**now I have seen with mine eyes**), and that has not happened yet. But what follows will yield more specifics on how this will come about.

> **9** Rejoice greatly, O daughter of Zion; shout, O daughter of Jerusalem: behold, thy King cometh unto thee: he *is* just, and having salvation; lowly, and riding upon an ass, and upon a colt the foal of an ass. **10** And I will cut off the chariot from Ephraim, and the horse from Jerusalem, and the battle bow shall be cut off: and he shall speak peace unto the heathen: and his dominion *shall be* from sea *even* to sea, and from the river *even* to the ends of the earth.

Through 9:1-8, Israel's enemies are in fear as one by one they fall in defeat. For a conqueror like Alexander, we should expect Israel also to be in fear as the army approaches. Yet it is not a Gentile conqueror that arrives in Jerusalem, but a Jewish king pronouncing peace. Understanding these two verses is critical to understanding the entire chapter. Fortunately, we have express statements of fulfillment of 9:9 in the New Testament to guide our way. But before turning there, we need to be mindful that the book of Zechariah, like all books of the Bible, is intended as a cohesive unit of thought to be read and understood as a unified whole and not in piecemeal fashion. To that end, let us review pertinent material preceding chapter 9.

We are introduced in chapter 1 to God's sovereignty over the nations (1:8-10), God's "good words and comfortable words" (1:13) that God will again bless Israel and deal with her enemies (1:14-17). Indeed, God will be a protector of Israel dwelling in the midst of Jerusalem (2:5) and Israel's enemies will be spoiled (2:8-9). This future time will be a time for Israel to "sing and rejoice" (2:10) because God will dwell in the midst of the Holy City and there will be peace with the Gentile nations who will also be God's people (2:11). In this future time, God will present to His people "my servant the Branch" (3:8) whose presence will be accompanied by the elimination of iniquity (3:9) and an age of peace and prosperity (3:10). The "man whose name is the Branch" will build "the temple of the LORD" (6:12) from which he shall "bear the glory" of God as he rules as a priest-king "upon his throne...he shall be a priest upon his throne" (6:13). People from around the world will come to Jerusalem to participate in the construction of "the temple of the LORD." Critically, all of these future blessings "shall come to pass, if ye [the Jewish people] will diligently obey the voice of the LORD your God." (6:15) Thus, there must be a spiritual revival before there will be physical peace and prosperity. In the hinge chapters 7-8 we see this principle presented as God admonishes the empty religion of the prior generation that brought about discipline (7:5-14), and foresees a return to righteousness coinciding with God's manifest presence "in the midst of Jerusalem" (8:3) that ushers in the Messianic Age of peace and prosperity (8:4-8). And once again, we have the promise of a future where God's people will come from all the nations of the world to experience His presence in Jerusalem (8:20-24). We must understand Zechariah 9 as building on what he previously says about this glorious future.

We are also aided by God's progressive revelation in the New Testament. What we often refer to as the Triumphal Entry is recorded in all four Gospels. Matthew expressly states that Jesus' riding into Jerusalem on a donkey fulfills Zechariah 9:9:

> **Matthew 21:4** All this was done, that it might be fulfilled which was spoken by the prophet, saying, **5** Tell ye the daughter of Sion, Behold, thy King cometh unto thee, meek, and sitting upon an ass, and a colt the foal of an ass.

Two key observations are that only Zechariah 9:9 is fulfilled at that time and that it is fulfilled literally. John's record of the same event is also important:

> **John 12:12** On the next day much people that were come to the feast, when they heard that Jesus was coming to Jerusalem, **13** Took branches of palm trees, and went forth to meet him, and cried, Hosanna: Blessed *is* the King of Israel that cometh in the name of the Lord. **14** And Jesus, when he had found a young ass, sat thereon; as it is written, **15** Fear not, daughter of Sion: behold, thy King cometh, sitting on an ass's colt. **16** These things understood not his disciples at the first: but when Jesus was glorified, then remembered they that these things were written of him, and *that* they had done these things unto him.

Like Matthew's account, John sees a literal fulfillment of Zechariah 9:9. Indeed, the disciples do not fully appreciate what they witness at the time, but after the resurrection "remembered they that these things were written of him." It is not merely that Jesus does something like that recorded in Zechariah 9:9, but what God says through Zechariah over 500 years before and inspires Zechariah to write are specifically written of Jesus Christ. And while the disciples do not appreciate all the details when they witness the Triumphal Entry, much of the populace welcomes Jesus as a king, even quoting from Psalm 118:25-26. While Mark and Luke do not quote Zechariah 9:9, both quote from Psalm 118 and recognize that the crowds welcome Jesus as the king who comes in the name of the LORD.

Apart from the New Testament revelation, we might misconstrue Zechariah's words in 9:9. Zechariah tells the people, **Rejoice greatly, O daughter of Zion; shout, O daughter of Jerusalem**. Instead of a foreign invader like Alexander, the people are called upon to greet their **King**. They are to **behold** or look as he approaches, for **thy King cometh unto thee**. The idiom **daughter of Jerusalem** simply means the inhabitants of Jerusalem. This requires a literal **king** and a literal rejoicing as the **King** is welcomed to the city, which we know is exactly what happens. In contrast to a man like Alexander, this **King...is just** or righteous **and having salvation**. It would be natural, at least looking at Zechariah 9:1-10 in isolation, to take **salvation** as physical deliverance from Israel's enemies, and quite probably the crowd at the triumphal entry took it that way. But we know that at the first Triumphal Entry, **King** Jesus comes to provide spiritual deliverance from sins, for that must precede physical blessing. As Matthew records at the outset of his Gospel, "And she shall bring forth a son, and thou shalt call his name Jesus: for he shall save his people from their sins." (Matthew 1:21) And this conforms to what Zechariah pronounces in the preceding chapters as outlined above. Jesus comes first to address our sin problem, **lowly** or humble, **and riding upon an ass, and upon a colt the foal of an ass**. There will be a second Triumphal Entry, to be sure, when Jesus arrives as a victor on a horse (Revelation 19), but here **King** Jesus arrives as no other king ever will or ever has in human history. He is in the lowly position of the one who is God's servant, the Branch, the one who will "give his life a ransom for many." (Matthew 20:28)

We should not think it odd that Zechariah puts no explicit separation of time between 9:9 and 9:10. When Jesus stands to read from the scroll of Isaiah in the synagogue in His home town of Nazareth, He says: "The Spirit of the Lord *is* upon me, because he hath anointed me to preach the gospel to the poor; he hath sent me to heal the brokenhearted, to preach deliverance to the captives, and recovering of sight to the blind, to set at liberty them that are bruised, To preach the acceptable year of the Lord." (Luke 4:18-19) Then "he closed the book" of Isaiah "and he gave it again to the minister and sat down." (Luke 4:20) Jesus reads from Isaiah 61:1-2, but stops mid-sentence and announces that what He reads is literally fulfilled at that time. But the words immediately after what Jesus reads state: "and the day of vengeance of our God; to comfort all that mourn; To appoint unto them that mourn in Zion, to give unto them beauty for ashes, the oil of joy for mourning, the garment of praise for the spirit of heaviness; that they might be called trees of righteousness, the planting of the LORD, that he might be glorified." (Isaiah 61:2-3) Jesus stops at precisely the place in the Isaiah scroll where the prophecy of His first advent ends. Specifically, Jesus stops with the prophecy of the "salvation" He would bring at His first advent, leaving the balance of the passage concerning the Messianic Age to be fulfilled later. And so it is here in Zechariah 9:9-10. One final remark on this point is that we should also observe the structural parallel between Zechariah 9 and 13. Zechariah 9:1-8 and 9:10-17 focus on events just before and at the time Jesus Christ returns, while Zechariah 9:9 concerns only the first advent. Similarly, Zechariah 13:1-6 and 13:8-9 focus on events during the day of the Lord, while 13:7 concerns the crucifixion of Messiah during the first century.

The prophet continues directly from the first advent in verse 9 to the second advent in verse 10. We can understand how the Jewish people who shouted "hosanna" at the triumphal entry expect verse 10 to be fulfilled right away, for Jesus' own disciples have that expectation. But they do not appreciate that Jesus must first be the suffering servant. We know from New Testament revelation that Jesus is presently building His church (Matthew 16:18) and after that is complete He will return. It is in connection with his second advent that God's march of liberation of Israel from her enemies expounded in verses 1-8 will occur. That liberation continues in verse 10 with the liberation of Israel from the enemies within its borders.

We may conjecture about what would have happened, and how Zechariah 9 would have been fulfilled, if the nation of Israel characteristically embraced Jesus as their Messiah in the first century. Hypothetically, in that event, there might not have been two advents at all and the entirety of Zechariah 9 would have been fulfilled in the first advent. But we must recall that while Jesus' offer of the Kingdom (e.g., Matthew 4:17: "Repent: for the kingdom of heaven is at hand") during His earthly ministry is genuine, it is met with much rejection, especially from the Jewish leadership. In Matthew's Gospel, this rejection comes to a head in Matthew 12, where the religious leadership accuses Jesus of casting out demons "by Beelzebub the prince of the devils." (Matthew 12:24) For this there could be no forgiveness (Matthew 12:31-32). And when they demand more signs, Jesus promises the sign of Jonah (Matthew 12:40 ff.), denoting His resurrection and the condemnation of that generation. Immediately preceding the famous Olivet Discourse, Jesus explicitly pronounces judgment on that generation in Matthew 23. All of this is to say that well before the Triumphal Entry, the hypothetical possibility of Jesus presenting Himself as king and immediately ruling and reigning over the world from the Temple is already lost. Of course, the disciples do not yet understand, which is why they are so concerned in Matthew 24 after hearing Jesus speak of the destruction of the Temple, prompting them to ask (my paraphrase), if not now, then when? The characteristic rejection of Jesus by the leadership sets in motion the events that will lead to the cross where the crowds will choose Barabbas over Jesus, inking in the saviour's blood their rejection. In association with Jesus' return, the balance of Zechariah 9 will be fulfilled, consistent with other prophecies. (e.g., Psalm 110:1-2; Daniel 2:44; Joel 3:1-17)

Notice how verse 9 describes the **king** in the third person, but verse 10 speaks in the first person and God the Father explains that the liberation of Israel from her enemies will include the removal of enemies from her national borders. Thus, God says, **I will cut off the chariot from Ephraim, and the horse from Jerusalem, and the battle bow shall be cut off**. The references to the **chariot, horse,** and **battle bow** are references to the historic Gentile weapons of war, here referred to as a metonymy for the Gentile enemies being removed from Israel. At this point we see again a change of person. Zechariah says **I will cut off...** speaking in the first person for God. He then says, **and he shall speak peace unto the heathen** or Gentiles. God removes the enemies, but the **king** will proclaim **peace unto the heathen**. How can this be? Because as we saw in verse 9:7, the march of God to Jerusalem has a purpose not only of removing enemies but refining the Gentiles so that those that remain are part of the family of God, a theme witnessed elsewhere in Zechariah. We know from New Testament revelation that the first advent and the work of the **king** on a Roman cross make this possible. (e.g., Romans 1:16; Ephesians 2:11-13)

What verse 10 makes abundantly clear is that Gentiles join the family of God and for that reason the **king shall speak peace unto** them. The era of Gentile domination and acrimony toward Israel ends and the reign of **king** Jesus will be worldwide. For **his dominion shall be from sea to sea, and from the river even to the ends of the earth**. This, of course, is the same global Kingdom of Daniel 2:44: "And in the days of these kings shall the God of heaven set up a kingdom, which shall never be destroyed: and the kingdom shall not be left to other people, *but* it shall break in pieces and consume all these kingdoms, and it shall stand for ever." This is the Kingdom of the "Son of man": "And there was given him dominion, and glory, and a kingdom, that all people, nations, and languages, should serve him: his dominion *is* an everlasting dominion, which shall not pass away, and his kingdom *that* which shall not be destroyed." (Daniel 7:14) Most expositors deny that there will be a literal worldwide Kingdom on this earth, but such theological commitments are forced on these passages. For the text plainly proclaims a **dominion...from sea to sea...to the ends of the earth**. We must ask, how else could God express a literal Kingdom on this planet earth than by these words? What additional verbiage must God employ to confirm a literal Kingdom is in view? The answer is none. God is not required in every unfulfilled prophecy concerning Israel's future to add a parenthetical, "I really mean this. Interpret the words literally." The words are plain and we need only believe God.

Finally, Zechariah revisits the matter of a coming **king** in Zechariah 14. There he says, "the LORD shall be king over all the earth: in that day shall there be one LORD, and his name one." (14:9) And the Gentiles that join to the LORD "shall even go up from year to year to worship the king, the LORD of hosts." (14:16) This **king** is the fulfillment of the priest-king type of Zechariah 3-4 and Zechariah 6, and is the Branch and the Messiah of God. This is, of course, Jesus Christ, the one the apostle John calls, "KING OF KINGS, AND LORD OF LORDS." (Revelation 19:16) God's judgments on the neighboring nations around Israel culminate in presenting the **king** who, according to Zechariah 14, draws the nations to battle in the Holy Land and routes them swiftly with a plague.

> **11** As for thee also, by the blood of thy covenant I have sent forth thy prisoners out of the pit wherein *is* no water. **12** Turn you to the strong hold, ye prisoners of hope: even to day do I declare *that* I will render double unto thee.

In these verses, God continues explaining the future victory over Israel's enemies, which results in the release of Jewish captives among the nations. God says, **as for thee** Israel, because of **the blood of thy covenant I have sent forth** or set free **thy prisoners out of the pit wherein is no water.** In other words, in accordance with the promises of God's covenant with Abraham, the **prisoners** are freed. The reference to **the pit wherein is no water** is to dry cisterns used to hold prisoners, a common ancient practice. (cf. Genesis 37:24) The **prisoners** are to return **you to the strong hold**, that is, to the land of Israel. They are no longer **prisoners** of despair but **of hope** both because they are freed and God promises them blessing: **even to day do I declare that I will render double unto thee.** All that they have lost to their enemies is not only returned, but doubled. This is a turn of fortunes only God can do.

> **13** When I have bent Judah for me, filled the bow with Ephraim, and raised up thy sons, O Zion, against thy sons, O Greece, and made thee as the sword of a mighty man. **14** And the LORD shall be seen over them, and his arrow shall go forth as the lightning: and the LORD God shall blow the trumpet, and shall go with whirlwinds of the south.

God uses metaphors to explain how those who were formerly prisoners of the Gentile nations will by the power of God rise against them. God says, **I have bent Judah for me, filled the bow with Ephraim.** This pictures the southern kingdom or **Judah** as the bow and the northern kingdom or **Ephraim** as the arrow. God will use the united Israel against her enemies. (see also Zechariah 14:14: "And Judah also shall fight at Jerusalem...") God will raise **up thy sons, O Zion**, that is, raise an army of the redeemed people of Israel, to do battle **against thy sons, O Greece**, a reference not to the singular nation of **Greece** but idiomatically to the Gentiles. Now **Zion**—representative not merely of Jerusalem but of the nation—is made...**as the sword of a mighty man**. In these metaphors we have **the bow**, the arrow, and the **sword**, comprised of an army from the reunited Israel. To this point, there has been no human element in God's march through Israel's enemies, but from the nation God will use His redeemed people to shake off the enemies. As a result, **the LORD shall be seen** or appear **over** or above **them** (His enemies), in a position to easily route them. And the victory will be swift as **his arrow shall go forth as the lightning**. Indeed, the LORD **God shall blow the trumpet** of war announcing the attack, and as a warrior **shall go with the whirlwinds of the south**. God's defeat of Israel's enemies is both sure and swift. What is perhaps implied here as these verses follow the arrival of King Jesus is made explicit in Zechariah 14, i.e., the moving agent that empowers and leads the Jewish remnant to victory of their enemies is the returning Messiah. (Zechariah 14:14)

> **15** The LORD of hosts shall defend them; and they shall devour, and subdue with sling stones; and they shall drink, *and* make a noise as through wine; and they shall be filled like bowls, *and* as the corners of the altar.

Consistent with the picture throughout Zechariah 9 of God as warrior, and the preceding verses about raising sons of Zion to fight, He is referred to as **the LORD of hosts** or armies, a common title for God throughout the book of Zechariah. We need to keep in mind that Zechariah 14 leaves no question that God's defense of Israel in the future day of the LORD is carried out by Messiah when he returns. (Zechariah 14:1-7, 12-15) What the LORD of hosts does here, He does through Messiah as his moving agent, which in a subtle way reinforces the deity of Messiah and the trinitarian notion of one Godhead (not two or three gods).

On the one hand, God **shall defend** or guard **them**—His people that He raises to fight. And the army He raises **shall devour** their enemies **and subdue with sling stones**. Zechariah mentions earlier the removal of the Gentile's weapons of war (chariots, horses, bows). The Jewish rebels have no such weapons. In the way David overcame Goliath with his courage and effort coupled with God's power assuring success, this future army will **subdue** their Goliath **with sling stones**. We need not take this to mean that their weapons will literally be, or only be, sling stones. The picture, rather, is of the seemingly inadequately armed forces of God seizing the victory by God's power. This final battle will not be a narrow victory but a complete routing of the enemies of Israel and of God. His army, figuratively, **shall drink** their enemies' blood and **make a noise** like a drunkard **as through wine**. Indeed, **they shall be filled** with the blood of their enemies **like bowls, and as the corners of the altar**. This last expression confirms it is the enemies' blood in view, and not literal **wine**. The bowls used for sprinkling the corners of the altar were always filled to the brim, and so the emphasis is on the completeness of the victory. God's people will be completely satisfied with the vengeance they achieve over their foes, and their blood will run deep.

> **16** And the LORD their God shall save them in that day as the flock of his people: for they *shall be as* the stones of a crown, lifted up as an ensign upon his land.

This verse is yet another critical interpretive indicator for the chapter. Zechariah explains that **the LORD their God shall save them in that day as the flock of his people**. The phrase **in that day** is a shorthand reference to the **day** of the Lord, a frequent Old Testament motif about the eschatological time of blessing and judgment. We have already seen such references in Zechariah. (e.g., Zechariah 2:11, 3:9-10) This further confirms, as does Zechariah 14:1, that the events surrounding the physical deliverance of Israel over its enemies and their regathering to the land will occur in the future and culminate with the second coming of the Messiah. At that time, God through His Messiah, Jesus, will **save** His redeemed people from their enemies and into the global Kingdom established under God's appointed king. Note also the reference to God's people **as the flock**. This alludes to a shepherd motif that the prophet emphasizes in Zechariah 11, speaking of the good shepherd whose services will be valued at 30 pieces of silver, a prophecy fulfilled by Jesus Christ at His first advent. Of course, the good shepherd is the promised king of this chapter. In the Kingdom, His people Israel **shall be** treasured **as the stones of a crown** by the Gentile peoples of the world instead of being enemies. Also, they shall be **lifted up as an ensign upon his land**. The latter expression describes redeemed Israel as a beacon or light to the world, a station they never attained. This concept is referenced in chapter 8 where God speaks of a future time when ten Gentiles will seek one Jewish person to lead them in pilgrimage to Jerusalem to see God. Zechariah returns to this theme in chapter 14.

> **17** For how great *is* his goodness, and how great *is* his beauty! corn shall make the young men cheerful, and new wine the maids.

In this last verse of Zechariah 9, the prophet takes a deep breath as it were and surveys in his mind all that God showed him. He is compelled to praise God, **for how great is his goodness** toward His people, **and how great is his beauty!** The **beauty** of God references His great deeds on behalf of His people. (see Psalm 27:4) The new Messianic Age ushered in by Messiah's victory over their enemies will bring about a complete restoration of the nation and a time of peace and prosperity, indicated by the words, the **corn** or grain **shall make the young men cheerful, and new wine the maids**. These words express abundance and rejoicing in God's bounty in the Kingdom.

Closing

This chapter presents God victorious over Israel's enemies but at the same time, empowering the people of Israel to fight. We see that pattern throughout Scripture—God does what only He can do but uses ordinary people to do what they are able to. In Joshua 6, for example, God brings down the walls of Jericho, but the people still had to walk around the city each day for seven days. In the book of Acts, Peter is a willing vessel but at the right moment he is "filled with the Holy Ghost" (Acts 4:8) for the ministry task at hand. God enables His people for the task, but their role is not passive. A common refrain among Christians in the face of challenging times is that "God is in control." I have frequently been told that God is in control and does not need us for anything. That is true but the implications sometimes drawn from this truth are problematic. Just because God will accomplish His purposes regardless of our cooperation is never an excuse for standing on the sidelines. God expects every one of us to be actively engaged in a local church and in ministering to other people. When we yield our members to righteousness (Romans 6:13) and become a living sacrifice (Romans 12:1), God enables our service (and rewards us at the bema). God does the part we cannot do, like softening the heart of someone we are ministering the gospel to. Do your part, with the future Kingdom in view, and give God the glory.

Application Points

- **MAIN PRINCIPLE:** The king and Messiah will bring spiritual deliverance at his first advent, then in connection with his second coming, God will bring judgment on Israel's neighbors and protect Israel, but at the same time there will be a refined Gentile remnant that is part of the family of God.

Discussion Questions

1. At the same time as God brings judgments on Israel's neighbors, we read that "he that remaineth...shall be for our God." (Zechariah 9:7) How is it that during this time there will be believing Gentiles? (think in terms of God's progressive revelation in the New Testament)

2. We know from the New Testament that Zechariah 9:9 is fulfilled at the Triumphal Entry recorded in all four Gospels. But what indicators in the text of 9:9-10 suggest two advents of the king?

3. How is the Triumphal Entry actually "triumphal"? Will there be a second Triumphal Entry of the king?

4. How will the coming king be like or unlike other rulers of nations?

5. What language in the text defines the scope of the Messianic Kingdom? Is there any indication in text of Zechariah 9 that this Kingdom is not a literal kingdom on this earth?

Chapter 12

New Exodus

The name "Zechariah" means "God remembers." He remembers His people and His promises to them. Over and again, Zechariah's messages remind the Jewish remnant, in need of "good words and comfortable words" (1:13), that God remembers. The book shows us the nation of Israel physically and spiritually revitalized in a glorious future where the promised Messiah lives in Jerusalem, transforming the nation and, indeed, the world. But in Zechariah's day, only a remnant returned home after the Babylonian captivity. While others would come, to this present time most of the Jewish people remain scattered among the nations. For the promised future blessings Zechariah presents to the people to be realized, there must be a future regathering of the Jewish people back to the Promise Land. This central theme—an exodus from the nations—is therefore prominent in Zechariah's ministry. (See Zechariah 2:6-7, 8:7-8) But now the prophet elaborates on the new exodus. It seems impossible in Zechariah's day, and even more so now, that the Jewish people scattered around the world would return to the Promise Land. Just as the original exodus from Egypt during the days of Moses required a people of faith (see Hebrews 11:29: "By faith they passed through the Red sea as by dry land..."), so also there will be a future revival as God calls His people home.

Scripture and Comments

Despite the chapter break we have between chapters 9 and 10, chapter 10 continues the same message (or burden) that began in 9:1, although the focus changes. Chapter 9 details the coming victory over Israel's enemies and the first and second comings of the king who will speak peace to the nations. Chapter 10 contrasts Israel's bad shepherds and consequent idolatry to the blessings to be experienced in the Kingdom with God as shepherd as the scattered Jewish people are regathered to the Holy Land. As Dennett notes: "This chapter is undoubtedly connected with chapter 9, but it would be a mistake to suppose that on this account there is a direct sequence in the narration of events."[140] Chapter 9 ends with Zechariah's statement of praise and general description of the prosperity of the new age. Chapter 10 does not sequentially follow but looks back to describe the new exodus of the Jewish people from the Gentile nations to the Promised Land where they will reign with the Messiah as he is installed as king.[141] Most expositors spiritualize away all such prophecies, denying a literal regathering of the Jewish people. One of the older commentaries aptly describes the problem with these fanciful interpretations of very plain passages like Zechariah 10 that promise a regathering:

> Of this, no man who believes the Scriptures can
> entertain a doubt. The passage before us, even
> if it stood alone, would be amply sufficient to
> warrant our expectation of this event. But it is

---

[140] Edward Dennett, *Zechariah the Prophet*, 117.
[141] Eugene H. Merrill, *An Exegetical Commentary - Haggai, Zechariah, Malachi*, 235.

one of many: for the prophets all, with one voice, agree in declaring that God has not finally cast off his people; but that they shall return to him, and enjoy under their Messiah a state of prosperity far exceeding any thing that they ever experienced since they became a nation. That that event is spoken of in the passage before us, will be evident to any one who will consult the context... In their present dispersion, they seem as if they were *cast off*: but, though scattered over the face of the globe, they are only "*sown*" there, as seed which the husbandman casts over his field, with a view to reap, and gather it to greater advantage at a future period. Their return will be a season of most sublime joy, both to them and their children: and the interpositions of God in their behalf will be as visible and as effectual as those which were vouchsafed at the Red Sea, on their departure from Egypt; or at the river Jordan, on their entrance into Canaan. Every obstacle shall be removed from before them, and every opposing enemy be destroyed.

Persons who are adverse to the idea of a literal restoration of the Jews to their own land, will satisfy themselves with saying, that the whole of this description is figurative: but if this be figurative, where, I would ask, shall any thing be found that is to be taken in a literal sense? or, supposing God to have ordained to accomplish any thing literally, by what plainer terms could he possibly declare it? There must, I think, be an end of all certainty in language, if the event here predicted be not to be understood in its literal and most obvious sense.[142]

---

[142] Charles Simeon, *Horae Homileticae: Hosea to Malachi*, 507–508.

Taken in a plain sense, God will restore the scattered nation to their land. More than that, God wants to bless them in the land.

> **Zechariah 10:1** Ask ye of the LORD rain in the time of the latter rain; *so* the LORD shall make bright clouds, and give them showers of rain, to every one grass in the field.

The burden that started in chapter 9 continues but the focus changes from the coming king to the blessings to be experienced in Messiah's Kingdom. To an agrarian culture, nothing speaks more of blessings than rain, and under Messiah's leadership, rain will be available in abundance for the asking. Recall the promises of Deuteronomy 11:

> **Deuteronomy 11:11** But the land, whither ye go to possess it, *is* a land of hills and valleys, *and* drinketh water of the rain of heaven: **12** A land which the LORD thy God careth for: the eyes of the LORD thy God *are* always upon it, from the beginning of the year even unto the end of the year. **13** And it shall come to pass, if ye shall hearken diligently unto my commandments which I command you this day, to love the LORD your God, and to serve him with all your heart and with all your soul, **14** That I will give *you* the rain of your land in his due season, the first rain and the latter rain, that thou mayest gather in thy corn, and thy wine, and thine oil. **15** And I will send grass in thy fields for thy cattle, that thou mayest eat and be full. **16** Take heed to yourselves, that your heart be not deceived, and ye turn aside, and serve other gods, and worship them; **17** And *then* the LORD's wrath be kindled against you, and he shut up the heaven, that there be no rain, and that the land yield not her fruit; and *lest* ye perish quickly from off the good land which the LORD giveth you.

In their dispersion from the land as a consequence of their rebellion and idolatry, the Jewish people lost these blessings just as Moses warned them. As Jeremiah says: "Are there *any* among the vanities of the Gentiles that can cause rain? or can the heavens give showers? *art* not thou he, O LORD our God? therefore we will wait upon thee: for thou hast made all these *things*." (Jeremiah 14:22) But with their return, God implores them to ask for blessings so that He may bless them. Thus, God says through Zechariah, **ask ye of the LORD rain in the time of the latter rain**. In response to such prayer and echoing the blessings of Deuteronomy 11, **the LORD shall make bright clouds, and give** you **showers of rain, to every one grass in the field**. Israel's rainy seasons begin in October (the early rain) and end in March to May (the latter rain). The latter rains are associated with bringing the crops to maturity for the harvest. The **showers of rain** will grow the crops and grass to feed the people and livestock, thus providing prosperity.

Many expositors that see a literal regathering nevertheless view verse 1 figuratively, construing the **showers** as spiritual blessings. I agree with David Baron's comment: "But it is perhaps necessary to repeat and emphasize that it is literal rain which is meant here, in the first instance, in which connection it is important to observe that Israel was taught to regard giving or withholding of this great temporal blessing, upon which the prosperity of the land the life of man and beast are dependent, as entirely in the hand of God."[143] While I do not think the first verse should be understood as spiritual blessings, admittedly, the point of the text extends beyond crops, showing a general prosperity in the land. We must not lose sight of the focus on the provider of the blessings, who is contrasted with the idols they formerly trusted for **showers of rain**. That they now turn to God and ask **the LORD** for **rain** indicates that a concomitant spiritual restoration occurs at the time of these blessings.

---

[143] David Baron, *Zechariah: A Commentary On His Visions And Prophecies*, 338.

2 For the idols have spoken vanity, and the diviners have seen a lie, and have told false dreams; they comfort in vain: therefore they went their way as a flock, they were troubled, because *there was* no shepherd.

In contrast to the LORD, the true and only source of blessings, **the idols have spoken vanity, and the diviners** or soothsayers **have seen a lie, and have told false dreams.** The term **idols** is the Hebrew *teraphim* and according to the NET translation notes, "refers to small images used as means of divination and other occult practices." These were "idols kept in the family rather than in a shrine" and "probably made in human form."[144] The **idols have spoken vanity**, which broadly refers to useless and powerless messages likely encouraging iniquity. The **diviners** refer to "people who claim to use supernatural power to interpret omens (strange or unusual events) in order to predict the future."[145] But similar to the idols' empty messages, **the diviners have seen a lie**, misleading the people through **false dreams**. Indeed, they tell the people what they want to hear—**they comfort in vain** but the **comfort** is empty or **vain** since it is rooted in **false dreams** and not truth. On how the **diviners** conjure their lies, Merrill explains: "As Ezekiel indicates, inspection of animal livers was one of the techniques of divination. Other means were the 'shaking of arrows' (Ezek. 21:21) and 'consulting the teraphim.' The first practice is well documented in ancient Near Eastern divination, but the last two are not, at least by this name."[146]

In this environment where **there was no shepherd**, the people like a confused **flock** of sheep **went their way** and **were troubled**. False prophets and teachers throughout history have led many people into sin and judgment. (Jeremiah 14:13-15;

---

[144] David J. Clark and Howard A. Hatton, *A Handbook on Zechariah*, 261–262.
[145] *Ibid.*, 262.
[146] Eugene H. Merrill, *An Exegetical Commentary - Haggai, Zechariah, Malachi*, 236–237.

Lamentations 2:14; Ezekiel 13:1-3; Revelation 2:20) The problem is that people can reach a point where false teaching is what they desire. (2 Timothy 4:3) And when the false teachers are dealt with, so are their followers. (Zephaniah 1:4-6) In contrast to the **diviners** Zechariah addresses, Jesus is the good shepherd:

> **John 10:11** I am the good shepherd: the good shepherd giveth his life for the sheep. **12** But he that is an hireling, and not the shepherd, whose own the sheep are not, seeth the wolf coming, and leaveth the sheep, and fleeth: and the wolf catcheth them, and scattereth the sheep. **13** The hireling fleeth, because he is an hireling, and careth not for the sheep. **14** I am the good shepherd, and know my *sheep*, and am known of mine.

Their idolatry is the result of having **no shepherd**, a reference to absent and/or bankrupt leadership. As Dennett comments, "Israel then in their unbelief had turned to idols and their prophets for succour, but found no relief or comfort; and the prophet depicts them as going their way as a flock, in their disappointment, troubled, because there was no shepherd— none to lead and to tend them; and thus since they had turned away from God, they were cast now in their sins upon their own resources."[147] Sadly, we know from the New Testament that this continues to be a problem in the first century: "But when he saw the multitudes, he was moved with compassion on them, because they fainted, and were scattered abroad, as sheep having no shepherd." (Matthew 9:36)

> **3** Mine anger was kindled against the shepherds, and I punished the goats: for the LORD of hosts hath visited his flock the house of Judah, and hath made them as his goodly horse in the battle.

---

[147] Edward Dennett, *Zechariah the Prophet*, 120.

Speaking for God in the first-person, Zechariah says, **mine anger was kindled** or burned **against the** faulty **shepherds, and I punished the goats**. The **shepherds** means leaders and broadly refers to religious and political leaders, and may refer to false prophets as well. The term **goats** appears to refer to persons among the **flock** that are not the sheep of God. (cf. Ezekiel 34:17; Matthew 25:32-33) It is notable that in Ezekiel 34:17-22, God says he will judge the flock and separate out the goats, who "feed on the good pasture" but "trample the rest of your pastures with your feet" so that "my sheep...must eat what you trampled with your feet and drink what you muddied with your feet." (see also Matthew 25:32-46) While the bad **shepherds** no doubt do some of the same evils as the **goats**, the **goats** are the wicked within the flock that harm the sheep. Through Ezekiel, God says: "Therefore will I save my flock, and they shall no more be a prey; and I will judge between cattle and cattle. And I will set up one shepherd over them, and he shall feed them, even my servant David; he shall feed them, and he shall be their shepherd." (Ezekiel 34:22-23) Ezekiel looks forward to a future time associated with the coming Messiah. We see the same parallel in the next verse where Zechariah connects these events to the coming Messiah.

Whereas the bad **shepherds** left the **flock** defenseless to wander, the LORD **of hosts** or armies **hath visited his flock the house of Judah, and hath made them as his goodly horse in the battle**. God's visit refers to His blessings on **Judah**, transforming them from wandering sheep without a shepherd to God's **goodly horse in battle**. These words indicate a trained horse of the highest quality. The God of armies, metaphorically, transforms the abandoned and defenseless **flock** into His **goodly horse** for **battle** to defeat Judah's enemies. This transformation is preparatory to battle, which Zechariah will expand on in the next verse. Notably, there is no indication that **Judah** deserves God's intervention on their behalf. The transformation is of His grace.

4 Out of him came forth the corner, out of him
the nail, out of him the battle bow, out of him
every oppressor together.

Zechariah continues the thought of God transforming Judah
into His battle horse to defeat Judah's enemies, explaining
that **out of him**, i.e., **out of** Judah, **came forth the corner** or
cornerstone, **out of him the nail, out of him the battle bow,
out of him every oppressor together.** I agree with Feinberg's
interpretation: "We prefer to understand the cornerstone, the
nail, and the battle bow of the Messiah, while the second
clause presents the result of His activities."[148] The term
cornerstone is used in the Old Testament to designate leaders
(see Judges 20:2, 1 Samuel 14:38), and is used specifically of the
Messiah in Isaiah 28:16 and Psalm 118:22, as well as in the New
Testament in Luke 20:17, 1 Corinthians 3:11, Ephesians 2:20
and 1 Peter 2:6. We read in Isaiah 28:16: "Therefore thus saith
the Lord GOD, Behold, I lay in Zion for a foundation a stone,
a tried stone, a precious corner *stone*, a sure foundation: he
that believeth shall not make haste." As in the Isaiah passage,
the cornerstone in view here is a proper shepherd, not like
those God judges in 10:3. Indeed, the cornerstone is the king
of Zechariah 9:9-10, Jesus Christ, who we know comes **out of**
Judah. As the cornerstone He is the foundation to Israel's
future Kingdom. He is the moving agent for God's promises in
10:3 to make Judah His "goodly horse in battle." But the
picture here is not the lowly king of Zechariah 9:9. This is all
about the second coming and reflects events we see so vividly
in Zechariah 14 and Revelation 19.

Zechariah continues, **out of him** (again, Judah) **the nail**. The
word **nail** may refer to a wall peg (see Ezekiel 15:3; Isaiah 22:22-
24) or tent peg (Judges 4:21-22). Valuables were hung on pegs,
and pegs were used for tents. We may again look to Isaiah to
understand the term **peg** in the context of a person. We find
interpretive assistance in Isaiah 22:15-25, where Isaiah

---

[148] Charles L. Feinberg, *God Remembers: A Study of Zechariah*, 144.

prophesied that Shebna the treasurer would be set aside from his position of honor and Eliakim would assume the governmental responsibilities. To Eliakim, the son of Hilkiah, would be given authority: "And I will fasten him as a nail in a sure place; and he shall be for a glorious throne to his father's house. And they shall hang upon him all the glory of his father's house..." (Isaiah 22:23-24) In like manner, the Messiah, "the dependable Nail, will have entrusted to Him all the glory of His Father's house in that coming day, and will not fail."[149] Thus, the term **peg** is metonymy for that which hangs on the **peg**, namely the honor and glory of God. The Son is that **peg**.

The **battle bow** pictures Messiah as a warrior and, relating it back to chapter 9, as a conquering king. We read in Revelation 19:11 of Jesus: "And I saw heaven opened, and behold a white horse; and he that sat upon him *was* called Faithful and True, and in righteousness he doth judge and make war." The term **oppressor** is an unusual word, used in Exodus 3:7 for the Egyptian taskmasters. Here, through the work of the Messiah, the Gentile oppressors will be removed from Judah.

> 5 And they shall be as mighty *men*, which tread down *their enemies* in the mire of the streets in the battle: and they shall fight, because the LORD *is* with them, and the riders on horses shall be confounded. 6 And I will strengthen the house of Judah, and I will save the house of Joseph, and I will bring them again to place them; for I have mercy upon them: and they shall be as though I had not cast them off: for I *am* the LORD their God, and will hear them. 7 And *they of* Ephraim shall be like a mighty *man*, and their heart shall rejoice as through wine: yea, their children shall see *it*, and be glad; their heart shall rejoice in the LORD.

---

[149] *Ibid.*, 146.

As we have seen in 9:13, God will lead and empower an army from Judah to fight victoriously over the Gentile invaders. This is elaborated here, with Messiah (the cornerstone, peg and battle bow of verse 4) fighting with and through this army, who **shall be as mighty men, which tread down their enemies in the mire of the streets in the battle**. Note that **their enemies** does not appear in the Hebrew text, and in most KJV's is written in italics to indicate as much; the interpretive wording was added. But the point here is that Judah will **tread down ...the mire** or mud **of the streets in the battle**. The **mire of the streets** symbolizes Judah's defeated enemies. We further read of Judah that **they shall fight** and prevail **because the LORD is with them** and not because of their own strength. Judah will so overcome her enemies that **the riders on horses shall be confounded**. We are reminded from 9:10 of the promise that God would remove the chariots and **horses** from the land. The picture here is of the infantry defeating the cavalry, confounding **the riders on horses**, which in the context of ancient warfare is quite unexpected. It is all because God is with them. We also read additional detail in Zechariah 14:13-15 that God will confuse the invaders and their animals.

Moreover, God will reunite the nation of Israel. After Solomon's rule, the kingdom split into two separate nations. Here, those separate kingdoms are referred to as **Judah** (the southern kingdom) and **Joseph** (recall that Joseph was the father of Ephraim and the Old Testament often referred to the northern kingdom as Ephraim). God **will strengthen the house of Judah, and ...save the house of Joseph, and ...bring them again to place them**. In other words, they both will be put back into the land, another reference to the regathering of the Jewish people. This is how God will show **mercy upon them**. But there is more than physical deliverance and victory here. Indeed, **they shall be as though I had not cast them off** in the first place. The healing will be so complete that it will be as if they were never exiled, but that is only possible if the iniquity is removed. (see Zechariah 5) To that end, God says, for I am the LORD **their God, and will hear** their prayers. This indicates a restored relationship. Zechariah focuses again on this future restoration in 13:9: "And I will bring the third part through the fire, and will refine them as silver is refined, and will try them as gold is tried: they shall call on my name, and I will hear them: I will say, It *is* my people: and they shall say, The LORD *is* my God."

In verse 7, **Ephraim** refers to the Northern Kingdom, which before Zechariah's time was defeated and scattered by the Assyrians. In the future when Messiah comes, the Northern Kingdom **shall be like a mighty man** or hero heading into battle, and their affliction will be reversed so that **their heart shall rejoice as through wine.** This echoes the imagery of rejoicing and prosperity of the young men and women in 9:17, and it is no temporary rejoicing. Thus, Zechariah adds that **their children shall see** their reversal of fortune and rejoicing **and** as a result the **children** also will **be glad.** This is consistent with other prophetic passages that speak of rejoicing in connection with God's deliverance of His people. (Isaiah 25:9, 65:13; Zephaniah 3:14) Again, we observe that their restoration includes spiritual restoration so that while in the past they would have rejoiced in the idols and diviners (v. 3), they give God the credit and **rejoice in the LORD.**

> 8 I will hiss for them, and gather them; for I
> have redeemed them: and they shall increase as
> they have increased.

Continuing the imagery of the good shepherd gathering his flock (9:16, 10:3), God **will hiss for** his people scattered abroad **and gather them.** The word **hiss** means to whistle and pictures God summoning His people home as a shepherd summons his flock. Baron provides a personal illustration that is helpful for those of us not familiar with shepherding sheep:

> On one occasion (it was in 1891) while camping
> for a few days with missionary friends in a wild
> part high up on the Lebanon, a picturesque-

looking young Bedouin shepherd was leading a small flock of sheep to some distant part in search of pasturage. Passing our encampment he stopped for a while to converse with us, and in the meantime his flock got scattered among the rocks; but by and by, when he was ready to start, he pulled out from under his burnoose a reed pipe, and began to play on it a not very melodious tune; and it was interesting and beautiful to notice how, as he was playing, his scattered sheep, some of which had wandered off to some distance, collected closer and closer around him, and formed into a flock; and when they were all there he started off again at their head.[150]

The regathering begins with God's whistle, which will be responded to because He **already redeemed** or ransomed **them.** The term **redeemed** is the word for purchasing from slavery and captivity. (Deuteronomy 13:5; 2 Samuel 7:23; Micah 6:4) Their spiritual redemption precedes their physical restoration in the land. Isaiah pronounced the same truth about the future redemption and regathering: "And the ransomed of the LORD shall return, and come to Zion with songs and everlasting joy upon their heads: they shall obtain joy and gladness, and sorrow and sighing shall flee away." (Isaiah 35:10) Likewise, Jeremiah said: "Hear the word of the LORD, O ye nations, and declare *it* in the isles afar off, and say, He that scattered Israel will gather him, and keep him, as a shepherd *doth* his flock. For the LORD hath redeemed Jacob, and ransomed him from the hand of *him that was* stronger than he." (Jeremiah 31:10-11) This redemption, of course, will happen as a future generation of Israel turns to Jesus: "For I say unto you, Ye shall not see me henceforth, till ye shall say, Blessed is he that cometh in the name of the Lord." (Matthew 23:39) It is all made possible by

---

[150] David Baron, *Zechariah: A Commentary On His Visions And Prophecies*, 363.

the coming king whose Triumphal Entry to address their sins is presented in Zechariah 9.

Israel's future redemption will be coupled with its multiplication, for **they shall increase as they have increased.** This is a common prophetic theme also. (Isaiah 54:2; Ezekiel 36:10; Hosea 1:10; Micah 2:12) Even in the diaspora God would **increase** or multiply His people, and then when they return to the land they will continue to **increase.** And we cannot help but see the parallel with Israel growing as a nation while in Egypt followed by an exodus from bondage to the Promise Land. Merrill aptly comments: "The Exodus of Israel from Egypt under Moses was not only the great saving event that made Israel a nation and brought her into fellowship with YHWH—it also became the paradigm of all God's redemptive work on behalf of all individuals and peoples who placed their confidence in Him. Thus, for example, the restoration of the exilic community is defined by Isaiah as a second exodus (Isa. 40:3–5; 43:1–7, 14–21; 48:20–22; 51:9–11)."[151] The dispersion is a new Egypt for God's people, but what is witnessed with the small return of people in Zechariah's day is a foretaste of a new exodus under God's blessing and protection. Indeed, Haggai, who ministers at the same time as Zechariah, encourages the people by likening God's promise that He is with them to His promises to the nation generations earlier during the exodus from Egypt. (Haggai 2:4-5) But the verse at hand looks to a future global exodus when God calls.

> **9** And I will sow them among the people: and they shall remember me in far countries; and they shall live with their children, and turn again.

Continuing to build on the future global exodus, Zechariah speaks for God in proclaiming He **will sow them among the people** or nations, but in the future **they will remember me in**

---

[151] Eugene H. Merrill, *An Exegetical Commentary - Haggai, Zechariah, Malachi,* 242.

far countries. Note that **sow** is not "scatter" as some new translations take it. It is **sow** as in sowing seeds. God is pictured here not as the one that scattered Israel, but rather, they are sown abroad as seeds to grow and multiply as a crop. Indeed, during the dispersion the people **shall live with their children**, indicating that God will multiply them as He multiplied the nation in Egypt. At some future point the people will **turn again**, meaning they will return to the land. The promised regathering will be a response to the Jewish people remembering God (**they will remember me**), indicating a spiritual turning to Him. This points to a future spiritual revival, which will be addressed in detail in Zechariah 12. Even in the first century in the ministries of John the Baptizer and Jesus, they preach repentance because the Kingdom is at hand. (Matthew 4:17) That generation did not **remember** God, but a future one will.

> 10 I will bring them again also out of the land
> of Egypt, and gather them out of Assyria; and I
> will bring them into the land of Gilead and
> Lebanon; and *place* shall not be found for
> them. 11 And he shall pass through the sea with
> affliction, and shall smite the waves in the sea,
> and all the deeps of the river shall dry up: and
> the pride of Assyria shall be brought down, and
> the sceptre of Egypt shall depart away.

As Zechariah notes in verse 8, God summons His people from the Gentile nations as a shepherd calls His sheep. While they are dispersed, God multiplies the people but they will eventually "remember me in far countries" and return. (Zechariah 10:9) Continuing the same thought, God says through Zechariah, **I will bring them again also out of the land of Egypt, and gather them out of Assyria**. Of course, both of these were long-time enemies of God's people, with them in bondage to **Egypt** early in their history and some portion of them in bondage in **Assyria** later. It is also to be observed that **Assyria** was a kingdom encompassing a large geographic area.

There is debate whether Zechariah means literally **Egypt** and **Assyria** or uses those as representative examples of all Gentile nations where God sows His people. Regardless of how you determine this narrow issue, the tenor of the passage as a whole is a complete return from the Gentile nations.

God **will bring them into the land of Gilead and Lebanon**. The term **Gilead** does not always have the same meaning. "Sometimes the name refers to all of Israelite Transjordan (e.g., Josh. 22:9), but often it is restricted only to the areas between the Jabbok and Arnon rivers to the south (i.e., Reuben and Gad; cf. Num. 32:29) or between the Jabbok and Yarmuk to the north (i.e., Manasseh; cf. Josh. 17:5). Gilead is a rugged highland area (cf. Gen. 31:21, 23, 25) cut by river valleys and bordered by Bashan to the north, Moab to the south, Ammon to the east, and the Jordan river to the west."[152] Given the context of a greatly multiplied nation returning to the Promise Land, we should take **Gilead** in its broadest sense. The region of **Lebanon** borders what we usually think of as Israel on the north. We must bear in mind that Israel never achieved the borders promised to it, and the Israel of today is much smaller than what God promised. What is in view in the future return to the land is a multiplied people filling the nation's originally intended borders, specified in Deuteronomy 1:7-8: "Turn you, and take your journey, and go to the mount of the Amorites, and unto all *the places* nigh thereunto, in the plain, in the hills, and in the vale, and in the south, and by the sea side, to the land of the Canaanites, and unto Lebanon, unto the great river, the river Euphrates. Behold, I have set the land before you: go in and possess the land which the LORD sware unto your fathers, Abraham, Isaac, and Jacob, to give unto them and to their seed after them." The reader should also carefully review Deuteronomy 29 and Deuteronomy 30:1-10.

---

[152] Allen C. Myers, *The Eerdmans Bible Dictionary* (Grand Rapids, MI: Eerdmans, 1987), 417.

Bringing His people to **Gilead** and **Lebanon** is a reference to fulfilling the promise of Israel's borders that had never been previously achieved. Baron notes this "probably represents the whole promised land east and west of the Jordan."[153] Indeed, Zechariah adds, **and place shall not be found for them,** suggesting the entire Promise Land cannot contain them. This may be hyperbole to emphasize the large population. We are reminded at once of the promise in Zechariah 2 of a restored Jerusalem that cannot contain the population and thus is "inhabited as towns without walls for the multitude." (Zechariah 2:4)

Drawing on exodus imagery, Zechariah says **God shall pass through the sea with** (or of) **affliction, and shall smite the waves in the sea, and all the deeps of the river shall dry up.** We at once remember God leading His people out of Egypt through the Red Sea, pushing back the **waves** to make an open path for His people. As God summons His sheep home He will once again make a way for them so that they may, figuratively, walk on **dry** land. In other words, God will remove the obstacles to their regathering in the Promise Land. The **deeps of the river,** meaning the Nile **River, shall dry up** just as the Jordan River did before the Ark of the Covenant. And **the pride of Assyria**—the Northern Kingdom's or Ephraim's enemy to the North—**shall be brought down** or humbled in defeat, **and the scepter** or domination **of Egypt**—Israel's enemy to the South—**shall depart away.** By implication, all of Israel's enemies are dealt with as God takes out Israel's enemies and clears a safe path of return home. At this time, those Gentiles left among the nations will not be against the Jewish people. (Zechariah 14:16)

> **12** And I will strengthen them in the LORD;
> and they shall walk up and down in his name,
> saith the LORD.

---

[153] David Baron, *Zechariah: A Commentary On His Visions And Prophecies,* 368.

The chapter closes with God's promise that He **will strengthen** Israel **in the** LORD, enabling their safe return to the Promise Land. And when they return home, **they shall walk up and down in his name.** The concept of walking **up and down** in the land symbolizes an exercise of dominion over the land that previously eluded them. This promise of blessing speaks not only of physical blessing, but also spiritual blessing. As Baron rightly explains, this "last expression may denote first their life, or walk and conversation, which shall all be rooted in God, and be in full accord with '*His Name*,' which stands for His revealed character, which shall then be fully and gloriously manifested in their midst in the person of their Messiah, the image of the invisible God."[154] The climax of this history future is God's redeemed people in the land He promised Abraham they would have, under the leadership of the coming king Jesus Christ. As Jesus says in the Olivet Discourse, which speaks to the time of tribulation leading to His return: "And he shall send his angels with a great sound of a trumpet, and they shall gather together his elect from the four winds, from one end of heaven to the other." (Matthew 24:31)

As an aside, I note that in relatively recent history (1948) Israel was politically restored as a nation, regained some of the land within its ancient boundaries, and some Jewish people returned to Israel. This is not in fulfillment of Zechariah 10 and other passages foreseeing the future regathering to the Promise Land because (1) Israel does not have all of its land yet, (2) the promises are to take place during the day of the Lord, and (3) the modest return to Israel thus far was not a return in belief, i.e., coupled with a spiritual revival based on accepting the Lord Jesus as the Christ (Messiah).

---

[154] *Ibid.*, 370.

Closing

Israel is the prodigal nation that in Zechariah 10 experiences a spiritual revival and then is welcomed home with God's blessing. As Christians, we sometimes come to a point in our lives where for a prolonged time we are not where we are supposed to be in terms of our walk with the Lord. A lot of choices and events (some bad and not our fault) may contribute to how we find ourselves where we are. But regardless of the path away from God, the result is that we are in a bad place spiritually and emotionally and we cannot fix it. If the new exodus of Zechariah 10 says anything, it says that nothing we can do can put us beyond God's promises. After centuries of disobedience, God welcomes the Jewish people home. And so it is for Christians who through choices and circumstances find themselves in a place that seems like exile from the joy of the Lord. If we will turn to the Lord and seek His face, we will find ourselves welcomed back into fellowship.

Application Points

- **MAIN PRINCIPLE:** A combination of Israel's idolatry and poor leadership leads to their dispersion among the nations, but God as their shepherd will summon His flock back to the Promise Land and through the coming Messiah will enable them to overcome their enemies.

- There must be a spiritual revival before Israel will experience God's promised material blessings.

Discussion Questions

1. Israel's sin of choice for centuries was idolatry. In what forms does idolatry exist today?

2. We read in 10:3 that God's "anger was kindled against the shepherds." What does the picture of a "shepherd" suggest about the type of leadership that is supposed to be

provided to God's people? What are the applications for those in leadership positions in a local church?

3. People today sometimes hijack the concept of Jesus to their liking to make a political statement and speculate about how Jesus would respond to this or that political issue. If you have seen this in the popular media or on social media, how does their "Jesus" compare to the coming king in Zechariah 10 who fights alongside the Jewish nation to defeat her enemies?

4. God promises in 10:8-12 that He will regather the Jewish people to the Promise Land. But this was 2,500 years ago. Why has God delayed so long?

5. What does the exodus of God's people from Egypt recorded in the book of Exodus have in common with the promised future regathering of the Jewish people to the land? And how is it different?

6. What must happen in the hearts of the Jewish people concerning Jesus Christ before the physical blessings in the Promise Land are realized?

Chapter 13

Two Shepherds

When Pontius Pilate asks who he should set free, the people answer, "Barabbas." (Matthew 27:21) This man participated in an "insurrection" and "committed murder in the insurrection." (Mark 15:7) John records that he is "a robber." (John 18:40) But the "chief priests and elders persuaded the multitude that they should ask Barabbas, and destroy Jesus." (Matthew. 27:20) With this little coaxing, "they cried out all at once...Away with this man [Jesus], and release unto us Barabbas." (Luke 23:18) And then almost prophetically, in response to Pilate's words, "I am innocent of the blood of this just person," the people respond, "His blood be on us, and on our children." (Matthew 27:25) And their request is honored shortly after when God uses the Romans to bring judgment on Israel. But who is this Jesus they adjudge worthy of a Roman cross?

Shortly before his birth to a young lady named Mary, the angel announces, "Hail, thou art highly favoured, the Lord is with thee: blessed art thou among women." (Luke 1:28) She will give birth to "a son" and "call his name JESUS" (Luke 1:31). Mary's son will "be great," "called the Son of the Highest," and "the Lord God shall give unto him the throne of his father David: And he shall reign over the house of Jacob for ever; and of his kingdom there shall be no end." (Luke 1:32-33) Jesus "shall be called the Son of God" (Luke 1:35) These matters are foretold in the Old Testament (including by Zechariah) and the Jewish nation should have recognized the Christ immediately by His words and deeds. The Son of God presents Himself as "the good shepherd...[who] giveth his life for the sheep." (John 10:11) But they would not have Him as Messiah: "O Jerusalem, Jerusalem, *thou* that killest the prophets, and stonest them which are sent unto thee, how often would I have gathered thy children together, even as a hen gathereth her chickens under *her* wings, and ye would not!" (Matthew 23:37) As a result, Jesus pronounces judgment on that generation: "Behold, your house is left unto you desolate." (Matthew 23:38)

Many argue that when Israel characteristically rejects Jesus, the promises to them in the Old Testament are nullified. But as we will see, Zechariah foretells of two shepherds, the good shepherd Jesus Christ that Israel will reject, and the evil one they will embrace. Notwithstanding Israel's rejection of the good shepherd, the glorious promises for Israel so pervasive in Zechariah's book remain. God works even through Israel's disobedience so that we might exclaim with the apostle Paul, "O the depth of the riches both of the wisdom and knowledge of God! how unsearchable *are* his judgments, and his ways past finding out!" (Romans 11:33)

Scripture and Comments

We now come to what may be the most challenging chapter in Zechariah, and is certainly the most debated. As Dennett concedes, "In this confessedly difficult chapter great care is needed in attending to the exact language employed by the

Spirit of God."[155] Similarly, Klein states: "Zechariah 11 may be the most difficult and controversial chapter of the entire book. In a famous comment, S. R. Driver took this point one step further, claiming that Zech 11:4–17 stands as the most enigmatic passage in the whole Old Testament."[156] Notwithstanding the challenges, careful study of this chapter in relation to the rest of the unit of which it is a part (chapters 9-11) and the next unit (chapters 12-14) to which it is a bridge, will permit us to arrive with confidence at the overall message. What unfolds through both of these large units of prophetic material is a focus on some central themes with each chapter adding more detail. These themes include God's scattering of His people, their return to the Land, the defeat of their enemies, a coming king who pronounces peace to the nations, and a Messianic Age of peace and prosperity.

While we might have preferred the prophet to give us a strictly chronological recitation of history future, God sees fit to deliver His messages through Zechariah with interspersing thematic emphasis. A key theme may be quickly mentioned in one place and expanded in another. Chapter 11 follows the same pattern while also providing a transition to the final unit in the book. While the coming king Messiah is presented in chapter 9, we find in chapter 11 Israel's future response to the Messiah. Sadly, Israel will reject the good shepherd in favor of hirelings.

> **Zechariah 11:1** Open thy doors, O Lebanon, that the fire may devour thy cedars. **2** Howl, fir tree; for the cedar is fallen; because the mighty are spoiled: howl, O ye oaks of Bashan; for the forest of the vintage is come down. **3** *There is* a voice of the howling of the shepherds; for their glory is spoiled: a voice of the roaring of young lions; for the pride of Jordan is spoiled.

---

155 Edward Dennett, *Zechariah the Prophet*, 131.
156 George L. Klein, *Zechariah*, 311–312.

These opening three verses are written in Hebrew poetry and rely on symbolic imagery. While commentators debate the details, there is little question that the language describes a judgment in relation to the Holy Land. But that said, many take the poem as a conclusion to the judgment on Israel's enemies from chapter 10, while others take the poem as a judgment on Israel or its bad leadership (**shepherds**) or both. And still others see the first two verses as foretelling a literal deforestation of the land. In addition, there is division over when this judgment occurs. The view advocated here is that the poem foretells a coming judgment on Israel with a special focus on the demise of the **shepherds** of Israel, which fits with the focus on **shepherds** in verses 4 – 17. The purpose of the placement of the poem is shock factor. The prior chapter presents the triumph of God's people over their enemies but then the next words from the prophet present defeat and destruction in the Holy Land. As Hartman rightly states, "The first six verses of Zechariah 11 picture such fierce judgment on the land of Israel that the contrast between this chapter and the previous one leaps off the page."[157] There will be defeat before the victory portrayed in chapter 10, and the determining factor of what happens next is Israel's response to the coming Messiah. This defeat before victory pattern parallels Zechariah 14:1-3.

An invasion of the Holy Land would typically come from the north, beginning in the region of **Lebanon**. Note that **Lebanon** does not refer to a country or kingdom but a region, and the name means "white mountain." One source describes the region: "A mountain range north of Israel and parallel to the Mediterranean Sea, named for its snowcapped peaks (Jer. 18:14). The range extends from the Nahr el-Kebir (the ancient Eleutheropolis river) near the Amanus mountains in the north nearly 160 km. (100 mi.) south to the Nahr el-Qāsimiyeh (the

---

[157] Fred H. Hartman, *Zechariah: Israel's Messenger of the Messiah's Triumph*, Zec 11.

Litani river gorge) at the northern border of Palestine."[158] We previously saw Zechariah reference the Promise Land by referencing **Lebanon** and Gilead. (Zechariah 10:10) Through the prophet, God calls upon **Lebanon** to **open thy doors** or gates. Regions do not have **doors** or gates, but in the ancient world cities had defensive walls and their gates were a critical part of their defense. Here, the reference is probably figurative of the dropping of their defenses so that the judgment may sweep through. Some have suggested that the **doors** may refer to the mountain passes between **Lebanon** and Israel, which are opened so that the judgment may sweep through. The prophet does not directly address any particular invader. But since chapter 10 ends with the Lord talking in the first person, and verse 11:4 also attributes the words to the Lord, we should understand the entire poem in 11:1-3 as God's words to Israel about what He will do, regardless of the instrument of judgment He employs. The destruction moves like a fire sweeping through the Holy Land leaving it desolate. The **doors** must open to permit **the fire** to **devour thy cedars** of **Lebanon**.

In the Bible, **cedars** are frequently associated with **Lebanon**. As one Bible dictionary explains: "The celebrated cedars of Lebanon are large, coniferous, evergreen mountain trees (*Cedrus libani* Loud). These cedars (Heb. *'erez*) were aptly named, as they did not grow in Israel. As young trees, cedars are cone-shaped, but as they age, the branches spread and flatten. Cedars of Lebanon grow up to 28 m. (90 ft.) tall and may live 3000 years. Many more cedar forests were in Lebanon in biblical times than exist there today. The wood of the tree was a popular commodity used in building. It carries a pleasant fragrance and resists insects."[159] These trees were highly prized for construction and were used in the construction of the Temple by Solomon. In the Old Testament, the tall and

[158] Allen C. Myers, *The Eerdmans Bible Dictionary*, 648.
[159] Megan Bishop Moore, "Cedar," ed. David Noel Freedman, Allen C. Myers, and Astrid B. Beck, *Eerdmans Dictionary of the Bible* (Grand Rapids, MI: W.B. Eerdmans, 2000), 227.

stately cedar trees are frequently used as metaphors for kings. (e.g., Judges 9:15; 2 Kings 14:9; Isaiah 14:8; Ezekiel 17:3; Amos 2:9) The **fir** tree may also be used in a similar sense. (e.g., Ezekiel 31:8) And oak trees also picture strength. (e.g., Amos 2:9) The **howl** of the trees in verses 1 and 2 is in parallel to **the howling of the shepherds** in verse 3, indicating that all three verses are focused on a judgment of **shepherds**, which provides a fitting bridge between the material in chapter 10 (see 10:2-3) and chapter 11 (especially 11:5, 8, 15-17). Merrill rightly concludes: "Attention to the following verses makes it rather apparent that the objects mentioned under the guise of trees and animals are the same as the shepherds. As already noted 'shepherd' is a common way of referring to kings in the ancient Near East and the OT, an epithet particularly favored by Zechariah (10:2, 3; 11:3, 5, 8, 15, 16, 17; 13:7). The lament of the poem, then, introduces the occasion for the lament, namely, the destruction of the evil shepherds (11:8, 17)."[160]

Accordingly, the **fire** devouring Lebanon's **cedars** pictures the downfall of the leadership. Similarly, God calls upon the **fir tree** to **howl** because **the cedar is fallen.** As the mightiest leaders fall **(because the mighty are spoiled)**, the next in line recognize their inevitable demise. God then turns to the **oaks of Bashan** and commands them to **howl** because **the forest of the vintage is come down.** "The name *Bashan* means 'fruitful', and the region was well known for its mighty oak trees (v. 2; cf. Ezek. 27:6) and *rich pastures* (cf. Jer. 50:19; Mic. 7:14)."[161] The region of **Bashan** was "an area of tableland north of Gilead and north-east of the Sea of Galilee."[162] The **oaks of Bashan**, like the **fir tree**, also see their inevitable fall because **the forest of the vintage** (the **cedars**), though long-established, already fell in judgment.

---

[160] Eugene H. Merrill, *An Exegetical Commentary - Haggai, Zechariah, Malachi*, 250.

[161] Andrew E. Hill, *Haggai, Zechariah and Malachi: An Introduction and Commentary*, 228.

[162] *Ibid.*, 227.

The next verse draws the critical parallels that help us understand the primary point of the poem (already noted above). Zechariah calls upon his audience to hear the **voice of the howling of the shepherds** because **their glory** or magnificence **is spoiled.** The fallen **trees** are equated to the loss of the **glory** that belonged to the **shepherds.** The **shepherds** refers broadly to the Jewish religious and political leadership, a point we will revisit in verse 8. This ties the poem to what preceded (see 10:2-3) and what follows (11:4-17), where "shepherd" also refers to the Jewish leadership.

Zechariah next calls upon his audience to listen to the **voice of the roaring of young lions; for the pride of Jordan is spoiled.** In the characteristically arid land, there is lush vegetation in the **Jordan** valley near the water and in ancient days there were **lions** there. As the land is destroyed to the point of the lush areas surrounding the **Jordan** River the **young lions** join in the lament for their lost habitat. The **young lions** are referred to in parallel with the **shepherds** and are another metaphor for the Jewish leadership. (Jeremiah 50:44; Ezekiel 19:1-9) By including both **shepherds** and **young lions** the prophet indicates that this judgment will impact various levels of the Jewish leadership. The judgment will be thorough and result in their loss of authority and affluence. They lose everything. The focus on **shepherds** provides a transition to the rest of the chapter where God presents the shepherd *par excellence* and another shepherd that is the antithesis of the good shepherd.

> 4 Thus saith the LORD my God; Feed the flock
> of the slaughter; 5 Whose possessors slay them,
> and hold themselves not guilty: and they that
> sell them say, Blessed *be* the LORD; for I am
> rich: and their own shepherds pity them not.

The remainder of the chapter is organized as follows: vv. 4-6 introduce the good shepherd, vv. 7-14 show the characteristic rejection of the good shepherd and the breaking of his two symbolic staffs, and vv. 15-17 address a new, worthless shepherd (and quite possibly a series of such shepherds) sent to the people. These verses explain the reason for the destruction in the first three verses. They also explain why there will be a future scattering of the Jewish people.

Zechariah begins with **thus saith the LORD my God**, marking the beginning of a new unit of thought that continues through verse 14. Here, God instructs Zechariah to **feed the flock of the slaughter**, in other words, **the flock** of sheep destined to be killed. The prophet relies on the metaphor of a **flock** of sheep sold by their shepherd to those who would **slaughter** them (the buyers or **possessors**). That **the flock** refers to the people of Israel is confirmed by God's statement in verse 6 that He **will no more pity the inhabitants of the land**. Of this **flock** of sheep, the prophet explains that their **possessors slay them, and hold themselves not guilty** for this crime. In contrast to the Jewish **shepherds**, the **possessors** likely refers to Gentiles who will rule over Israel and kill the people with impunity. They will own them as chattel and destroy or **sell them** in order to profit by them. They will sarcastically attribute their financial success to God, saying, **blessed be the LORD; for I am rich**. This merchandising of God's people by Gentile nations is made possible because **their own shepherds pity them not**. The task of the **shepherds** is to protect and feed the **flock**, but these **shepherds** fail entirely because they do not care.

Before moving forward, we must ask in what way Zechariah is supposed to **feed the flock of the slaughter**? It seems unlikely that his immediate audience comprises the **flock of the slaughter**, given the emphasis throughout the book on God's returned blessings upon them (e.g., Zechariah 1:13-14, 16) and their charge to rebuild the Temple, which is completed shortly *after* Zechariah's message. There is no indication that they rebel against God, or that the generation Zechariah ministers to is destroyed (see 11:9). It is, of course, possible that Zechariah could minister to his present audience as representative of a future generation, but once again, we are told the **flock of the slaughter** will not value his ministry (11:12-

13) and will suffer judgment as a result (11:9-10), which is not hinted at anywhere else in the book. Finally, that Zechariah is already feeding **the flock** of God as a faithful prophet delivering the prior visions and messages makes it unlikely that in the eleventh chapter he is told to **feed the flock** as if that were a new activity on his part. Accordingly, I reject that Zechariah 11 is about the prophet actually ministering to the current generation in Jerusalem, being rejected and then pronouncing judgment on them.

Certainly, there is ample precedent for God's prophets playing out divine object lessons before the people. (see 1 Samuel 15:27-28; Isaiah 20:2; Jeremiah 27:2-12; Ezekiel 12:1-16, 37:15-23; Hosea 1:2-3) The difficulty here is that it does not seem possible that Zechariah could do, even in symbolic acts, all that is indicated in this passage. In particular, in verse 8 the prophet writes, "three shepherds also I cut off in one month." One possibility is that Zechariah performs part of the symbolic acts indicated in the passage and explains the other parts to his audience. However, the passage gives no indication of such a distinction, and instead reads as if Zechariah did it all literally. For example, he agreed to **feed the flock** (11:7), takes up the tools of a **shepherd** (11:7), and then says in a matter of fact fashion that he kills three other **shepherds** whom he "lothed" and who "abhorred me" (11:8). Whether we view Zechariah as ministering to the people or taking hire to care for literal sheep, it is difficult to see how he could do all that is recorded here, and there is no indication in the text of a mixture of play acting and explanations. Accordingly, a more viable alternative, as Baron and other older commentators understood the passage, is that Zechariah participates in a vision as he does in Zechariah 3 in order to experience and better understand the rejection of the good shepherd from God's perspective.[163] On this point there is no room for being dogmatic about what exactly the prophet did, but of the overall meaning of his message there can be little doubt, as we will see.

---

[163] David Baron, *Zechariah: A Commentary on His Visions and Prophecies*, 388-89.

Before leaving these verses, we must address the timing issue. Merrill makes a reasonable case for the shepherd role-play looking back to God's gentle care of His people before the exile and the rebelliousness that led to God giving them over to the Babylonians: "Actually what he said he did is what YHWH had done in the past, before the exile. Zechariah enters into the experience of YHWH and shares the emotion and heart of YHWH, so that man, as much as possible, might understand what motivated Him to act as He did in judgment."[164] Merrill reasons that **shepherds** must refer to kings, and since Israel had no kings in Zechariah's time, or thereafter, the passage must look to the past.[165] While the prophet previously calls upon the people to remember the past, he did so in explicit terms, which are not found here. (e.g., Zechariah 1:2-6, 8:10-15) Moreover, in chapter 11, it is Israel's rejection of the good shepherd that causes God to give them a bad shepherd. It would be odd, indeed, if God is saying that because of a prior generation's rejection of Him as the good shepherd, although they are presently the recipients of His divine blessings, He will at a future time send a bad shepherd. (e.g., Zechariah 8:11, "But now I will not be unto the residue of this people as in the former days, saith the LORD of hosts."). It seems more probable that, in contrast to the blessings God pours out on His people during Zechariah's day, dark days are ahead when Israel will be the **flock of the slaughter**. They will be without good **shepherds** and God will respond by sending the good shepherd *par excellence,* the Son of God and promised king (Zechariah 9:9). In this vision, Zechariah plays the role of the good shepherd *par excellence* and experiences the rejection of the Son of God.

I note that this view fits what God affirms in His progressive revelation. For example, Matthew writes that when "Jesus saw the multitudes, he was moved with compassion, because they

---

164 Eugene H. Merrill, *An Exegetical Commentary - Haggai, Zechariah, Malachi,* 253.
165 *Ibid.*

fainted, and were scattered abroad, as sheep having no shepherd." (Matthew 9:36) Jesus also explains in John 10, using shepherd / sheep parables, that He is the good shepherd:

> **John 10:1** Verily, verily, I say unto you, He that entereth not by the door into the sheepfold, but climbeth up some other way, the same is a thief and a robber. **2** But he that entereth in by the door is the shepherd of the sheep. **3** To him the porter openeth; and the sheep hear his voice: and he calleth his own sheep by name, and leadeth them out. **4** And when he putteth forth his own sheep, he goeth before them, and the sheep follow him: for they know his voice. **5** And a stranger will they not follow, but will flee from him: for they know not the voice of strangers.

The quoted parable is a continuation of Jesus' address to the Pharisees at the end of John 9. The religious leadership during Jesus' earthly ministry are the "thief and a robber." Only the true shepherd, Jesus, will come by the door. The door is guarded by the porter, John the Baptist, who will only open for the Messiah, the true shepherd. The sheep know the shepherd's voice and follow Him, which we see played out in John 1 when Jesus calls disciples to follow Him. (John 1:39-40) We also know that the generation Jesus ministers to will value Him at 30 pieces of silver in their rejection of Him as Messiah, in fulfillment of Zechariah 11:12-13. (see Matthew 26:15, 27:3) For these reasons, it is best to understand that Zechariah likely participates in a vision from God to experience and understand the future rejection of the good shepherd and coming Messiah so that he can then explain it to the people. As with so much of the book, God's message focuses on the future, filling in the details about the coming Messiah.

> **6** For I will no more pity the inhabitants of the land, saith the LORD: but, lo, I will deliver the

men every one into his neighbour's hand, and
into the hand of his king: and they shall smite
the land, and out of their hand I will not
deliver *them*.

God continues about what He will do through the good
shepherd, which Zechariah will in vision experience firsthand.
With regard to the flock destined for slaughter, God says, **For I
will no more pity the inhabitants of the land**. The **land** refers to
the land of Israel. We should ask why it is that God will not
pity His people any longer? This verse is proleptic of Israel's
characteristic rejection of the coming Messiah Jesus, whom
God will send to them as promised. Despite their suffering
under poor shepherds, they will reject the Messiah that God
sends to shepherd them. Accordingly, instead of God having
pity for His people, He says, **lo, I will deliver the men every one
into his neighbor's hand, and into the hand of his king**. Because
Israel will reject the good shepherd and Messiah, God will hand
them over to their **neighbor's hand**, a reference to the
surrounding Gentile nations. The **hand of his king** refers to
Gentile leaders, the "possessors" alluded to earlier. That Israel's
enemies **shall smite the land** is fulfilled when the Romans quash
the Jewish rebellion in 70 A.D., as the note below explains:

> After A.D. 6 Jerusalem was under Roman
> procurators, with the exception of the years 41–
> 44 under Herod Agrippa I. Judea was apparently
> the least desirable post in government service,
> and the province's procurators were among the
> worst Roman officials. The Jews were
> increasingly restive under Roman control and
> the procurators were increasingly violent, cruel,
> and dishonest. Open rebellion broke out in
> A.D. 66. Two years earlier Gessius Florus, the
> procurator, had sent his troops on a mad
> rampage in Jerusalem, and the extreme Zealot
> faction of the Jews had reacted violently. The

war began when the Zealots seized Masada and then, under Menahem, marched on Jerusalem. Simultaneously Jews in the gubernatorial city of Caesarea were massacred, and news of this atrocity spread throughout the country. New coins were marked Year 1 through Year 5 of the revolt (A.D. 66–70; *see* Plate 41). The emperor Nero dispatched Vespasian to Judea to put down the revolution; in 68 Vespasian had isolated Jerusalem and was ready to begin a siege. The empire, however, was in turmoil, with unrest in the east and revolt in the west. Nero committed suicide. Vespasian, who was acclaimed emperor in 69, left for Rome to secure his throne and gave his son Titus responsibility for ending the Jewish war.

Titus had four legions. The Tenth had moved from Jericho to the Mt. of Olives, destroying the Qumrân community on its way. The Twelfth had come from Caesarea and was encamped W of the city, along with the Fifth and Fifteenth that had come from the north. In the spring of 70 the offensive was launched. The Jewish forces were under Simon bar-Giora and Yohanan of Gush-Halab (John of Gischala). The Romans breached the third wall on the west and then the second wall, but their attempt to take Antonia failed. Titus thereupon decided on a siege, and a circumvallation was thrown up, according to Josephus almost 8 km (5 mi) long, built in three days (BJ v 12.1f [491–511]). According to some scholars, the "third wall" of Sukenik and Mayer was part of this circumvallation (but see S. Ben-Arieh, "The 'Third Wall' of Jerusalem," in *Jerusalem Revealed*, pp. 60–62). The horrors of the six-

month siege are graphically told by Josephus (BJ
v.12.3 [512–18]). Antonia was taken, and the Jews
barricaded themselves in the temple. On 9 Ab
(Aug. 5, A.D. 70) the temple was burned and the
Roman soldiers carried out a campaign of
slaughter along the entire east ridge. The Jews
made their last stand in Herod's palace but the
end was inevitable. Titus ordered the entire city
razed to the ground except for the three large
towers at the northwest corner. Many Jews were
executed, others were carried off as slaves, the
Tenth Legion was quartered in Jerusalem, and
Titus held a triumphal procession in Rome in
which he displayed the golden candelabra from
the temple. The Arch of Titus in Rome was
built to commemorate the triumph and on one
of its panels is carved in high relief the scene of
his soldiers carrying the candlestand.[166]

Of the destruction of Jerusalem, the Jewish Encyclopedia
states: "The suffering in the city must have been terrible.
Many of the inhabitants were carried off and sold as slaves in
the Roman markets. According to Josephus ("B. J." v. 13, § 7),
as many as 115,880 dead bodies were carried out through one
gate between the months of Nisan and Tammuz; and even
before the siege was ended, 600,000 bodies had been thrown
out of the gates."[167] Zechariah adds that **out of their hand I
will not deliver them**. God does not intervene on Israel's
behalf, and as a consequence Rome quashes the rebellion,
retakes the land of Israel, and mercilessly destroys Jerusalem
and butchers large numbers of people.

---

[166] W. S. Lasor, "Jerusalem," ed. Geoffrey W Bromiley, *The International Standard Bible Encyclopedia, Revised* (Wm. B. Eerdmans, 1979–1988), 1029–1030.

[167] Isidore Singer, ed., *The Jewish Encyclopedia: A Descriptive Record of the History, Religion, Literature, and Customs of the Jewish People from the Earliest Times to the Present Day, 12 Volumes* (New York; London: Funk & Wagnalls, 1901–1906), 127.

> 7 And I will feed the flock of slaughter, *even* you, O poor of the flock. And I took unto me two staves; the one I called Beauty, and the other I called Bands; and I fed the flock.

In verse 6, God instructs Zechariah to "feed the flock of the slaughter" in the role of good shepherd, and here Zechariah responds obediently, **I will feed the flock of the slaughter, even you, O poor of the flock**. As Feinberg explains, "[i]n vision the prophet performs the commission of the Lord which he states both at the beginning of the verse and at the end."[168] Zechariah's role looks forward to when Messiah comes to **feed the flock of the slaughter**. At that time Messiah will especially focus on the **poor of the flock**, which verse 11 confirms are the faithful ("the poor of the flock that waited upon me knew that it was the word of the LORD"). As Baron explains, the word **poor**, or needy, weak, or afflicted, "is almost invariably used in the Hebrew Bible of the pious or *godly* in the nation who are persecuted and oppressed by the godless— of those whom the wicked in his pride 'hotly pursue,' or persecute, but who, knowing God to be their refuge, can look up to Him and say: 'But I am *poor* and needy, yet the Lord thinketh upon me.'"[169] That there will be a **poor of the flock** tells us that not everyone will reject the Messiah, yet characteristically they will reject him and are rightly **the flock** destined to **the slaughter**.

Zechariah comments on his role in delivering this prophecy. To understand his statement, we must be reminded that shepherds traditionally carried two staffs (or **two staves**), one for walking support and one for fighting off predators. One staff is called **Beauty** or Favor and the other is called **Bands** or Union. The staff called **Beauty** signified God's grace toward His people, and the staff called **Bands** symbolized the union of the two nations (Israel and Judah). Hill explains: "The *two staffs* allude

---

[168] Charles L. Feinberg, *God Remembers: A Study of Zechariah*, 159.
[169] David Baron, *Zechariah: A Commentary on His Visions and Prophecies*, 391.

to the tools of shepherding, the rod and the staff (cf. Ps. 23:4). The staff or crook was a symbol of leadership in the biblical world. In ancient Egypt, the ornamental shepherd's crook held by the Pharaoh represented his just rule of the people. Unlike the prophet Ezekiel who joined two sticks into one, symbolizing the reunification of the two Hebrew kingdoms (Ezek. 37:15–19), Zechariah dramatized the reversal of YHWH's covenant relationship and Israelite unity by breaking the two staffs (vv. 10, 14)."[170] Merrill similarly states: "Closer to Zechariah's experience was that of Ezekiel who also took two wooden poles, one standing for Judah and the other for Israel (Ezek. 37:15–23). Ezekiel took the two poles and joined them together as one signifying that in the time of eschatological restoration there will no longer be division between Israel and Judah, for they will be one people with one king and one God. In a sense what Ezekiel did in his dramatization was to effect a reversal of what Zechariah is about to do."[171] We will further address the **two staves** below when the prophet breaks them. But we note here that with his tools in hand, the prophet carries out his assigned task and feeds **the flock**.

> **8** Three shepherds also I cut off in one month;
> and my soul lothed them, and their soul also
> abhorred me.

In the course of feeding the flock, Zechariah states that **three shepherds also I cut off in one month**. The identification of the three shepherds has been debated for centuries. Baron correctly notes: "There is, perhaps, not another scripture in the Old Testament which has been more variously interpreted than the first part of the 8th verse of this chapter...."[172] Similarly, Feinberg writes: "Perhaps no other passage in the Old

[170] Andrew E. Hill, *Haggai, Zechariah and Malachi: An Introduction and Commentary*, 232.
[171] Eugene H. Merrill, *An Exegetical Commentary - Haggai, Zechariah, Malachi*, 257.
[172] David Baron, *Zechariah: A Commentary on His Visions and Prophecies*, 393.

Testament has been so variously interpreted as this."[173] The reason for such varied interpretations is that commentators search for **three** specific individuals and then try to make sense of the **one month**, i.e., that they literally died within a 30-day period or else explaining how **one month** is not limited to a 30-day period, thus opening the possibilities.

Rather than understanding these as specific people, the better view is that they are the three classes of shepherds (prophets, priests, civil authorities or rulers) that Messiah brings judgment upon when He comes because they reject him. Of this view, Feinberg explains: "The oldest, and probably the correct, view is that of Cyril and Theodoret, which is followed by Hengstenberg, Chambers, Baron, Dods, Gaebelein, and others. This interpretation sees in the three shepherds not three individuals, but three orders or classes of individuals: the king, the priest, and the prophet (compare Jer. 2:8, 26)."[174] This verse will be fulfilled in the first century in relation to the Messiah's earthly ministry. Note what Zechariah says: **and my soul lothed them, and their soul also abhorred me.** Even the most casual reader of the Gospels cannot miss the disdain of the first century Jewish leadership for Jesus. We see vehement opposition from the scribes and lawyers, the Pharisees, Sadducees, priests, and ultimately the civil authorities who try and execute Him. At the same time, Jesus pronounces judgment on that generation. We may remember the familiar words, "but woe unto you, scribes and Pharisees, hypocrites." (Matthew 23:13-15) See Jesus' words:

> **Matthew 23:29** Woe unto you, scribes and Pharisees, hypocrites! because ye build the tombs of the prophets, and garnish the sepulchres of the righteous, **30** And say, If we had been in the days of our fathers, we would not have been partakers with them in the

---

[173] Charles L. Feinberg, *God Remembers: A Study of Zechariah*, 160.
[174] *Ibid.*, 160-161.

> blood of the prophets. **31** Wherefore ye be
> witnesses unto yourselves, that ye are the
> children of them which killed the prophets.
> **32** Fill ye up then the measure of your fathers.
> **33** *Ye* serpents, *ye* generation of vipers, how
> can ye escape the damnation of hell?

The reader will do well to read Matthew 23. Jesus concludes: "Behold, your house is left unto you desolate." (Matthew 23:38) But the judgment will not be the end of the Jewish people, for in His next breath Jesus promises: "For I say unto you, Ye shall not see me henceforth, till ye shall say, Blessed is he that cometh in the name of the Lord." (Matthew 23:39) The phrase **one month** indicates a quick destruction, which befalls the nation in 70 A.D. under the Romans and is, as argued above, the destruction announced in the opening verses of chapter 11. That destruction on the shepherds (viewed as trees and lions earlier) is in view in verse 8.

> **9** Then said I, I will not feed you: that that
> dieth, let it die; and that that is to be cut off,
> let it be cut off; and let the rest eat every one
> the flesh of another.

Continuing his role, Zechariah announces he **will not feed you**. His shepherding the flock destined for slaughter will come to an abrupt end, and as a result, **that that dieth, let it die; and that that is to be cut off, let it be cut off**. For so long as the Messiah continues as shepherd during his earthly ministry, the flock is safe. But now, the good shepherd **will not feed** them nor deliver them from the Romans and the coming destruction. Again, this is the destruction announced in the opening poem in 11:1-3. So terrible will this destruction be that the prophet concludes, **let the rest** or those that survive the onslaught **eat every one the flesh of another**. This pictures a resulting famine and cannibalism. The Jewish historian Josephus made a record of this event in connection with the Roman siege (see *War*, VI, 193-213), which though somewhat lengthy should be reviewed in connection with the fulfillment of the prophecy at hand:

> Now of those perished by famine in the city, the number was prodigious, and the miseries they underwent were unspeakable; for if so much as the shadow of any kind of food did anywhere appear, a war was commenced presently; and the dearest friends fell a fighting one with another about it, snatching from each other the most miserable supports of life. Nor would men believe that those who were dying had no food; but the robbers would search them when they were expiring, lest any one should have concealed food in their bosoms, and counterfeited dying: nay, these robbers gaped for want, and ran about stumbling and staggering along like mad dogs, and reeling against the doors of the houses like drunken men; they would also, in the great distress they were in, rush into the very same houses two or three times in one and the same day. Moreover, their hunger was so intolerable, that it obliged them to chew everything, while they gathered such things as the most sordid animals would not touch, and endured to eat them; nor did they at length abstain from girdles and shoes; and the very leather which belonged to their shields they pulled off and gnawed: the very wisps of old hay became food to some; and some gathered up fibers, and sold a very small weight of them for four Attic [drachmae]. But why do I describe the shameless impudence that the famine brought on men in their eating inanimate things, while I am going to relate a matter of fact, the like to which no history relates, either among the Greeks or Barbarians!

It is horrible to speak of it, and incredible when heard. I had indeed willingly omitted this calamity of ours, that I might not seem to deliver what is so portentous to posterity, but that I have innumerable witnesses to it in my own age; and, besides, my country would have had little reason to thank me for suppressing the miseries that she underwent at this time.

There was a certain woman that dwelt beyond Jordan, her name was Mary; her father was Eleazar, of the village Bethezub, which signifies the House of Hyssop. She was eminent for her family and her wealth, and had fled away to Jerusalem with the rest of the multitude, and was with them besieged therein at this time. The other effects of this woman had been already seized upon; such I mean as she had brought with her out of Perea, and removed to the city. What she had treasured up besides, as also what food she had contrived to save, had been also carried off by the rapacious guards, who came every day running into her house for that purpose. This put the poor woman into a very great passion, and by the frequent reproaches and imprecations she cast at these rapacious villains, she had provoked them to anger against her; but none of them, either out of the indignation she had raised against herself, or out of the commiseration of her case, would take away her life; and if she found any food, she perceived her labors were for others, and not for herself; and it was now become impossible for her anyway to find any more food, while the famine pierced through her very bowels and marrow, when also her passion was fired to a degree beyond the famine itself; nor did she consult with anything but with her passion and the necessity she was in. She then attempted a most unnatural thing; and snatching up her son, who was a child sucking at her breast, she said, "O, thou miserable infant! For whom shall I preserve thee in this war, this famine, and this sedition? As to the war with the Romans, if they preserve our lives, we must be slaves! This famine also will destroy us, even before that slavery comes upon us:— yet are these seditious rogues more terrible than both the other. Come on; be thou my food, and be thou a fury to these seditious varlets and a byword to the world, which is all that is now wanting to complete the calamities of us Jews." As soon as she had said this she slew her son; and then roasted him, and ate the one half of him, and kept the other half by her concealed. Upon this the seditious came in presently, and smelling the horrid scent of this food, they threatened her, that they would cut her throat immediately if she did not show them what food she had gotten ready. She replied, that she had saved a very fine portion of it for them; and withal uncovered what was left of her son. Hereupon they were seized with a horror and amazement of mind, and stood astonished at the sight; when she said to them, "This is mine own son; and what hath been done was mine own doing! Come, eat of this food; for I have eaten of it myself! Do not you pretend to be either more tender than a woman, or more compassionate than a mother; but if you be so scrupulous and do abominate this my sacrifice, as I have eaten the one half, let the rest be reserved for me also." After which, those men went out trembling, being never so much affrighted at anything as they were at this, and with some difficulty they left the rest of that meat to the mother. Upon which the whole city was full of this horrid action immediately; and while everybody laid his miserable case before their own eyes, they trembled, as if this unheard-of action had been by themselves. So those that were thus distressed by the famine were very desirous to die; and those already dead were esteemed happy, because they had not lived long enough either to hear or to see such miseries.

Let us now move to verses 10-11 of this prophecy.

10 And I took my staff, *even* Beauty, and cut it asunder, that I might break my covenant which I had made with all the people. 11 And it was broken in that day: and so the poor of the flock that waited upon me knew that it *was* the word of the LORD.

Continuing his participation in the vision as the good shepherd, Zechariah says, **I took my staff, even Beauty** or Favor, **and cut it asunder, that I might break my covenant which I had made with all the people**. We must remember that the **covenant** God made with **the people** through the mediator Moses carries with it blessings and curses. That is, generally speaking, if **the people** are faithful to God they will be protected and prospered. But if they are rebellious, they will face escalating judgments culminating in God allowing a Gentile invader to overtake them. We see these blessings and curses outlined in Deuteronomy 28, of which a sample is quoted below:

Deuteronomy 28:49 The LORD shall bring a nation against thee from far, from the end of the earth, *as swift* as the eagle flieth; a nation whose tongue thou shalt not understand; **50** A nation of fierce countenance, which shall not regard the person of the old, nor shew favour to the young: **51** And he shall eat the fruit of thy cattle, and the fruit of thy land, until thou be destroyed: which *also* shall not leave thee *either* corn, wine, or oil, *or* the increase of thy kine, or flocks of thy sheep, until he have destroyed thee. **52** And he shall besiege thee in all thy gates, until thy high and fenced walls come down, wherein thou trustedst, throughout all thy land: and he shall besiege thee in all thy gates throughout all thy land, which the LORD thy God hath given thee. **53** And thou shalt eat the fruit of thine own body, the flesh of thy sons and of thy daughters, which the LORD thy God hath given thee, in the siege, and in the straitness, wherewith thine enemies shall distress thee.

Note that in verse 53 the destruction causes a famine leading to cannibalism, which is consistent with Zechariah 11:9, "let the rest eat every one the flesh of another." It should be noted that the destruction of Jerusalem by Nebuchadnezzar in 586/587 B.C. also led to famine and cannibalism, as confirmed in Lamentations. But as argued previously, the current vision is not looking to a past destruction but a future one (from Zechariah's vantage point). Finally, we must not miscomprehend that the breaking of the **covenant** means God is through with His people when everything Zechariah says points to future blessings for Israel *after* their rejection of the good shepherd. As Eugene Merrill rightly explains:

> For YHWH to break His covenant with His people is not to suggest an irreparable breach,

for the OT witness pervasively attests to the inviolability of that fundamental relationship (Ps. 89:34 [HB 89:35]; Isa. 54:9–10; Jer. 31:35–37; 33:19–26). What is meant is that the benefits of that covenant—in this case, the benefit of protection from conquest and deportation—have been withheld. In that sense, YHWH has exercised His right as Suzerain to bring to bear the curses of the covenant upon His disobedient vassal Israel, something He had threatened to do at the onset of the covenant arrangement (Lev. 26:14–33; Deut. 28:15–68). He broke His covenant by allowing His people to break it and thus to invite the suspension of its privileges.[175]

Thus, what we read here symbolizes the fact that God's protection and blessing of the people temporarily ends, as it had before the Babylonians took Israel. Note that when the destruction comes, the **poor of the flock** will recognize the fulfillment of Scripture as they **knew it was the word of the LORD**.

> 12 And I said unto them, If ye think good, give *me* my price; and if not, forbear. So they weighed for my price thirty *pieces* of silver. 13 And the LORD said unto me, Cast it unto the potter: a goodly price that I was prised at of them. And I took the thirty *pieces* of silver, and cast them to the potter in the house of the LORD.

Further continuing in vision as the good shepherd, but having completed his duties as the shepherd, Zechariah asks for his

---

[175] Eugene H. Merrill, *An Exegetical Commentary - Haggai, Zechariah, Malachi*, 259.

compensation. He requests his severance pay because he is fired by the flock. But instead of demanding a specific wage, he puts it to the sheep to determine the value of his services rendered. **If ye think good, give me my price; and if not, forbear.** Their response is that they **weighed for** the shepherd's **price** or compensation **thirty pieces of silver.** As many commentators observe, this is the value of a slave under the Law. (Exodus 21:32) The point is not that this is a paltry sum of money, as some assume, for it is a considerable sum.[176] Rather, the point is that the Son of God is valued as a mere servant. At this point, **the LORD said unto** Zechariah, further confirming all of this is in a participatory vision, to **cast** the money **unto the potter.** Note God's sarcasm about the compensation: **a goodly price that I was prised** or valued **at by them.** The **goodly price** is literally "splendor of splendor," language to draw attention to the fact that God considers the sum completely inappropriate.

Following God's instructions, Zechariah **took the thirty pieces of silver, and cast them to the potter in the house** or Temple **of the LORD.** The reference to the Temple, in light of the fact that it was not completed for three years after the last reported date in the book (7:1), indicates the project will be standing when the rejection occurs. The **potter** likely produces the vessels needed for the Temple operations. As Feinberg explains, "[t]he temple was chosen so that the act of repudiation by God might be as public as possible."[177] Of course, the meaning of this prophecy is settled in the progressive revelation of God in the New Testament. Jesus is betrayed for **thirty pieces of silver** and the traitor Judas Iscariot returns the money to the Jewish leaders, who in turn purchase a potter's field for burying foreigners since in their perverted sense of righteousness they do not want blood money in the Temple treasury:

---

[176] David Guzik, *Zechariah*, Zec 11:12–14.
[177] Charles L. Feinberg, *God Remembers: A Study of Zechariah*, 164.

> **Matthew 27:3** Then Judas, which had betrayed
> him, when he saw that he was condemned,
> repented himself, and brought again the thirty
> pieces of silver to the chief priests and elders,
> **4** Saying, I have sinned in that I have betrayed
> the innocent blood. And they said, What *is*
> *that* to us? see thou *to that.* **5** And he cast down
> the pieces of silver in the temple, and departed,
> and went and hanged himself. **6** And the chief
> priests took the silver pieces, and said, It is not
> lawful for to put them into the treasury,
> because it is the price of blood. **7** And they
> took counsel, and bought with them the
> potter's field, to bury strangers in. **8** Wherefore
> that field was called, The field of blood, unto
> this day. **9** Then was fulfilled that which was
> spoken by Jeremy the prophet, saying, And
> they took the thirty pieces of silver, the price of
> him that was valued, whom they of the children
> of Israel did value; **10** And gave them for the
> potter's field, as the Lord appointed me.

Some commentators believe there are irreconcilable
discrepancies between the Matthew passage and Zechariah
11:12-13, but this is misguided. Zechariah foretells what will
happen from God's vantage point. The focus is not the precise
details of what the good shepherd will do in shepherding the
flock, but instead reveals God's heart for His people, the
rejection of the good shepherd, and the heart of those that
reject the shepherd. The picture of the shepherd and His sheep
reveals the goodness of God toward His people through the
Messiah. The matter of the **thirty pieces of silver** poignantly
reveals the hearts of those that reject Him, valuing him as a
servant and not the promised Messiah, God with us. The vision
concerns the heart and not the precise mechanics, and so there
is no basis for concluding that there is a disconnect between
the vision and the supposed fulfillment in Matthew because the
wages are paid to Judas and not Jesus. Nor would it make sense

that the good shepherd, the Son of God, would literally request of the Jewish people in the first century His wages as their shepherd since they are not literally sheep and He is not literally a shepherd of real sheep. Moreover, to whom would He demand payment? As already mentioned, the passage at hand does not say exactly how the good shepherd will fulfill his role as the good shepherd. We know from Jesus' words: "I am the good shepherd: the good shepherd giveth his life for the sheep." (John 10:11) The story of all four Gospels is that the shepherd dies for the salvation of the people, and it is fitting that the matter of the **thirty pieces of silver** would be bound up with the death of the good shepherd for the flock. I also note that Zechariah is hardly ignorant of the future demise of the shepherd, for he later reveals (13:7) the death of the good shepherd as he continues to provide more details about history future. Those more precise details are not necessary to the purpose of the vision in chapter 11.

Finally, when Matthew says this prophecy is fulfilled, he ascribes it not to Zechariah but Jeremiah. Some see this as a contradiction or error in the text and numerous explanations have arisen to explain it. One is that Matthew draws from both Jeremiah (especially chapter 19) and Zechariah, and so he names the more prominent prophet. Another explanation that is also satisfactory is that in Jewish tradition, the prophetic writings were organized with Jeremiah coming first, and thus Matthew quotes the passage from the roll of the prophets and cites the first book, Jeremiah.

> **14** Then I cut asunder mine other staff, *even* Bands, that I might break the brotherhood between Judah and Israel.

Because his good shepherd role is concluded, Zechariah **cut asunder** his **other staff, even Bands** or union, **that I might break** or annul **the brotherhood between Judah and Israel.** Since this staff represents the unity of the two nations (Judah and Israel), the breaking of the staff indicates disunity or strife between them. But the point cannot be the political division between Judah and Israel that already exists—the nation had been long divided (following the reign of King Solomon). Rather, the reference is to a worsening internal strife that characterizes the situation during and especially after Jesus' earthly ministry. There is political strife as different groups vie for power (e.g., Pharisees, Sadducees, Zealots, Herodians), as well as the antagonism of Judah toward Samaria. During the First Jewish-Roman War, or the Great Revolt, and especially during the period from 66-70 A.D. leading to the destruction of Jerusalem, civil government falls apart and more radical factions take over, killing those who advocate surrender to the Romans.

> **15** And the LORD said unto me, Take unto thee yet the instruments of a foolish shepherd. **16** For, lo, I will raise up a shepherd in the land, *which* shall not visit those that be cut off, neither shall seek the young one, nor heal that that is broken, nor feed that that standeth still: but he shall eat the flesh of the fat, and tear their claws in pieces.

Having participated in vision in the role of the good shepherd, Zechariah is told to experience the villain. **The LORD said unto** Zechariah, **Take unto thee yet the instruments** or gear **of a foolish shepherd**. Recall that in verse 7, Zechariah as the good shepherd says, "I took unto me two staves; the one I called Beauty, and the other I called Bands; and I fed the flock." There he takes up the **instruments** appropriate to his intent to be a good shepherd. We see no indication here that in his role as **a foolish shepherd** he will take up similar tools. Rather, it is **the instruments of a foolish shepherd**. While those **instruments** are not specifically identified, they may be inferred by the actions of **the foolish shepherd**—and they are the opposite of the tools of the good **shepherd**. Loving care, protection, and unifying leadership are replaced with self-promotion, exploitation and persecution. We dare not ask how the Jewish people could spurn the good **shepherd** in favor of the evil **foolish shepherd** unless we are willing first to look in our own mirrors. And while me might readily criticize the miserable lot we have in Washington, D.C., we must take responsibility as a nation for our addiction to **foolish shepherd**[s]. We vote for beauty, "presidential" appearances, the ability to give a "verbal beatdown" in a debate, and grandiose promises of free stuff. These kinds of shepherds are not only elected, but greedily so by a public with an insatiable appetite for wickedness and wealth.

Accordingly, there should be no surprise that a future generation of Israel will welcome the **foolish shepherd**. As Jesus said in John 5:43: "I am come in my Father's name, and ye receive me not: if another shall come in his own name, him ye will receive." Indeed, as we saw in the introduction above, the generation of Israel that Jesus ministers to prefers the murderer Barabbas over the good **shepherd**. And consistent with many other commentators, I think it likely Zechariah looks forward not only to one **foolish shepherd**, but many and these will undoubtedly culminate in the Anti-Christ so frequently mentioned in the prophetic literature. God will permit the ultimate **foolish shepherd** because in His timing and wisdom, this will result in a largescale national revival where the people finally receive the good **shepherd**. As previously covered, the prophecy in Zechariah 9:9-10 looks to two comings of the king. Merrill rightly explains that Israel will place themselves under bad leaders "culminating at last in that very epitome of godless despotism, the individual identified in the NT as the Antichrist (1 John 2:18, 22; 4:3; 2 John 7; cf. Matt. 24:5, 24; 2 Thess. 2:3-4). It is only when that leadership is seen to be what it truly is—foolish and antithetical to God—that it will be discarded by the people and destroyed by YHWH who Himself will then assume the reins of government (Rev. 13:1–18; 14:9–12; 19:19–21; cf. Dan. 11:36–45)."[178]

[178] Eugene H. Merrill, *An Exegetical Commentary - Haggai, Zechariah, Malachi*, 266.

Next, we cannot miss the descriptor **foolish**. This is a leader that neither knows nor fears God. (Proverbs 1:7) We see this testified by his actions. As Guzik explains: "This foolish shepherd is allowed and appointed by God as judgment because His people forsook the true shepherd. This was fulfilled in Israel's rejection of Jesus. They rejected the Good Shepherd (John 10:1–18) but received another shepherd (John 5:43)."[179] God says, **For, lo, I will raise up a shepherd in the land** of Israel, **which shall not visit those that be cut off** (either separated for slaughter or gone astray), **neither shall seek the young one** that is lost. Of course, a good **shepherd** does **visit those that be cut off** and **seek the young one** that has wandered away. As Jesus says in Matthew 18:12: "How think ye? if a man have an hundred sheep, and one of them be gone astray, doth he not leave the ninety and nine, and goeth into the mountains, and seeketh that which is gone astray?" Similarly, the **foolish shepherd** will not **heal that that is broken, nor feed that that standeth still**. In other words, he does not tend to the injured nor the healthy. He does not care for their well-being.

I pause to add that we need to realize this future leader likely says he cares but his actions say otherwise. That too should seem familiar today. His true intent is revealed in that he **shall eat the flesh of the fat, and tear their claws in pieces**. He will devour them completely, even removing their hooves to get every last morsel, bleeding the stone at it were. The wicked **shepherd** is a future leader that God will raise up and who will exploit them to the fullest and then some. It is not clear that Zechariah's prophecy has one specific ruler in mind, but it does seem that many bad shepherds fit the bill, and they all portend the coming Anti-Christ. He is the coming leader prominent in books like Daniel and Revelation that is both a counterfeit of the good **shepherd** but also counter or against the true Messiah.

---

179 David Guzik, *Zechariah*, Zec 11:15–16.

> **17** Woe to the idol shepherd that leaveth the
> flock! the sword *shall be* upon his arm, and
> upon his right eye: his arm shall be clean dried
> up, and his right eye shall be utterly darkened.

Although God will raise up the wicked shepherd, God will also
bring judgment on him. Thus, we read, **woe to the idol
shepherd that leaveth the flock!** "The word *woe* (Heb.
hôy) is a technical interjection in prophetic literature, usually
introducing an announcement of malediction in the form of a
curse or judgment oracle (e.g. Ezek. 34:2; Amos 6:1; Mic. 2:1;
Nah. 3:1; Zeph. 2:5)."[180] Indeed, **the sword** of judgment **shall be
upon his arm, and upon his right eye: his arm shall be clean
dried up, and his right eye shall be utterly darkened.** The image
is that of a **shepherd** wounded so that he is unable to continue.
This **shepherd** has **his arm** injured so that he cannot defend
with a staff, and then **his right eye** is injured so that he cannot
see. But of course, these are not so much literal descriptions of
his injuries as symbolic of his incapacitation as a shepherd.
Guzik rightly states: "The worthless shepherd feels the sword
of God's judgment against **his arm** and **his right eye**. The **arm**
expresses strength and the **eye** expresses intelligence, so this
will be a harsh blow against the worthless shepherd."[181] God
will render him unable to defend himself, then (by implication)
God will slay him. The destruction of the Anti-Christ is
addressed in other places in Scripture. (see Daniel 7:8-11, 26;
2 Thessalonians 2:8; Revelation 19:19-21, 20:10)

Closing

The Bible says a great deal about leadership and presents many
examples of good (not perfect) leaders. One obvious facet of
these leaders is that the people under their care follow their

---

[180] Andrew E. Hill, *Haggai, Zechariah and Malachi: An Introduction and
Commentary*, 237.
[181] David Guzik, *Zechariah*, Zec 11:17.

leadership. In Moses we find exemplified the rare but necessary quality of humility. (Numbers 12:3) In Joshua we find another needful quality for good leadership, namely courage. (Joshua 10:25) In Nehemiah, we find wisdom in carrying out the task of rebuilding the walls of Jerusalem and dealing with adversity. In David, we find these and other qualities so that he was considered a man after God's own heart. (Acts 13:22)

Despite the substantial revelation God provides on leadership, Christians are adept at picking bad shepherds. A primary reason for this is that the Biblical content is set aside in favor of familiar secular means of selecting leaders in the manner that management is hired in the corporate context. The result is that we would never hire the apostle Peter to pastor our church because he lacks the credentials. Nor would we hire the apostle John because he lacks the experience with a church our size. And of course, Paul is out of the question because he is not a really dynamic orator. But none of these men were selected by God to be a CEO, nor for that matter to be a manager. They were selected to shepherd—to lead—and that is altogether different.

It is foolish to try work within a secular framework to find a non-secular, non-worldly leader. It is easy to look down at Israel's devastating decisions in rejecting the good shepherd and embracing a series of bad ones, but when you get down to where the rubber hits the road, they could not recognize the Son of God in their midst because they were looking for a Messiah that was nothing like God at all. And likewise, we easily make similar mistakes in selecting church leaders and political leaders, not knowing from God's Word what the genuine article should look like (or just not caring). And like Israel, we pay a price for it. We are well-served to learn from Scripture about leadership.

Application Points

- **MAIN PRINCIPLE:** God will send the Messiah to be the good shepherd *par excellence* to the nation of Israel and he will be characteristically rejected, yet they will embrace a series of bad leaders culminating in the Anti-Christ.

- The critical distinction between good and bad leaders is that good ones seek the best interest of the people and bad ones view the people as a commodity to be spent in pursuit of their personal agendas.

Discussion Questions

1. Why does Israel characteristically reject the good shepherd, Jesus Christ?

2. What purpose do you think was served in Zechariah experiencing, at least in vision, the roles of the good and bad shepherd as opposed to some other means of conveying God's message to the people?

3. How does the payment of Judas Iscariot of 30 pieces of silver fulfill Zechariah's prophecy that the good shepherd's request for wages is answered with 30 pieces of silver?

4. What do you think are the qualities to look for in the hiring of a preacher and what is the best way to find that person? What practices, if any, do you think should be borrowed from the secular employment context in finding and hiring a preacher?

5. What are the qualities that show a church leader is a "foolish shepherd"?

Chapter 14

Revival

There have been a number of great revivals throughout history. A notable early revival came under the leadership of King Josiah. He was only 8 years old when he became king (2 Chronicles 34:1), and in the eighth year of his reign "he began to seek after the God of David his father; and in the twelfth year he began to purge Judah and Jerusalem from the high places, and the groves, and the carved images, and the molten images." (2 Chronicles 34:3) He also initiated restoration work in the Temple. (2 Kings 22:3-5) During this time, the high priest Hilkiah discovered a copy "of the law in the house of the LORD" (2 Kings 22:8) and it was read to Josiah (2 Kings 22:10). The Bible says that "it came to pass, when the king had heard the words of the book of the law, that he rent his clothes." (2 Kings 22:11) In some way every great revival begins with conviction under the Word of God, which is why it is so critical today that Bible teachers present the whole counsel of God with boldness and clarity. The United States experienced its First Great Awakening in the 1730's and 1740's as Christians were impacted by the preaching of God's Word. A Second Great Awakening followed in the early 1800's and others after that. But the greatest revival in history is yet to come.

During the first advent, Jesus Christ presents himself as Israel's promised Messiah but most of the Jewish people, and especially the religious leadership, reject Him. There have always been Jewish Christians, but it remains the case even now that most Jewish people reject Jesus as the Messiah. The Bible is clear that during the day of the Lord (the tribulation period) there will be an unprecedented revival among the Jewish people when many will place their faith in Jesus. This miraculous turn of events will come about because of an outpouring of God's Spirit (Zechariah 12:10), the work of the 144,000 Jewish Christian evangelists active during the tribulation (Revelation 7:3-8, 14:1-5), and the ministry of God's "two witnesses" (Revelation 11:3-13). Zechariah 12 vividly presents the future revival of Israel as the people turn to Jesus, and to this day this passage continues to prompt many Jewish people to faith in Christ.

Scripture and Comments

We come now to the final section of the book of Zechariah. Just as chapter 9 through 11 form a single unit (a "burden of the word of the LORD"), chapters 12 through 14 also form a single unit presenting another burden. The theme is Israel's future and the day of the LORD when Jesus returns. This final section is not only critical to the overall message of the book of Zechariah, but critical to a fulsome Biblical understanding of end times events. As Charles Feinberg aptly states: "As a portion of the prophetic Scriptures, it is second to none in importance in this book or in any other Old Testament book. It is indispensable to an understanding of the events of the last days for Israel—the time of the Great Tribulation and the establishing of God's Kingdom on earth."[182] This last unit will touch on several end times events, both local (Israel) and global (worldwide) in scope. Charles Feinberg summarizes the scope of this final unit well:

> The actual events, world-embracing in character, which are presented include the world confederacy against Jerusalem; the victory of God's people, empowered of the Lord; the conviction of Israel nationally by the Spirit of God; the presentation of Christ as their rejected Messiah; the national Day of Atonement; the cleansing of the hearts of the nation; the purging of the land from idolatry and false prophets; parenthetically, the crucifixion of the Messiah; the time of Jacob's trouble; the partial success of the nations invading Palestine and besieging Jerusalem; the appearance of the Messiah for His people; their rescue and His coming with His saints; the changed and renovated Holy Land; the establishment of the Messianic kingdom; the punishment of the nations for their futile assault on Israel; the celebration of the kingdom feast, the Feast of Tabernacles; and the complete restoration of the people of God to a holy nation.[183]

In chapters 12 and 13, which need no chapter break, we see both physical and spiritual deliverance for Israel. These must go hand in hand for a restored Israel. As Duane Lindsay explains: "Two conditions are necessary for the establishment of Israel's future messianic kingdom: (a) the overthrow of the Gentile world powers that oppose the establishment of this kingdom and (b) the regeneration of individual Jews who will

---

[182] Charles L. Feinberg, *God Remembers: A Study of Zechariah*, 169.
[183] *Ibid.*, 169-170.

constitute the nation when God fulfills the Abrahamic and Davidic Covenants. Both of these conditions will be accomplished by the Lord, as seen in chapters 12–13. He will deliver Israel physically from her enemies (12:1–9) and He will deliver her spiritually (12:10–13:9)."[184]

> **Zechariah 12:1** The burden of the word of the LORD for Israel, saith the LORD, which stretcheth forth the heavens, and layeth the foundation of the earth, and formeth the spirit of man within him.

We read that Zechariah receives a **burden of the word of the LORD for Israel**. It stands out at once that this **burden** is **for Israel**. In Zechariah's time, there is no united **Israel** and there had not been a united **Israel** for two centuries because the northern tribes went into exile as a result of the Assyrian invasion, and because centuries before that the nation split. These opening words, therefore, point us to a future fulfilment when there will be a united **Israel**.

Zechariah emphasizes that it is God's message, the God of Israel that created the universe (**stretcheth forth the heavens**), the planet earth (**layeth the foundation of the earth**), and humanity. Regarding the creation of humanity, the focus is not on the physical or material aspect of man, but the immaterial aspect of man. The message Zechariah has **for Israel** is from the God that **formeth the spirit of man within him**. These phrases allude to the creation event in Genesis 1 and 2, and the reference to the **spirit of man** specifically alludes to Genesis 2:7: "And the LORD God formed man of the dust of the ground, and breathed into his nostrils the breath of life; and man became a living soul." The Bible frequently refers back to the creation event because the supernatural creation shows the majesty and power of God. Here it speaks to His ability to detail for Zechariah (and us) history future and ensure it comes to pass.

[184] F. Duane Lindsey, "Zechariah," in *The Bible Knowledge Commentary: An Exposition of the Scriptures*, 1566.

Dennett explains the scope of what follows: "After the introduction of Antichrist, at the close of the preceding chapter, the prophet is occupied with the events of the last days, or those events which circle around Jerusalem, and which are connected with her siege and deliverance. Looking in the power of the Spirit into the future, he depicts event after event, until he sees, at the end of the book, the kingdom established, with Jerusalem as the religious metropolis of the whole earth, and all nations owning the authority of the King in Zion."[185] It is no surprise, given the weight of his message, that Zechariah reminds his audience (and us) before delivering it that God is capable. As Guzik states, "The section begins with praise for God's creative power, reminding us that He is in control and completely able to accomplish what He predicts."[186]

> **2** Behold, I will make Jerusalem a cup of trembling unto all the people round about, when they shall be in the siege both against Judah *and* against Jerusalem.

In contrast to chapter 11 that opens with the devastation of the Holy Land, this chapter opens with God giving Israel the victory. These prophecies are not inconsistent, however, because the material in chapter 11 centers on the first coming of Messiah and events that occur in the first century, including Rome defeating the Jewish rebellion, overtaking Jerusalem, and destroying the second Temple in 70 A.D. The material in chapter 12 looks beyond those events to Israel's victory over its enemies associated with the second coming of Messiah. Some commentators build their eschatology on the premise that after Israel crucifies Jesus, the Old Testament blessings promised to them of a regathering to the Holy Land and establishment of an earthly Messianic Kingdom centered in Jerusalem were forever lost, and such blessings are instead

---

[185] Edward Dennett, *Zechariah the Prophet*, 150.
[186] David Guzik, *Zechariah*, Zec 12:1–4.

fulfilled in some spiritual sense in the "church." But Zechariah foretells Israel's rejection of Messiah at his first advent, the crucifixion of Messiah, and a subsequent regathering of Israel and Messianic blessings at the second advent. Any eschatology that denies these future blessings to Israel nullifies most of the book of Zechariah.

God **will make Jerusalem a cup of trembling unto all the people round about, when they shall be in the siege both against Judah and against Jerusalem.** Zechariah looks to a future time when **Jerusalem**, and indeed all of **Judah**, is under **siege**. To its attackers, **Jerusalem** will be a **cup of trembling**. The **cup** often pictures God's wrath (e.g., Lamentations 4:21, Revelation 16:19). Here, it is God's wrath against Israel's enemies, described as **all the people**, a reference to Gentile nations. The **cup** holds wine or some strong drink. The word **trembling** or staggering describes drunkenness that results from too much alcohol, but here, there is **trembling** because God will make Israel's enemies drink of His wrath to the point of figurative inebriation so that they stumble in defeat. I note that Zechariah does not explicitly state why the nations have gathered **in the siege** against **Judah and...Jerusalem**, just the fact of it.

> **3** And in that day will I make Jerusalem a burdensome stone for all people: all that burden themselves with it shall be cut in pieces, though all the people of the earth be gathered together against it.

This verse presents the first of sixteen references in chapters 12-14 to **that day**, a shorthand for "the **day** of the Lord." [187] This phrase "**day** of the Lord" generally refers to a future time when Messiah returns, bringing judgment to Israel's enemies and blessing to Israel (see, e.g., Daniel 9:24-27, 12:1-7; Joel 3:1-3, 9-21; Zephaniah 3:6-17; Haggai 2:20-23). The shorthand **that day**

---

[187] F. Duane Lindsey, "Zechariah," in *The Bible Knowledge Commentary: An Exposition of the Scriptures*, 1568.

is an extremely common phrase in the prophetic books of the Old Testament. In the **day** of the LORD, God **will make Jerusalem a burdensome stone for all people** or Gentile nations. Specifically, those Gentile nations who try to take **Jerusalem** will find it a **burdensome stone,** that is, like an unmovable **stone.** Global forces **(the people of the earth)** will gather to **burden themselves with** the stone—to destroy **Jerusalem**—and as a result **shall be cut in pieces.** This will be a complete routing of Israel's enemies, and in chapter 14 the prophet will correlate this defeat of Israel's enemies with the second coming of the king, Messiah Jesus.

This gathering of the nations against **Jerusalem** is popularly referred to as the Battle of Armageddon (see Revelation 16:13-16). This battle occurs at the Messiah's return (see Revelation 19:11-21). The purpose of the invasion will be an uprising against Anti-Christ (introduced in the last chapter as the ultimate "foolish shepherd"), whose headquarters is established in **Jerusalem** (see Daniel 11:36-45) after he breaks the peace treaty he makes with Israel and invades (see Daniel 9:24-27). The judgment on those invading nations described in Zechariah 12 will be carried out by Messiah, and the specifics of his victory over Israel's enemies are set forth in Zechariah 14.

> **4** In that day, saith the LORD, I will smite every horse with astonishment, and his rider with madness: and I will open mine eyes upon the house of Judah, and will smite every horse of the people with blindness.

In that day, again a reference to the future "day of the Lord," the LORD...**will smite every horse with astonishment, and his rider with madness.** The Lord will deal directly with the invaders, confusing both the horses and the riders. Although it is certainly conceivable that the invaders might utilize a cavalry, most people today would imagine an invasion to utilize the weapons of modern warfare like tanks and aircraft. But we have to understand that Zechariah describes the future in the terminology of his time. Whether or not an actual cavalry will be used in the invasion, the point is that God will **smite** the enemies **with madness**. In contrast, He **will open His eyes upon the house of Judah**, that is, He will take notice of the enemy attack and intervene on Judah's behalf and **smite every horse of the** enemies **with blindness**. This will incapacitate the invading soldiers and their weapons. The prophet elaborates on this "plague" in 14:12-15.

> **5** And the governors of Judah shall say in their heart, The inhabitants of Jerusalem *shall be* my strength in the LORD of hosts their God.

The prophet next gives us insight into the future **governors** or leaders **of Judah**. They **shall say in their hearts**, in other words, think to themselves that **the inhabitants of Jerusalem shall be my strength in the LORD of hosts their God**. In contrast to the bad shepherds Zechariah addresses in chapter 11 who seek to exploit the flock, these leaders see the people **of Jerusalem**, and by extension the people of **Judah**, as a source of **strength** against their enemies because they are empowered by **the LORD of hosts**.

> **6** In that day will I make the governors of Judah like an hearth of fire among the wood, and like a torch of fire in a sheaf; and they shall devour all the people round about, on the right hand and on the left: and Jerusalem shall be inhabited again in her own place, *even* in Jerusalem.

Continuing to detail what will happen **in that day**, and building on verse 5, God says, **I will make the governors of Judah like an hearth of fire among the wood, and like a torch of fire in a sheaf**. Whereas verse 5 indicates God will empower the people to stand against their enemies, here he empowers the leaders or **governors** of **Judah** against the invaders. They will be like fire among dry wood or a fire among dry wheat (a **sheaf**) as they rapidly **devour all the enemies** or invaders **round about**,

on the right hand and on the left. Other scriptures also use the idea of Judah's enemies being burned up. (e.g., Isaiah 47:14; Obadiah 18; Malachi 4:1) As a consequence of Judah's victory over her enemies, **Jerusalem shall be inhabited again in her own place,** meaning the Jews will again dwell in Jerusalem.

> 7 The LORD also shall save the tents of Judah first, that the glory of the house of David and the glory of the inhabitants of Jerusalem do not magnify *themselves* against Judah.

God will begin by liberating the outlying areas of Judah (**the tents of Judah first**) and then liberate **Jerusalem** itself. That this liberation is necessary indicates that invaders gain control over Judah before God brings deliverance, which is consistent with other passages. (e.g., Zechariah 14:1-2; Matthew 24:15-22) God will liberate in this order so that those in **Jerusalem** and those of the **house of David** do not become prideful, **that the glory of the house of David and the glory of the inhabitants of Jerusalem do not magnify themselves against Judah.** For it is critical that all Jewish people recognize their deliverance is from God and not of their own strength. As Lindsay notes, "The priority of Judah's deliverance over that of Jerusalem will assure the entire nation's unity with the inhabitants of the capital city."[188] We cannot disconnect the physical deliverance pictured in 12:1-9 from the spiritual deliverance beginning in 12:10 that focuses first on the **house of David,** i.e., the rulers of Israel at this future time.

> 8 In that day shall the LORD defend the inhabitants of Jerusalem; and he that is feeble among them at that day shall be as David; and the house of David *shall be* as God, as the angel of the LORD before them.

---

[188] F. Duane Lindsey, "Zechariah," in *The Bible Knowledge Commentary: An Exposition of the Scriptures*, 1567.

In the **day** of the LORD, God will **defend the inhabitants of Jerusalem**. Not only will God intervene on their behalf as we see in chapter 14, but He will supernaturally strengthen the general populace so that **he that is feeble among them...shall be as David**, the giant slayer and great warrior. God will also supernaturally strengthen the leadership so that **the house of David shall be as God, as the angel of the LORD before them**. Thus, God will confuse the enemies (12:4) while simultaneously empowering the people of Judah to defend themselves. I note that the **angel of the LORD before them** takes us back to the prominent role of the **angel of the LORD** as protector of Israel and captain of God's armies in chapters 1 and 6 in the night visions. As I noted there, the **angel of the LORD** is the pre-incarnate Christ. That they will be empowered as the **angel of the LORD** is unsurprising because Jesus Christ will, as chapter 14 shows, fight alongside them to route their enemies.

> **9** And it shall come to pass in that day, *that* I will seek to destroy all the nations that come against Jerusalem.

Concluding the unit (12:1-9) on Israel's future physical deliverance from the invading **nations**, the prophet writes that **it shall come to pass in** the **day** of the LORD **that** God **will seek to destroy** all of the Gentile **nations** that attack **Jerusalem**. As previously noted, this event is referred to as the Battle of Armageddon, and in chapter 14, Messiah's role in the Battle is expounded. I note here that the book of Revelation includes additional detail about this final climactic battle with Israel's enemies:

> **Revelation 16:14** For they are the spirits of devils, working miracles, *which* go forth unto the kings of the earth and of the whole world, to gather them to the battle of that great day of God Almighty. **15** Behold, I come as a thief. Blessed *is* he that watcheth, and keepeth his

garments, lest he walk naked, and they see his shame. **16** And he gathered them together into a place called in the Hebrew tongue Armageddon.

While from the perspective of Israel's enemies, they are coming to the Holy Land to wage war, the Bible says God "gathered them together into a place called in the Hebrew tongue Armageddon." They will apparently invade Israel to wage war with the Anti-Christ (Daniel 11:36-45), but find themselves dealing with the "king of kings" and "Lord of Lords" who will "in righteousness...judge and make war" and "smite the nations...[and] treadeth the winepress of the fierceness and wrath of Almighty God." (Revelation 19:11-16)

> **10** And I will pour upon the house of David, and upon the inhabitants of Jerusalem, the spirit of grace and of supplications: and they shall look upon me whom they have pierced, and they shall mourn for him, as one mourneth for *his* only *son*, and shall be in bitterness for him, as one that is in bitterness for *his* firstborn.

Zechariah turns from physical deliverance to spiritual deliverance, a subject that continues into chapter 13. As a preliminary matter, that this deliverance comes **upon the inhabitants of Jerusalem** implies that some of the regathering to the land up to future time occurs in unbelief. The Bible teaches a regathering of Jewish people to Israel prior to the Lord's return and a regathering after his return. Whereas this verse confirms that during the day of the Lord there will be non-believing Jews in Israel, passages like Zechariah 10:8-12 address a regathering in belief after the Lord returns.

There is no question that mourning results from the pouring out of **the spirit of grace and supplications**. Zechariah states that God **will pour upon the house of David, and upon the inhabitants of Jerusalem the spirit of grace and of supplications**. The **house of David** refers to the Jewish leadership, while the **inhabitants of Jerusalem** refers to the general populace of **Jerusalem** and by extension of Israel. God motivates a national repentance evidenced by mourning. As Merrill explains concerning the **grace**: "Grace (חֵן, ḥēn) essentially has to do with a favorable disposition or act in the OT. When God or even men show grace, they act without reciprocating for a previous gesture of kindness. As in the language of Christian theology it is an expression of unmerited favor."[189] The concept of **supplications** is a reference to prayers requesting God's favor or help. The reference to **the spirit** indicates the work of the third person of the Godhead, the Holy Spirit, whose ministry in this time bestows favor (**grace**) upon the people and moves them to earnestly seek God in prayer. This is consistent with the pouring out of the Spirit during the day of the LORD predicted by the prophet Joel:

> **Joel 2:28** And it shall come to pass afterward, *that* I will pour out my spirit upon all flesh; and your sons and your daughters shall prophesy, your old men shall dream dreams, your young men shall see visions: **29** And also upon the servants and upon the handmaids in those days will I pour out my spirit.

In light of Acts 2, where the apostle Peter quotes from Joel 2, there can be no question that Joel 2:28-29 has in mind a work of the Holy Spirit. And for that reason, there is little question that Zechariah also speaks of a future work of the Holy Spirit. Lindsay agrees, explaining: "This is most probably a reference to the Holy Spirit (see NIV marg.), so called because He will minister graciously to Israel in her sinful condition and will lead her to supplication and repentance."[190]

---

[189] Eugene H. Merrill, *An Exegetical Commentary - Haggai, Zechariah, Malachi*, 279.

[190] F. Duane Lindsey, "Zechariah," in *The Bible Knowledge Commentary: An Exposition of the Scriptures*, 1567.

The result is a national revival that begins as the Jewish people **look upon me whom they have pierced**. The word **look** is not physical sight but a spiritual **look** in the sense of a realization of what they have done. The word **pierced** indicates "piercing to death." [191] In chapter 11, God presents himself as the good shepherd, but we know from New Testament revelation that the ministry of the good shepherd is carried out by the second member of the Godhead, the Son. Here also, God says the people will turn to **me whom they have pierced**, and again the reference is to the Son. There can be no doubt of this in light of the apostle John's commentary on the crucifixion quoting Zechariah 12:10: "And again another scripture saith, 'They shall look on him whom they pierced.'" (John 19:37)

There will be a realization during the day of the LORD that they murdered the Son at the first advent, and as a result **they shall mourn for him, as one mourneth for his only son**. This is genuine conviction of sin, a change of mind or repentance about who Jesus is, and an acknowledgment about what the nation did to Him on Calvary. We see a foretaste of this in Acts 2, in response to Peter's preaching: "Therefore let all the house of Israel know assuredly, that God hath made that same Jesus, whom ye have crucified, both Lord and Christ." (Acts 2:36) We read that "[n]ow when they heard this, they were pricked in their heart, and said unto Peter and to the rest of the apostles, Men and brethren, what shall we do?" (Acts 2:37) But what we read about at Pentecost is not the national revival Zechariah foresees.

That the people will mourn as **for his only son** indicates the deep and sincere nature of their mourning. Indeed, they **shall be in bitterness for him, as one that is in bitterness** over the death of their **firstborn**. Merrill elaborates on the significance of the language here:

191 *Ibid.*, 1567.

The description of the reaction to the pierced one is also suggestive of messianic language. When the people see what they have done in their spiritual blindness, they will lament as one laments for his "only son" (הַיָּחִיד, hayyāḥîd), his "first-born" (הַבְּכוֹר, habběkôr). יָחִיד (from יָחַד, hāḥad, "be united") conveys the idea of a one and only. It is the term YHWH chose when speaking to Abraham about Isaac whom he was about to slay on Moriah: "Take your son, your only son (יְחִידְךָ, yěḥîděkā), whom you love" (Gen. 22:2). The LXX renders the Hebrew word yāḥîd as ἀγαπητός (agapētos, "beloved"), the same word the NT writers use to describe Jesus, "the beloved Son" of God (e.g., Matt. 3:17; 17:5; Luke 9:35). The NT dependence here is obvious."[192]

The mourning summarized in verse 10 is elaborated in what follows.

> **11** In that day shall there be a great mourning in Jerusalem, as the mourning of Hadadrimmon in the valley of Megiddon. **12** And the land shall mourn, every family apart; the family of the house of David apart, and their wives apart; the family of the house of Nathan apart, and their wives apart; **13** The family of the house of Levi apart, and their wives apart; the family of Shimei apart, and their wives apart; **14** All the families that remain, every family apart, and their wives apart.

Their **great mourning** reveals on a national level a conviction over their sin of murdering ("me whom they have pierced") the second member of the Godhead, the Son of God and their

---

[192] Eugene H. Merrill, *An Exegetical Commentary - Haggai, Zechariah, Malachi*, 282.

Messiah. This genuine **mourning** is a necessary prerequisite for their spiritual deliverance, which we see in 13:1-6. For "in that day there shall be a fountain opened to the house of David and to the inhabitants of Jerusalem for sin and for uncleanness." (Zechariah 13:1)

Again, Zechariah includes the time-marker, **in that day**, referencing the future **day** of the LORD associated with the second advent of Messiah. At this time, **there** will **be a great mourning in Jerusalem** just **as** there was **the mourning of Hadadrimmon in the valley of Megiddon**. This references the mourning over the death of the good King Josiah who was killed in battle with Pharaoh Neco in 609 B.C. (see 2 Kings 23:29-30; 2 Chronicles 35:22-27) The entire nation will mourn. The emphasis is on how widespread and complete the revival is as the Jewish nation turns to Messiah. The revival includes people from all levels of society, from the ruling class (**house of David**), the Levites (**house of Levi** and the **family of Shimei**), and every other family (**all the families that remain**). Concerning the **house of Levi** and **house of Shimei**, Merrill explains the reference is to the Levites but likely includes the priests: "The "clan of Levi" (v. 13) refers to the whole priestly or religious side of Israel's life, just as "clan of David" spoke of the political. The Shimeites, then, were the descendants of Levi who presumably dominated the Levitical classes in the postexilic era. Shimei was, according to the genealogies, the grandson of Levi through Gershom (Ex. 6:16–17; cf. Num. 3:17–18). He was not a priest inasmuch as the priests traced their lineage back to Gershom's brother Kohath (1 Chron. 6:1–3), so he represents specifically the Levites. Yet the priests and their wives would also be included under the general Levitical umbrella, for the purpose here is to suggest a general repentance embracing the totality of political and religious life."[193]

---

[193] *Ibid.*, 285.

LOOKING FORWARD, LIVING NOW

Some believe the **house of Nathan** refers to prophets because there was the prophet **Nathan** that ministered to **David**. But **David** also had a son named **Nathan**. Again, as Eugene Merrill explains, the reference is likely to a branch of the Davidic lineage to emphasize the comprehensive scope of the mourning over the murder of Messiah:

> Nathan was the third son of David born in Jerusalem, apparently an elder brother of Solomon by a different wife (2 Sam. 5:14; 1 Chron. 3:5). Though the kings of Judah from Solomon to the tribe of the Exile were descendants of Solomon (1 Chron. 3:10–16), it is quite apparent that a change occurred at that point and that royal descent began to be traced through Nathan. This is hinted at in the OT genealogical and dynastic records and made explicit in the NT. Zerubbabel, as we have noted already (see pp. 146ff.) was of royal blood but was not of the line of Solomon. Though in one list he is called the son of Pedaiah (1 Chron. 3:17–19), he is usually considered to be the son of Shealtiel (Ezra 3:2, 8; 5:2; Neh. 12:1; Hag. 1:12, 14; Matt. 1:12; Luke 3:27). Probably he was, in fact, the grandson of Shealtiel. Jehoiachin, however, left no male heir (Jer. 22:3) and yet had "sons" (1 Chron. 3:17). These sons may have been offspring of a daughter who, according to Luke's genealogy, married Neri, a descendant of David in a parallel line through Nathan (Luke 3:27). Luke also records that Zerubbabel was of the Nathan lineage, as was Jesus Himself (Luke 3:23–31). Because the prophet Zechariah was a contemporary of Zerubbabel, he would naturally refer to the Davidic house of his own time as the "clan of

Nathan," for by then the line of descent had already shifted from Solomon to Nathan.[194]

When Zechariah says **the land shall mourn** he means **the land** of Israel, i.e., all the people and **every family** that constitute the remnant at that time. (Zechariah 13:9) Also note the references to **every family apart...and their wives apart**. While the nation will mourn, the depth of this time of conviction and repentance is such that people will isolate themselves from others to individually reckon with their own sin.

This is the fulfillment of the national Day of Atonement (or Yom Kippur) of Leviticus 16. Recall that every year on the tenth day of the seventh month (Tishri), the people would celebrate this feast by "afflicting the soul" and participating in an elaborate ritual involving two goats. One goat was sacrificed for the sins of the nation (goat for Jehovah) and the other released to carry away the sins from the people (the Azazel). In Hebrews 10, the writer explains that there is no longer a need for the people to continue this feast in the same way year after year because Jesus provided a sacrifice once that is sufficient for all time. Just as the sacrifice of the goat on the Day of Atonement only had value to those that afflicted their souls, so also Jesus' sacrifice will not save the Jewish people until they mourn. The true Yom Kippur will occur in **that day** based on the sacrificial atonement of the Son of God that occurred at the first advent. The Son is presently at the right hand of God awaiting the time of His return when Israel's enemies will be destroyed, which is what we see occur in the earlier portion of this chapter. (Hebrews 10:12-17)

Closing

There is knowing about Jesus Christ and there is knowing Jesus Christ. One application that comes out of Zechariah 12

---

[194] *Ibid.*, 284–285.

is that when they mourn in the realization that they pierced God on a Roman cross in the first century, it is not merely a corporate time of mourning but a time when each individual separately and personally experiences "bitterness" over this sin. There are those today that would check a box identifying themselves as Christians, but they never made a personal decision for Christ. They may think of themselves as Christians because they were raised in a Christian family or live in a "Christian" nation, or even because they go to church or raised their hand at a church camp. But being a Christian requires a personal decision to place trust in Jesus Christ alone for the forgiveness of sins based on his provision for sin by his death, burial and resurrection. The idea of a national revival is exciting, but for it to have individual implications there must be individual decisions.

Application Points

- **MAIN PRINCIPLE:** In the day of the LORD, God (through Messiah) will deliver Israel from Gentile invaders and bring spiritual revival by a pouring out of the Holy Spirit resulting in a realization among the Jewish people that they killed the Messiah.

Discussion Questions

1. Why do you think Zechariah 12 begins by emphasizing God as Creator?

2. The chapter opens with God delivering Israel from invading Gentile nations. Do you think the United States has a place in this prophecy?

3. Why do the Gentile nations invade Israel during the day of the LORD?

4. In 12:9, God says He "will seek to destroy all the nations that come against Jerusalem." How do you synthesize this truth with the message that Gentile nations will be joined to the Lord in the day of the Lord (e.g., 2:11, 14:16)?

5. Why would God pour out "the spirit of grace and of supplications"? In other words, why are both "grace" and "supplication" necessary for God's purposes?

6. What does the level of mourning among those that "look upon me whom they have pierced" tell you about the condition of their hearts at this time?

7. What do we need to see revival in our nation? In our church?

Chapter 15

Take Away Sins

The writer to Hebrews explains that "the law" of Moses is "a shadow of good things to come, and not the very image of the things." The reason the Law is a "shadow" or sketch of "good things to come" is that the Jewish people could "never with those sacrifices which they offered year by year continually make the comers thereunto perfect." (Hebrews 10:1) That harsh reality is evident because "in those sacrifices there is a remembrance again made of sins every year." (Hebrews 10:3) The sacrifices were annually repeated because "it is not possible that the blood of bulls and of goats should take away sins." (Hebrews 10:4) Note the last three words—take away sins. That is the greatest need the Jewish people have (and Gentiles also), and the Law provides no solution for it. We can understand the significance in John the Baptizer's words when he "seeth Jesus coming unto him, and saith, Behold the Lamb of God, which taketh away the sin of the world." (John 1:29) Turning back to Hebrews, the writer says of Jesus: "Wherefore when he cometh into the world, he saith, Sacrifice and offering thou wouldest not, but a body hast thou prepared me." (Hebrews 10:5) While the offerings of the priests in the Old Testament "can never take away sins" (Hebrews 10:11), "by one offering [Jesus] hath perfected for ever them that are sanctified" (Hebrews 10:14). At the cross, Jesus opened a fountain that washes sins away. Zechariah speaks to that fountain.

Scripture and Comments

This chapter continues the explanation of the spiritual deliverance of Israel that occurs in the day of the LORD. In Zechariah 12:10, the prophet says that God "will pour upon" Israel "the spirit of grace and of supplications" with the result that "they shall look upon me whom they have pierced, and they shall mourn for him." There will be a time of national revival where the Jewish people realize they murdered the Messiah at his first advent and under great conviction there will be a time of deep mourning. "The lamentation of repentance that results when Judah sees the one whom they have pierced by their apostate disobedience will in turn result in their forgiveness, an act described in the present unit as a purification or cleansing."[195] This great conviction results in changing their thinking about who Jesus is. No longer would they view Him as a blasphemer worthy of death (Matthew 24:64-66), but they will recognize Him as the Messiah and in their hearts say, "Blessed is he that cometh in the name of the Lord." (Matthew 23:39) At that time there will be a true national Day of Atonement and their sins will be washed away.

> **Zechariah 13:1** In that day there shall be a fountain opened to the house of David and to the inhabitants of Jerusalem for sin and for uncleanness.

---

[195] *Ibid.*, 287.

The verse begins with **in that day**, a phrase repeatedly used in chapter 12. (see 12:3, 4, 6, 8, 9, 11) This is one of those instances where a chapter break is awkwardly placed splitting a cohesive unit of thought. As before, **in that day** is shorthand for "the day of the Lord" and refers to a future time when Messiah returns, bringing judgment to Israel's enemies and blessing to Israel (see, e.g., Daniel 9:24-27, 12:1-7; Joel 3:1-3, 9-21; Zephaniah 3:6-17; Haggai 2:20-23). The phrase **in that day** occurs twenty times in Zechariah. This verse is a continuation of the future national revival experienced by Israel as introduced in Zechariah 12:10-14. A **fountain** is **opened**, and its waters wash sin away. This idea is pictured elsewhere in the Old Testament. For instance, Ezekiel wrote: "Then will I sprinkle clean water upon you, and ye shall be clean: from all your filthiness, and from all your idols, will I cleanse you." (Ezekiel 36:25) Other passages use the idea of water as cleansing and life-giving. (Numbers 31:23; Ezekiel 47:1-12; Isaiah 12:2-3) Jesus offers living waters to the woman at the well in John 4. To be saved, a person must be cleansed of their sin.

Zechariah says **there shall be a fountain opened to the house of David and to the inhabitants of Jerusalem for sin and for uncleanness**. Zechariah pinpoints the recipients of this blessing as **the house of David** (leadership) **and the inhabitants of Jerusalem** (general populace) just as he did in 12:10 in relation to the "spirit of grace and supplications." But as Eugene Merrill notes, "[t]hey, however, are only representative of the whole redeemed people as 12:12–14 puts beyond doubt."[196] Some see in 13:1 a reference to the cross or the "gospel age." [197] But while it is true that the **fountain** was **opened** at Calvary for all people, the present oracle points to an occurrence **in that day**, a time marker repeated in verses 2 and 4. Zechariah looks to a specific "final work of YHWH" regarding His people Israel.[198] The **fountain** is an artesian well continuously spewing forth living

---

[196] *Ibid.*, 288.
[197] Roger Ellsworth, *Opening Up Zechariah*, 125.
[198] Eugene H. Merrill, *An Exegetical Commentary - Haggai, Zechariah, Malachi*, 287–288.

waters that will remove both **sin** and **uncleanness**. While **sin** concerns a failure to conform to God's will, which for the Jewish people in Zechariah's time was set forth in the Mosaic Law, **uncleanness** is a state of defilement or impurity that occurs when a person breaches God's "principles of holiness."[199]

As Duane Lindsey succinctly explains, "On the day of Christ's crucifixion the fountain was opened *potentially* for all Israel and the whole world. At the Second Advent of Christ, the **fountain will be opened** *experientially* for the Jewish nation."[200] This future event is associated with the fulfillment of the New Covenant with Israel, a concept frequently referenced in the prophets. (e.g., Jeremiah 31:33-34; Ezekiel 36:25) As the writer of Hebrews affirms, Jesus is the "mediator of a better covenant, which was established upon better promises" (Hebrews 8:6) and "mediator of the new testament" (Hebrews 9:15). Because there is "fault" with the covenant God made with Israel through Moses, in that it could not cleanse people of sin, God promised to "make a new covenant with the house of Israel and with the house of Judah." (Hebrews 8:7-8) This New Covenant will not be like the one God made with Moses (Hebrews 8:9):

> **Hebrews 8:10** For this *is* the covenant that I will make with the house of Israel after those days, saith the Lord; I will put my laws into their mind, and write them in their hearts: and I will be to them a God, and they shall be to me a people: **11** And they shall not teach every man his neighbour, and every man his brother, saying, Know the Lord: for all shall know me, from the least to the greatest. **12** For I will be merciful to their unrighteousness, and their sins and their iniquities will I remember no more.

---

[199] *Ibid.*, 287–288.
[200] F. Duane Lindsey, "Zechariah," in *The Bible Knowledge Commentary: An Exposition of the Scriptures*, 1568.

This New Covenant is inaugurated in Jesus' blood: "this is my blood of the new testament, which is shed for many for the remission of sins." (Matthew 26:28) But the fulfillment of the promises of the New Covenant to Israel, summarized in the Hebrews passage quoted above, has not yet occurred. The apostle Paul specifically associates that fulfillment with the second advent of Messiah as does Zechariah in the passage at hand. (Romans 11:25-27)

At that future time, the **fountain** provided at Calvary will be **opened** to Israel experientially with a great national revival. And with the righteousness of God written in their hearts, the nation will be cleansed of sins.

> **2** And it shall come to pass in that day, saith the LORD of hosts, *that* I will cut off the names of the idols out of the land, and they shall no more be remembered: and also I will cause the prophets and the unclean spirit to pass out of the land.

Again emphasizing the time period is **in that day**, Zechariah says, **it shall come to pass**. Despite God's assurance that **it shall** happen, I note here that most expositors teach the opposite—these blessings are spiritualized away as "church" blessings so that the plain sense of the verses as they would have been understood both by Zechariah's immediate audience and the Jewish people for centuries after that will not **come to pass**. But any notion that Israel forfeited these blessings is misguided because the book of Zechariah foresees both Israel's future failures and God's return of blessing to them after those failures. The question of whether these things **shall come to pass** depends not upon Israel, but on the veracity of God Himself.

The **LORD of hosts** says that He **will cut off the names of the idols out of the land, and they shall no more be remembered**. I noted above that this passage captures the fulfillment of the

New Covenant blessings to Israel. It is not just that a future generation of Israel will experience a national revival, but they will have God's "law in their inward parts" and God will "write it in their hearts; and will be their God, and they shall be my people." (Jeremiah 31:33) As a result, the nation will be characteristically righteous in a way that never previously occurred. The LORD of hosts will remove sin from the land and from the daily experience of the people. This is no doubt what Zechariah sees symbolically in his vision 5:5-11 where wickedness is carried back to Shinar, cleansing the land. The sin here is typified by two of its most serious manifestations, idolatry and false prophecy. These serious issues are addressed in many other places in Scripture (e.g., Jeremiah 23:13-14, 30; 27:8-10; Ezekiel 13:1-14:11; Lamentations 2:14, 4:13).

That God will **cut off** or remove **the names of the idols** means idolatry will with finality be removed and forgotten. Israel's history reveals its persistent engagement in idolatry up until the exile. But some argue that in post-exilic Israel idolatry is gone, from which they conjecture that Zechariah wrote the subject passage prior to the exile into Babylonian captivity. Even if there was an historical respite within Israel of this particular sin after the exile, that does not mean Israel will not again engage in idolatry. As Lindsey notes, "Idolatry near the time of the Second Advent of Christ will include worship of the image of the beast in the temple in Jerusalem (Dan. 9:27; 11:31; Matt. 24:15; 2 Thes. 2:4; Rev. 13:4), though other types of idolatry will also be present (Rev. 9:20)."[201]

Further, we know from Jesus' preaching in the Olivet Discourse that false prophets will remain until His return. (Matthew 24:4-5, 11, 23-24) And in the Revelation, during the Tribulation period, the false prophet leads and deceives the world in worshipping the beast (anti-Christ) and his animated image. Thus, it is entirely fitting that **in that day** God **will cause the**

---

201 *Ibid.*, 1568.

prophets and the unclean spirit to pass out of the land of
Israel. Concerning the reference to **the unclean spirit** we note
that demonic activity has always been around. We see it in the
Gospels where Jesus and His disciples cast out demons. (e.g.,
Matthew 10:1; Mark 5:9-13) We also see **unclean** spirits at work
during the Tribulation period. (e.g., Revelation 16:13-14, 18:2)
But as the Kingdom is implemented, Satan and his demons are
bound for a thousand years. (Revelation 20:1-3) What is
recorded in the Revelation is the fulfillment of God's promise
here to remove **the unclean spirit** from **the land**.

> **3** And it shall come to pass, *that* when any shall
> yet prophesy, then his father and his mother
> that begat him shall say unto him, Thou shalt
> not live; for thou speakest lies in the name of
> the LORD: and his father and his mother that
> begat him shall thrust him through when he
> prophesieth.

Emphasizing the spiritual changes that will occur and result in
a removal of false prophets, God says **it shall come to pass that
when any shall yet prophesy, then his father and his mother
that begat him shall say unto him, Thou shalt not live**. The
Law required the execution of false prophets. (Deuteronomy
13:1-5) False prophets frequently led the people of Israel into
idolatry. For such a grave crime, the death penalty was
imposed even if it involved family:

> **Deuteronomy 13:6** If thy brother, the son of
> thy mother, or thy son, or thy daughter, or the
> wife of thy bosom, or thy friend, which *is* as
> thine own soul, entice thee secretly, saying, Let
> us go and serve other gods, which thou hast
> not known, thou, nor thy fathers; **7** *Namely,* of
> the gods of the people which *are* round about
> you, nigh unto thee, or far off from thee, from
> the *one* end of the earth even unto the *other*
> end of the earth; **8** Thou shalt not consent

> unto him, nor hearken unto him; neither shall thine eye pity him, neither shalt thou spare, neither shalt thou conceal him: **9** But thou shalt surely kill him; thine hand shall be first upon him to put him to death, and afterwards the hand of all the people. **10** And thou shalt stone him with stones, that he die; because he hath sought to thrust thee away from the LORD thy God, which brought thee out of the land of Egypt, from the house of bondage.

Consistent with this, the spiritual environment of Israel after the pouring out of "the spirit of grace and supplications" (12:10) and opening of "a fountain...to the inhabitants of Jerusalem for sin and for uncleanness" will be such that the false prophet's own parents will insist on his execution. They will make the charge, **for thou speakest lies in the name of the LORD**. The false prophet says "God said" when He did not. As a result, **his father and his mother that begat him shall thrust him through when he** falsely **prophesieth**. They will **in that day** revere their relationship with God more than all other relationships. Some may protest that this is too severe to be accepted at face value, or that the punishment (death) does not fit the crime. But we must remember that false prophets proliferate deception and cause nothing but despair and death, pushing those under their influence away from God with eternal consequences. And again, the people of God at this time experience the blessings of the New Covenant and have the righteousness of God written in their hearts in a way that never happens until this time. Their attitude toward sin now reflects God's attitude toward sin, which is vastly different than how most people today (Christians included) perceive sin.

> **4** And it shall come to pass in that day, *that* the prophets shall be ashamed every one of his vision, when he hath prophesied; neither shall they wear a rough garment to deceive:

There is a tremendous difference between regret and remorse. We routinely hear apologies from public figures caught in some criminal or immoral activity (usually after they denied wrongdoing and then the indisputable evidence of their guilt in a video or secret recording surfaces). Of course, they regret what they did because they were caught, but that is not remorse. In the same way, **it shall come to pass in that day** that the false **prophets** will get outed. They **shall be ashamed every one of his** false **vision, when he hath prophesied**. This, of course, is the opposite of what they did previously, spreading their venom with impunity. The **prophets shall be ashamed** of their false teaching because of the severity of the punishment, and thus they try to hide their crime. To evade the penalty, they will remove their **rough garment** that they wore as the traditional garb of a prophet **to deceive** the people. (1 Kings 19:13, 19; 2 Kings 2:8, 13-14; Matthew 3:4)

> **5** But he shall say, I *am* no prophet, I *am* an husbandman; for man taught me to keep cattle from my youth.

When the false **prophet** is interrogated, **he shall say, I am no prophet**, openly denying his guilt. He will claim some other trade than that of prophet, for example, a farmer (**husbandman**) or rancher (**for man taught me to keep cattle from my youth**). Zechariah's words partially quote, and then paraphrase, the genuine prophet Amos' testimony of his own background: "Then answered Amos, and said to Amaziah, I was no prophet, neither was I a prophet's son; but I was an herdman, and a gatherer of sycomore fruit." (Amos 7:14) In contrast to Amos, who used his background to give validity to his calling, the false prophets will lie about their background to evade the charge of being false prophets. They will claim it **from my youth,** that is, that they have always had the same trade and never worked as a **prophet**.

> **6** And *one* shall say unto him, What *are* these wounds in thine hands? Then he shall answer,

> *Those* with which I was wounded *in* the house
> of my friends.

The false prophets' testimony that they are really farmers and ranchers will not be believed because visible evidence gives them away. In particular, their self-inflicted wounds (1 Kings 18:28) will give them away. The wounds are indicative of self-mutilation commonly practiced by idolatrous prophets and priests, but strictly forbidden among God's true prophets. (Deuteronomy 14:1) The wounds provide irrefutable evidence that they are false prophets. Yet when questioned, **What are these wounds in thine hands**, they will lie about the source of the wounds. Representative of the absurd lies they will concoct to cover the truth, they **answer, Those with which I was wounded in the house of my friends**. In other words, the **wounds** are the result of an accident. But their lies are to no avail, as 13:2 confirms.

> 7 Awake, O sword, against my shepherd, and against the man *that is* my fellow, saith the LORD of hosts: smite the shepherd, and the sheep shall be scattered: and I will turn mine hand upon the little ones.

Zechariah now presents a new oracle that returns to the **shepherd** motif seen in 9:16, 10:2-3 and 11:4-17. In chapter 11, the Messiah (the good shepherd) is rejected and his services (ministry) valued at 30 pieces of silver. While we know from the New Testament that this looked forward to the crucifixion, Zechariah now makes the death of the good **shepherd** explicit. Here, **my shepherd**, meaning God's **shepherd**, is not only rejected but killed. As shown below, this is undisputedly about the crucifixion of Jesus. But one may question the abrupt change in focus from the future day of the Lord in 12:1-13:6 associated with the second advent of the Messiah to the first advent. Charles Simeon is correct in saying: "This is generally thought to be the beginning of a distinct prophecy: yet it seems not only to be connected with, but in a measure to arise out of, the preceding context."[202] As he further explains, "Then in our text God says, As the false prophet shall be *slain by his own father* for endeavouring to turn you from God, so shall the true prophet be *slain by his father* in order to turn you to God...."[203] Thus, Zechariah goes back to the **shepherd** theme to elaborate on Israel's condition, their need for God's intervention, and how the fountain of 13:1 is made possible. I also note that the general structure of Zechariah 13 mirrors that of Zechariah 9. Both chapters focus on events during the day of the LORD with one verse dividing the material with a focal point on the first advent. In Zechariah 9, verse 9 is the focal verse that points to the presenting of Messiah to Israel during Jesus' earthly ministry in the event we call the Triumphal Entry. In Zechariah 13, this seventh verse is the focal verse that points to the death of Christ during his earthly ministry.

God says through the prophet, **awake, O sword, against my shepherd, and against the man that is my fellow, saith the LORD of hosts.** The use of **sword** does not mean a literal **sword** but a violent death. God's **shepherd** is **the man that is my fellow.** That he is **the man** indicates his humanity, while **my fellow** indicates a peer or equal to God, thus proving his deity. As Lindsey confirms, "In Zechariah 13:7 the Lord is claiming identity of nature or unity of essence with His Shepherd, thus strongly affirming the Messiah's deity."[204] That God awakens **the sword** indicates that it is His will that the **shepherd** die, consistent with His command, **smite** or strike **the shepherd.** As we read the Gospels, we realize both that Jesus cannot be taken to that rugged cross except that He permit it (Matthew 26:53), and that it is the Father's will that Jesus permit Himself to be placed on the tree (Matthew 16:21). From a human perspective, the Jewish leadership and Roman officials think

---

[202] Charles Simeon, *Horae Homileticae: Hosea to Malachi*, 528.

[203] *Ibid.*, 528–529.

[204] F. Duane Lindsey, "Zechariah," in *The Bible Knowledge Commentary: An Exposition of the Scriptures*, 1569.

they determine Jesus' fate, but it was always the Father's will that Jesus the priest-king offer Himself on a Roman cross as the once for all time sacrifice for sin.

As a result of the death of the **shepherd...the sheep shall be scattered.** And God **will turn** His **hand upon the little** or insignificant **ones** in the flock. Jesus applies this passage to Himself, leaving no doubt as to its fulfillment: "Then saith Jesus unto them, All ye shall be offended because of me this night: for it is written, I will smite the shepherd, and the sheep of the flock shall be scattered abroad" (Matthew 26:31; see also Mark 14:27). Israel **shall be scattered** as a result of its rejection of Jesus. Charles Feinberg observes of this event: "God has overruled the smiting for blessing, but still the consequences must follow for rejection of Messiah by Israel...The sheep were not only scattered on the night of His betrayal, but have been scattered over the world since the destruction of Jerusalem."[205] But the phrase **I will turn my hand upon the little ones** can be easily misunderstood. The **littles ones** correspond to the "poor of the flock" of 11:11, those "that wait upon me" and "knew that it was the word of the LORD." The idea of God turning His **hand upon** someone, as Charles Feinberg explains, "is usually employed for infliction of judgment and chastisement, as in Amos 1:8 and Psalm 81:15 (Heb.). Here it is employed for the salvation of God's people. Compare Isaiah 1:25."[206] That God will bless a believing remnant is further confirmed in what follows.

> 8 And it shall come to pass, *that* in all the land,
> saith the LORD, two parts therein shall be cut
> off *and* die; but the third shall be left therein.

Whereas verse 7 concerns the first advent, this verse looks forward again to "that day" just before the Lord's return. We see this in Zechariah 9:9-10, where verse 9 finds fulfillment at

---

205 Charles L. Feinberg, *God Remembers: A Study of Zechariah*, 191.
206 *Ibid.*, 191.

the Triumphal Entry but verse 10 awaits the return of the king. There is no explicit statement in 13:7 or 13:8 that there will be a gap of time between the two, but in light of New Testament revelation there can be no question of this. **The LORD says it shall come to pass, that in all the land** of Israel, **two parts therein shall be cut off and die; but the third shall be left therein.** This speaks to a refined remnant of Israel and is reminiscent of Ezekiel 5:1-12 where God commands the prophet to shave his head and divide the hair into three equal portions, burning and destroying two-thirds of the hair and throwing the rest to the wind so that it is scattered, thereby killing two-thirds of the "house of Israel" as judgment for their refusal to obey God's statutes and keep His judgments. While Ezekiel may only have been looking forward to Nebuchadnezzar's victory over Jerusalem, the parallel is obvious. With Ezekiel's prophecy, even the one-third that were not destroyed were relegated to further trials, and ultimately they were refined and a refined remnant were returned to the land. In the next verse, we see God's purpose in the refining of His people.

> **9** And I will bring the third part through the fire, and will refine them as silver is refined, and will try them as gold is tried: they shall call on my name, and I will hear them: I will say, It *is* my people: and they shall say, The LORD *is* my God.

God **will bring the third part through the fire**. God's purpose in permitting them to experience the trials ahead is to **refine them as silver is refined, and...try them as gold is tried.** This refers to melting down the metals and removing the dross or impurities. And this process plays a role in turning them to the Lord. For it will be the refined remnant of Jewish people that **shall call on my name**, God says, **and I will hear them.** God's response to the refined remnant will be, **It is my people**, to which **they shall** affirm, **The LORD is my God.** Duane Lindsey summarizes this portion of Zechariah well:

The surviving remnant will have been purged and purified by the persecutions in the Tribulation, as well as by God's judgment on living Israel at the Second Advent (cf. Ezek. 20:33–38; Matt. 25:1–30). They will **call on** the **name** of the Lord in faith (Zech. 12:10–13:1) and become a restored nation (Rom. 11:26–27). Their renewed covenant relationship with the Lord (Hosea 1–2; Jer. 32:38–41; Ezek. 37:23–28) will be reflected in God's words, **They are My people** (cf. Zech. 8:8), and the people's response, **The LORD is our** (lit., "my") **God** (cf. Hosea 2:21–23).[207]

During the tribulation, the remnant will **call on** God's **name** in prayer and He will physically deliver them, as we see in Zechariah 12. The apostle Paul writes of this physical deliverance in Romans 10:13: "For whosoever shall call upon the name of the Lord shall be saved." This deliverance will be in connection with the second coming of the king. What follows in the final chapter of Zechariah provides the details of this glorious deliverance.

Closing

Although God will deliver Israel from her enemies in the day of the LORD, He will not deliver every Jewish person. Instead, He will preserve a refined remnant through various trials. Zechariah likens the refining process that produces this remnant to the refining of silver or gold to remove impurities. Note that it does not say God keeps them out of the trials. In a similar way, God uses the trials of life to refine the faith of Christians today. Peter writes that we are "begotten...again" of the Father for a "lively hope" (or living hope), namely "an

---

[207] F. Duane Lindsey, "Zechariah," in *The Bible Knowledge Commentary: An Exposition of the Scriptures*, 1569.

inheritance incorruptible, and undefiled, and that fadeth not away, reserved in heaven for" us. (1 Peter 1:3-4) As Christians there is a "salvation ready to be revealed in the last time" (1 Peter 1:5) when we receive our inheritance, but Peter's immediate audience is enduring persecution and other trials and so he writes, "Wherein ye greatly rejoice, thou now for a season, if need be, ye are in heaviness through manifold" trials. (1 Peter 1:6) The purpose of "the trial [or testing] of your faith, being much more precious than of gold that perisheth, though it be tried with fire" is that your faith "be found unto praise and honour and glory at the appearance of Jesus Christ." (1 Peter 1:7) The "faith" Peter writes of is not faith in the gospel message, for he assumes they are already "begotten...again" or born again children of God. Rather, it is believing God's Word in general and living life on that basis that is in issue, for Peter explains we should "as newborn babes, desire the sincere milk of the word, that ye may grow thereby." (1 Peter 2:2) The trials of life refine our faith—like refining gold—as we respond to those trials on the basis of God's Word. This is how we experience growth. And this refined grown-up faith, Peter says, is more valuable than earthly gold because this quality of faith appropriates our portion of the inheritance. When we stand before Jesus our refined faith will result in our "praise and honour and glory."

Application Points

- **MAIN PRINCIPLE:** In the day of the LORD, the fountain for washing away sins made available by Jesus Christ when He dies on a Roman cross becomes experientially realized by a refined remnant of the Jewish people as they experience revival and receive the New Covenant blessing of having the righteousness of God written in their hearts.

- Idolatry and false prophets will be permanently removed from Israel.

Discussion Questions

1. Jesus dies on a Roman cross in the first century, but Zechariah says a fountain is opened to the Jewish people "for sin and for uncleanness" in the day of the LORD. In what way is the fountain opened in the first century and in what way is it opened in the day of the LORD?

2. Do you think there is idolatry in the nation where you live? If so, what form does it take and what are some of the idols?

3. Do you think there are false prophets in the nation where you live? Do you think any of them teach in church pulpits, on Christian radio or on Christian television? Based on the Bible, how can we know a false prophet?

4. Should we tolerate a false teacher in a church? If the answer is not "yes" or "no," what is the standard and how is that standard impacted by Zechariah 13?

5. Why do you think God must refine the Jewish people before a remnant will "call on my name" and "say, the LORD is my God"?

6. What does Zechariah 13:7 say about the humanity and deity of Christ?

Chapter 16

Victory

D-Day, the beginning of the end of World War II in Europe (1939-1945). The famous Battle of Normandy began on D-Day, June 6, 1944, as approximately 156,000 American, British, and Canadian soldiers landed on the beaches along the coast of the region of Normandy in France. The Allied forces came by ship and landed on the beaches in the largest amphibious military battle in history. The battle continued into August 1944 and resulted in the liberation of Western Europe from Germany's control. The battle liberated northern France and by the following spring the Allied forces defeated the Germans.

There is another D-Day on the horizon. The long war against God that began with the Fall in Genesis 3 will come to a close. The earthly epicenter of this conflict is Israel, the victim of multiple Gentile nations throughout history. In the coming D-Day, the largest international military force in history will lay siege to Israel. But unknown to them, God draws them to this final battle. It is not their D-Day, but Israel's, because their assault puts a fire to the fuse that will inevitably bring their destruction. This international force will achieve initial success, but when it appears they are accomplishing their objectives, there will be a revival in Israel that results in a Jewish remnant calling upon Jesus to deliver them. Jesus will at first provide a way of escape for those fleeing Jerusalem, and then He will destroy the invaders and every enemy soldier will die. Jesus, their promised Messiah, will deliver victory. The book of Zechariah, with all of its challenges, is a book of victory for the people of God. This final chapter in Zechariah is the exciting climax that closes with Jesus' worldwide Kingdom in place, characterized by peace, prosperity and holiness.

Scripture and Comments

Chapters 9 through 11 comprise a single "burden" Zechariah receives from God, and chapters 12 through 14 comprise the final "burden" Zechariah receives and is inspired to write. To summarize what Zechariah says to this point, chapter 9 foretells the coming of the King-Messiah who will fight for and free His people. Chapter 10 presents the conditions during the Millennial reign of the King-Messiah. Chapter 11 presents the Messiah as God's good shepherd, whom the people will reject and value at 30 pieces of silver, for which they will suffer under a bad shepherd who will devour them. Whereas the rejection of Messiah in Chapter 11 looks to the first advent of Jesus, chapter 12 looks to His second coming and a time of national revival for Israel. Chapter 13 continues describing the revival that is associated with Messiah's return and explains the spiritual cleansing that will be poured out on the Jewish nation, but ends with the prophecy that 2/3 of the inhabitants of Israel will be killed as God refines a Jewish remnant that will pray for deliverance and be delivered in the day of the LORD. Building on Zechariah 13:8-9, in this final chapter of the book, specific details are given of the plundering of Jerusalem by Gentile invaders, Messiah's return and victory over Israel's enemies, the establishment of Messiah's Kingdom, and a description of worship during the Kingdom. As Merrill succinctly comments, "The second great oracle and the entire prophecy of Zechariah end on the grand and glorious note of the sovereignty of YHWH and the establishment of His universal and eternal kingdom."[208]

> **Zechariah 14:1** Behold, the day of the LORD cometh, and thy spoil shall be divided in the midst of thee.

Note that this verse builds on 13:8-9: "And it shall come to pass, that in all the land, saith the LORD, two parts therein shall be cut off and die; but the third shall be left therein. And I will bring the third part through the fire...they shall call on my name, and I will hear them: I will say, It is my people: and they shall say, The LORD is my God." Zechariah writes, **behold, the day of the LORD cometh.** Although Zechariah previously referenced "that day" some twenty times, this is the only occurrence in the book of the phrase, **the day of the LORD.** As with the shortened expression, "that day," this refers not to a 24-hour **day** but a future time of blessing and judgment upon Israel and the nations. Hixson and Fontecchio provide a general description:

> A general definition of the Day of the Lord is that period of time when God intervenes directly in the affairs of mankind in power and great glory to accomplish a specific or divine purpose. It does not always have eschatological implications, especially in the Old Testament. Theologically, in its broadest sense, it refers to that period of time in the eschaton beginning with the Rapture and continuing until the creation of the new heavens and new earth.

---

[208] Eugene H. Merrill, *An Exegetical Commentary - Haggai, Zechariah, Malachi,* 299.

* * *

A primary element of the Day of the Lord will be the judgment and persecution of the nation of Israel. Israel will be presented with one final chance to receive Messiah during the Tribulation....A second element is the judgment of the Gentile nations. The coming judgment is broader than Israel. It is judgment on all of mankind, and the culmination of human history.[209]

Arnold Fruchtenbaum explains its relationship to Israel during the Tribulation:

There are five "Day of Jehovah" passages that directly relate the Great Tribulation to Israel: first, Ezekiel 13:1-7 describes the Day of Jehovah in relationship to the false Jewish prophets in the Tribulation. The multiplication of false prophets among Israel will require a massive cleansing, described in Zechariah 13:2-6. Second, in Joel 2:1-11, the Day of Jehovah is depicted as a time of darkness and invasion. Third, in Joel 3:14-17, the Day of Jehovah is described as the time of refuge for Israel. Fourth, in Amos 5:18-20, the Day of Jehovah is again depicted as the time of darkness. Fifth, the Day of Jehovah is portrayed as being especially heavy against Jerusalem.[210]

During this future time, **thy spoil shall be divided in the midst of thee.** The reference to **thy** is to Israel (see 13:8: "all the land") but especially to Jerusalem (14:2), consistent with

---

[209] J.B. Hixson and Mark Fontecchio, *What Lies Ahead: A Biblical Overview Of The End Times* (Lucid Books: Brenham, Texas 2013), 238-239.

[210] Arnold G. Fruchtenbaum, *Israelology: The Missing Link In Systematic Theology* (Tustin, CA: Ariel Ministries, 2001), 771.

Fruchtenbaum's comment above that this period of time will be "especially heavy against Jerusalem." While the events portrayed are not limited to Jerusalem, that city is the focal point. What this verse confirms is that Gentile invaders find initial success in overtaking Israel and even take Jerusalem and plunder it. This deadly invasion, perhaps in conjunction with other judgments during the Tribulation, reduces the Jewish population in Israel by two-thirds as described in the preceding verses in Zechariah 13.

We know from other passages that Anti-Christ will appear on the world scene and rapidly ascend to worldwide domination. He will make peace with Israel by a seven-year treaty, and then defy that treaty in the middle of the seven years and persecute the Jewish people. Meanwhile, some nations will move against him in rebellion and will bring their forces to Jerusalem where Anti-Christ will be. (see Daniel 7:15-28, 9:20-27, 11:21-45; Revelation 13:1-10, 16:12-16, 19:11-21) They will be in for a rude awakening when they discover that it is not their **day** but the Lord's.

> **2** For I will gather all nations against Jerusalem to battle; and the city shall be taken, and the houses rifled, and the women ravished; and half of the city shall go forth into captivity, and the residue of the people shall not be cut off from the city.

Continuing the description of the day of the LORD, God says through the prophet, **I will gather all nations against Jerusalem to battle; and the city shall be taken, and the houses rifled, and the women ravished**. This gathering of the nations against Jerusalem is usually referred to as the Battle of Armageddon. These nations believe they are coming against Anti-Christ but, in fact, God draws them there to judge them. As Merrill writes, "It is important to note that it is YHWH who gathers the nations, for His design is not only to purify His people in tribulation (cf. 13:8–9) but to provide an occasion for the destruction of their enemies.... Micah also describes the assembling of the nations against Zion and says that they little realize why they are there, namely, to be sheaves on the threshing-floor of YHWH's judgment (Mic. 4:11–13)."[211] Dennett similarly concludes: "Here we have the revelation that at first, before Jehovah appears, the enemy will triumph and capture the city. Jehovah permits this for the punishment of the apostates of Judah under the influence of the antichrist....The scripture makes it also plain that Jehovah will suffer Jerusalem to be taken before He intervenes."[212] The book of Revelation confirms that much of the world will be deceived into worshiping the Anti-Christ, and so there will be apostates within Israel. But at the same time, as Zechariah prophesies in chapter 12, there will also be a great revival in Israel before the Lord returns.

Passages like Revelation 16:12-16 and Joel 3 also address this gathering of the **nations** for judgment. **Jerusalem** will be overtaken, the **houses** sacked for plunder, and the **women** raped. These are typical descriptions of warfare, both in the ancient world and now, as the media reporting that comes to our televisions confirms. There are no atrocities that mankind is incapable of doing. The terrible deeds that will be done at this time are the reason that Jesus warned the Jewish people to flee the city without even taking time to gather their belongings after the abomination of desolation (some sort of defiling of the Temple by Anti-Christ) takes place in the middle of the Tribulation period. (Matthew 24:15-22)

Continuing the description of Israel's defeat, we read that **half of the city** of Jerusalem **shall go forth into captivity** or into exile, **and the residue** or remainder **of the people shall not be cut off** or removed **from the city.** In other words, about **half of the city** will escape, but the other half will not. God's hand in their escape is outlined in Revelation 12:12-17.

[211] Eugene H. Merrill, *An Exegetical Commentary - Haggai, Zechariah, Malachi,* 300.
[212] Edward Dennett, *Zechariah the Prophet,* 179–181.

> 3 Then shall the LORD go forth, and fight
> against those nations, as when he fought in the
> day of battle.

There will be a turning point, however, when **the LORD will go forth, and fight against those nations, as when he fought in the day of battle**. Although the Gentiles will be permitted initial success in taking Israel, their aggression will be brought to a halt as God intervenes to fight the invading armies. This, of course, speaks of Jesus' return or second triumphal entry. The first triumphal entry at Mt. Olivet is at the beginning of the Passion Week. As predicted in Zechariah 9, Jesus enters the city on a donkey, humble and having salvation. His victory is over sin and death. The second triumphal entry also involves Mt. Olivet, but this time the victory will be over the nations that oppose God and His people. This victory is also detailed in Revelation 19:11-21. It is, in fact, Jesus the King of Kings and Lord of Lords who intervenes for His people **as when he fought in the day of battle**. Probably the better translation, which makes sense of the context here, is "as when he fights in the day of battle." This is not a reference to a prior battle, but an emphasis on the Lord's personal participation in the battle to come. His return will come in response to the great national revival that is recorded in Zechariah 12-13. Some of the details of this deliverance are recorded in Zechariah 2:8-9, 9:10-17 and 12:1-9. The present chapter expands on this deliverance and focuses particularly on Messiah's (Jesus') role.

> 4 And his feet shall stand in that day upon the
> mount of Olives, which *is* before Jerusalem on
> the east, and the mount of Olives shall cleave in
> the midst thereof toward the east and toward
> the west, *and there shall be* a very great valley;
> and half of the mountain shall remove toward
> the north, and half of it toward the south.

The text says **his feet shall stand in that day upon the mount of Olives, which is before Jerusalem on the east**. First, there can be no reasonable interpretation here but the literal one as the verse doubles down on the geographic location, adding **which is before Jerusalem on the east.** There also can be no dispute that this is the Messiah, Jesus Christ. When He ascended from **the mount of Olives** with the disciples watching, the angels said, "Ye men of Galilee, why stand ye gazing up into heaven? this same Jesus, which is taken up from you into heaven, shall so come in like manner as ye have seen him go into heaven." (Acts 1:11) Zechariah 14:4 records the event the angels announced in Acts 1:11. Jesus will **stand...upon the mount of Olives** and split the mountain to create **a very great valley.** The prophet explains that **the mount of Olives shall cleave in the midst thereof.** At that moment, **half of the mountain shall remove toward the north, and half of it toward the south.** This may result from a great earthquake. It will form a new valley that will permit the Jewish remnant in **Jerusalem** to escape the city and will also be the place where Jesus will draw the Gentile invaders to destroy them. Joel likely refers to this new **valley** when he connects Armageddon with the **valley** of Jehoshaphat ("God judges") in Joel 3:2, 12. This newly formed set of two mountains with the **great valley** between them is probably the two bronze mountains of the climactic eighth night vision in Zechariah 6.

> 5 And ye shall flee *to* the valley of the mountains; for the valley of the mountains shall reach unto Azal: yea, ye shall flee, like as ye fled from before the earthquake in the days of Uzziah king of Judah: and the LORD my God shall come, *and* all the saints with thee.

When the new valley is formed, the remnant still in the city (others already left, see 14:2) **shall flee to the valley of the mountains** for safety. Describing the length of this **valley,** the prophet says **the valley of the mountains shall reach unto Azal.** The location of Azal is uncertain. The people **shall flee, like as ye fled from before the earthquake in the days of Uzziah king**

of Judah. That **earthquake** occurred during the reign of king **Uzziah** (792-740 B.C.) over two centuries before Zechariah's ministry but is apparently an event still within Israel's collective memory. When they **flee...the LORD my God shall come, and all the saints with thee**. The word **saints** means "holy ones" and refers to "the *armies of heaven* described in Revelation 19:14."[213] These are angels and resurrected believers, as Walvoord explains in his commentary on Revelation 19:14:

> Accompanying Christ on His second coming are those described as "the armies which were in heaven." Some...have limited this army to the church, the Bride of Christ, on the basis that it is described as clothed in fine linen, white and clean. There is, however, no reason to limit this to the church, though the church is arrayed in fine linen. The church is not alone in having righteousness in the form of righteous deeds, and it is more probable that here not only the saints but also the holy angels are meant. It is well not to impose limitations upon a Scripture text which are not implicit in the text itself. The spectacle, however, of Christ on a white horse with a vesture dipped in blood accompanied by innumerable heavenly beings clothed in fine linen is a demonstration that now at long last the filthy, blasphemous situation in earth is going to be wiped clean with a divine judgment of tremendous character.[214]

This interpretation is also consistent with the active role of God's angels seen in the eighth night vision.

[213] David Guzik, *Zechariah*, Zec 14:3–5.
[214] John F. Walvoord, *The Revelation of Jesus Christ* (Moody Press: Chicago, 1989), 277.

> 6 And it shall come to pass in that day, *that* the
> light shall not be clear, *nor* dark: 7 But it shall
> be one day which shall be known to the LORD,
> not day, nor night: but it shall come to pass,
> *that* at evening time it shall be light.

When Jesus returns with the armies of heaven, **it shall come to pass in that day, that the light shall not be clear nor dark.** Instead, **it shall be one day which shall be known to the Lord, not day, nor night.** In the Olivet Discourse, Jesus describes a cosmic event that brings darkness: "Immediately after the tribulation of those days shall the sun be darkened, and the moon shall not give her light, and the stars shall fall from heaven, and the powers of the heavens shall be shaken." (Matthew 24:29) Other texts also present a future time of darkness, which may be the result of earthquakes and volcanic activity. (Joel 2:30-31; Revelation 6:12, 8:12) But the passage here speaks of both a removal of natural lighting and yet **it shall come to pass, that at evening time it shall be light.** One modern translation reads as follows: "On that day there will be no light—the sources of light in the heavens will congeal." (14:6, NET) Because of the loss of natural lighting, there will not be **day, nor night** in the usual sense. Yet when Jesus returns, **light** shall be restored **at evening time.** This **light** may emanate from Jesus just as there was **light** in the Creation event before there were natural lights (stars) in the heavens. Guzik articulates the point well: "The lights we guide our lives by **will diminish,** but God will bring His own light."[215] I think it likely that this is the sign Jesus said would accompany his return: "And then shall appear the sign of the Son of man in heaven: and then shall all the tribes of the earth mourn, and they shall see the Son of man coming in the clouds of heaven with power and great glory." (Matthew 24:30) When the Lord returns light breaks away the darkness. As Lindsey comments, "the time of Christ's Second Advent will be accompanied by

---

[215] David Guzik, *Zechariah*, Zec 14:6–11.

unparalleled natural phenomena (Isa. 13:10; 34:4; Joel 2:10, 30-31; 3:15; Matt. 24:29)."²¹⁶

> **8** And it shall be in that day, *that* living waters shall go out from Jerusalem; half of them toward the former sea, and half of them toward the hinder sea: in summer and in winter shall it be.

Also when Jesus returns, again **in that day, living waters shall go out from Jerusalem.** We see in chapter 13 that the Lord opens a spiritual fountain to His people to cleanse the land, and now a physical one opens. Essentially, two rivers form, one that flows **toward the former** or eastern **sea** and the other **toward the hinder** or western **sea.** One flows to the Dead Sea (the eastern **sea**) and the other to the Mediterranean Sea (the western **sea**). The phrase **in summer and in winter shall it be** means these two newly formed rivers flow year around. The **living waters** are not sourced in melting snow from mountain tops, but from the LORD himself. It stands to reason that the current topography of Israel will not permit these rivers to flow. But we will see in 14:10 that Jesus also alters the topography resulting in a renewed fertile land that flows with milk and honey. (e.g., Exodus 3:8) The "dead" sea will no longer be dead, but alive with vegetation and other animal life.

> **9** And the LORD shall be king over all the earth: in that day shall there be one LORD, and his name one.

Jesus will be, as Revelation 19:16 states, King of Kings and Lord of Lords. He will not simply be **king** of Jerusalem or Israel, but **king over all the earth.** He will become **king** by routing Israel's enemies, which are all of the other kings in the world that oppose him. When Jesus presents himself as **king** he will be **king over all the earth**, just as in the night visions

---

²¹⁶ F. Duane Lindsey, "Zechariah," in *The Bible Knowledge Commentary: An Exposition of the Scriptures*, 1570.

where He is "Lord of the whole earth." (4:14; 6:5) This fulfills the dominion promise of Zechariah 9:10: "and he shall speak peace unto the heathen: and his dominion shall be from sea even to sea, and from the river even to the ends of the earth." This also fulfills Jesus' prayer in Matthew 6:9-10: "Our Father which art in heaven, Hallowed be thy name. Thy kingdom come. Thy will be done in earth, as it is in heaven."

The prophet adds that **in that day shall there be one LORD, and his name one.** This refers to the Shemah in Deuteronomy 6:4: "Hear, O Israel: The LORD our God is one LORD." In Mark 12:29, we read in response to a question about the greatest commandment: "And Jesus answered him, The first of all the commandments is, Hear, O Israel; The Lord our God is one Lord." Recall that in chapter 13, which describes the reign of Messiah that occurs at the time described in this verse, the land will be cleansed of idolatry. Instead of people following after many gods, there is just one Lord. Merrill comments on the significance of this passage to the nature of God: "It is generally held by scholars of all persuasions that this is a confession not only of YHWH's self-consistency but of His uniqueness, His exclusivity. In terms of comparative religion, it is a statement of monotheism. It was as the climax to the basic principles of the Deuteronomic Covenant that the Shema was first articulated (Deut. 5:1–6:3). In that more limited context it was an encapsulation of Israel's faith alone ("our God"), so that any nuance about His oneness in terms of exclusivity must be understood accordingly."[217]

> 10 All the land shall be turned as a plain from Geba to Rimmon south of Jerusalem: and it shall be lifted up, and inhabited in her place, from Benjamin's gate unto the place of the first gate, unto the corner gate, and *from* the tower of Hananeel unto the king's winepresses.

217 Eugene H. Merrill, *An Exegetical Commentary - Haggai, Zechariah, Malachi*, 310.

When Jesus returns, He will create two new rivers of living waters (14:8) and alter the topography of **the land** into a **plain** so that the living waters will feed all of it. The mostly mountainous **land shall be turned as a plain from Geba to Rimmon south of Jerusalem**. The town of **Geba** was 6 miles north of Jerusalem on the northern border (Joshua 21:17) and **Rimmon** was 35 miles southwest of Jerusalem on the southern border (Joshua 15:32). In addition, **Jerusalem shall be lifted up** or elevated, consistent with Isaiah 2:2 and Micah 4:1-5, **and inhabited in her place**. As Eugene Merrill observes, Jesus establishes His rule both by his victory over Israel's enemies and His transformation of the land: "But in the eschaton He is king not merely in Jerusalem but from Jerusalem and over all the earth (cf. Isa. 2:2-4; Mic. 4:1-3). He has established His claims as sovereign by conquest and by recreation (Isa. 65:17-19; 66:18-21)."[218]

Recall that the third night vision focuses on the future substantial population that exceeds the ancient boundaries. The city will be **inhabited...from Benjamin's gate unto the place of the first gate, unto the corner gate, and from the tower of Hananeel unto the king's winepress**. These landmarks emphasize Jerusalem's specific inclusion within this future blessing. The **first gate, Benjamin's gate** (Jeremiah 38:13, 38:7), and the **Tower of Hananeel** (Nehemiah 3:1), were in the northeastern quadrant of the city. The **corner gate** was on Jerusalem's west wall close to the **corner** formed with the north wall. The **king's winepresses** were on the southern side of the city.

> 11 And *men* shall dwell in it, and there shall be no more utter destruction; but Jerusalem shall be safely inhabited.

People will **dwell** safely **in** Jerusalem, consistent with earlier statements in the book. (2:5; 8:4-5; 9:8) From this point

---

218 *Ibid.*, 310.

forward, **there shall be no more utter destruction** of the Holy City, **but Jerusalem shall be safely inhabited**. This allows for the utopian-like environment seen in 8:3-5: "...Jerusalem shall be called a city of truth...There shall yet old men and old women dwell in the streets of Jerusalem, and every man with his staff in his hand for very age. And the streets of the city shall be full of boys and girls playing in the streets thereof." We must recognize that while there were times of relative peace and prosperity in the history of Jerusalem, what is described here is not fleeting. It will sustain throughout the Millennium.

> **12** And this shall be the plague wherewith the LORD will smite all the people that have fought against Jerusalem; Their flesh shall consume away while they stand upon their feet, and their eyes shall consume away in their holes, and their tongue shall consume away in their mouth.

This verse reverts back to the subject matter of verse 3. In the Battle of Armageddon, Jesus destroys His enemies with the sword that proceeds from His mouth. (Revelation 19:21) The idea is likely that Jesus, in His sovereignty and power, simply speaks their deaths and it happens. Jesus will send a **plague wherewith the LORD will smite all the people that have fought against Jerusalem**. The plague is directed to the armies of the nations that attack **Jerusalem**. In the third night vision, God says: "for he that toucheth you toucheth the apple of his eye." (Zechariah 2:8) During the Tribulation, an international military force tests God in this regard, with catastrophic consequences. The prophet explains in graphic terms that **their flesh shall consume** or decay **away while they stand upon their feet, and their eyes shall consume away in their holes** or sockets, **and their tongue shall consume away in their mouth**. This flesh-eating **plague** spreads so swiftly that it will kill the soldiers **while they stand** and before their bodies hit the ground.

> 13 And it shall come to pass in that day, *that* a
> great tumult from the LORD shall be among
> them; and they shall lay hold every one on the
> hand of his neighbour, and his hand shall rise
> up against the hand of his neighbour.

Continuing to explain Jesus' defeat of the armies that invade
Jerusalem, the prophet writes that **it shall come to pass in that
day, that a great tumult** or confusion **from the LORD shall be
among them.** Because verse 12 describes a plague that kills the
enemy troops where they stand, this **tumult** presumably
precedes the final plague. Jesus confuses the enemy so that
**they shall lay hold every one on the hand of his neighbor, and
his hand shall rise up against the hand of his neighbor.** In this
imposed confusion, the enemy troops will turn upon and kill
one another. This is reminiscent of the battle fought by
Gideon's army in Judges 7:22: "And the three hundred blew the
trumpets, and the LORD set every man's sword against his
fellow, even throughout all the host: and the host fled to
Bethshittah in Zererath, *and* to the border of Abelmeholah,
unto Tabbath." This also fulfills Haggai 2:22: "And I will
overthrow the throne of kingdoms, and I will destroy the
strength of the kingdoms of the heathen; and I will overthrow
the chariots, and those that ride in them; and the horses and
their riders shall come down, every one by the sword of his
brother." It bears repeating that these arrogant armies picked
the wrong time to touch the "apple [pupil] of God's eye."

> 14 And Judah also shall fight at Jerusalem; and
> the wealth of all the heathen round about shall
> be gathered together, gold, and silver, and
> apparel, in great abundance.

This passage parallels Haggai 2:7: "And I will shake all nations,
and the desire of all nations shall come: and I will fill this
house with glory, saith the LORD of hosts." **Judah** obtains a
complete reversal of fortune. Instead of being the one
plundered and defeated as in 14:1-2, **Judah** is the victor that

gets the spoils of the Gentile nations. First, **Judah also shall fight at Jerusalem**. The sequence of events is that a Gentile invasion meets with initial success in taking Israel (14:1-2), but a remnant seeks the Lord and He returns to the Mount of Olives with the armies of heaven and creates a great valley to allow the remnant still in **Jerusalem** to flee the city (14:4-5), then Jesus confuses the invaders and empowers the remnant to **fight** at His side (see also 9:13, 12:8-9), and this battle culminates in all of the enemy invaders dying. As a result of Judah's victory, **the wealth of all the heathen** or Gentile nations **round about shall be gathered together, gold, and silver, and apparel, in great abundance**. This parallels Israel spoiling Egypt during the time of the Exodus. At that time, Egypt could have permitted God's people to leave the first time Moses told Pharaoh to let the people go, but he refused. Pharaoh's pride was his undoing. So also in the day of the LORD, the armies that assault Israel and Jerusalem make poor choices and face the consequences. Those who come against God's people will pay with their lives and their wealth. This spoil may be used to build the Millennial temple.

> **15** And so shall be the plague of the horse, of the mule, of the camel, and of the ass, and of all the beasts that shall be in these tents, as this plague.

In the same way as Jesus confuses the enemy troops, **so also shall be the plague on the horse, on the mule, on the camel, and on the ass, and on all the beasts that shall be in these tents** or camps of the enemy invaders. The **plague** will disable even the enemies' animals. Such animals were critical equipment for the armies of the ancient world, and still play a role in modern warfare. But they will be of no use when the **plague** hits, either to aid in fighting or fleeing.

> **16** And it shall come to pass, *that* every one that is left of all the nations which came against Jerusalem shall even go up from year to year to worship the King, the LORD of hosts, and to keep the feast of tabernacles.

When the fight is over, **it shall come to pass, that every one that is left of all the** Gentile **nations which came against Jerusalem shall even go up from year to year to worship the king, the** LORD **of hosts.** But which Gentiles constitute **every one that is left?** The short answer is that this is limited to Gentile Christians. That only believers will enter Jesus' Kingdom when it is implemented is confirmed elsewhere. (Matthew 25:32-46) This is evident from prior verses in Zechariah as well. In Zechariah 2:11, for example, we read that "many nations shall be joined to the LORD in that day, and **shall be my people**." (Zechariah 2:11) Similarly, "many people and strong nations **shall come to seek** the LORD of hosts in Jerusalem, and to pray before the LORD." (Zechariah 8:22) And in the verse at hand, these believing Gentiles **shall even go up from year to year to worship the King, the** LORD **of hosts, and to keep the feast of tabernacles**. The future pilgrimages by believing Gentiles during the Messianic Kingdom are also foretold in Zechariah 8:23: "In those days *it shall come to pass*, that ten men shall take hold out of all languages of the nations, even shall take hold of the skirt of him that is a Jew, saying, We will go with you: for we have heard *that* God *is* with you." The foregoing comments do not mean there are no non-believers in the Kingdom. We know that near the end of the Millennium, for example, "when the thousand years are expired, Satan shall be loosed out of his prison, and shall go out to deceive the nations...to gather them together to battle." (Revelation 20:7-8) But when the Kingdom begins, there will only be believers.

The seven day feast called the **feast of tabernacles** or **feast of booths** begins on the fifteenth day of Tishri with a day of holy convocation treated as a Sabbath day. Special offerings are required each day, and it is celebrated by the people building and dwelling in booths or **tabernacles** to commemorate the forty years of wilderness wonderings with God's manifested presence from the Tabernacle. This was a time of rejoicing that followed the Day of Atonement (Yom Kippur), and it symbolized the people of God dwelling in His presence with

Him providing for them (Leviticus 23:33-36, 39-43; Exodus 23:14-17; Numbers 29:12-38; Deuteronomy 16:13-16, 31:9-13). What we see at this future time is a fulfillment of this feast because the people of God, Jew and Gentile, enjoy the physical presence of God the Son in Jerusalem.

This verse has prompted debate concerning how the **feast of tabernacles** is kept, and in particular, whether the animal sacrifices are done. If the mechanics of the feast are altered in the Kingdom, there is no hint of that here or anywhere else. Accordingly, there will apparently be animal sacrifices. That raises the next question, namely why? That is, because Jesus died for the sins of the world once and for all, why continue the animal sacrifices? The probable answer is that these are memorials just as the Lord's Supper is today. I included a more extended analysis of this issue in Appendix A that follows these notes.

One final critical observation is needed here. The **families of the earth** hearkens to the language of the Abrahamic Covenant where Abraham was promised that "in thee shall all families of the earth be blessed." (Genesis 12:3) Of course, this is fulfilled in Christ, who is our substitutionary atonement for sins. But this blessing is further experienced as believing Gentiles enjoy the Kingdom. Also, they will **worship the King**. There is no question the **King** refers here, as it does in Zechariah 9:9, to Jesus Christ, the second member of the Godhead. That God permits this **worship** affirms the deity of Jesus, as does the apposition of **king** to **LORD of hosts**. The worshipers will see Jesus, the Son of God, in Jerusalem. Recall Jesus' words to Philip: "he that hath seen me hath seen the Father." (John 14:9)

> **17** And it shall be, *that* whoso will not come up of *all* the families of the earth unto Jerusalem to worship the King, the LORD of hosts, even upon them shall be no rain. **18** And if the family of Egypt go not up, and come not, that

have no *rain*; there shall be the plague, wherewith the LORD will smite the heathen that come not up to keep the feast of tabernacles. **19** This shall be the punishment of Egypt, and the punishment of all nations that come not up to keep the feast of tabernacles.

The book of Revelation affirms that the Kingdom Jesus establishes will have an initial one thousand year period (the Millennium) after which this material universe will be replaced with the new heavens and new earth. (Revelation 20:6, 21:1) During the Millennial reign of Jesus, everyone will be required to make the trip to Jerusalem—no exceptions. Thus, **it shall be, that whoso will not come up of all the families of the earth unto Jerusalem, to worship the King, the LORD of hosts, even upon them shall be no rain.** Once again we find affirmation of the deity of Jesus Christ in that the **families of the earth** are required to **worship** him. But if a nation refuses, it will meet with immediate temporal judgment, namely a **drought**. For example, **if the family of Egypt** (meaning the Egyptians) **go not up** to Jerusalem to **worship the king**, and **come not** unto him, **that** they will **have no rain.** If they continue to refuse, **there shall be the plague, wherewith the** LORD **will smite the** Gentiles **that come not up to keep the feast of tabernacles.** He adds, again using **Egypt** hypothetically, **this shall be the punishment of Egypt, and the punishment of all nations that come not up to keep the feast of tabernacles.**

While it is difficult to imagine such a refusal, we know that near the end of the Millennial period, Satan will be loosed and will deceive many and raise a rebellion against Jesus, which will be met with swift judgment. (Revelation 20:7-10) This is possible because while the Kingdom will initially be composed only of believers, they will procreate during the 1,000 period (recall the earlier reference to the Kingdom being populated with happy children, Zechariah 8:5). Thus, it is possible that people, or even a nation, will at some point refuse. Regardless, we have already seen that Jesus' Kingdom will be characterized by righteousness. Rebellion will not be tolerated. We must bear in mind that no one will refuse to come to Jerusalem due to lack of evidence for who Jesus is. But Jesus is the king of kings and lord of lords, and any rejection of His authority will have consequences. The next two verses further explain why these consequences, which some may think severe, must follow.

> **20** In that day shall there be upon the bells of the horses, HOLINESS UNTO THE LORD; and the pots in the LORD'S house shall be like the bowls before the altar. **21** Yea, every pot in Jerusalem and in Judah shall be holiness unto the LORD of hosts: and all they that sacrifice shall come and take of them, and seethe therein: and in that day there shall be no more the Canaanite in the house of the LORD of hosts.

Simply put, Jesus' Kingdom will be characterized by holiness. For the Jewish people, horses were not considered "clean" animals, but in Jesus' Kingdom everything must be holy, even the things least associated in a Jewish mindset with holiness. Therefore, **in that day shall there be upon the bells of the horses** the inscription, **holiness to the LORD**. This is the same inscription that is on the mitre worn by the high priest and its use here is no coincidence. (Exodus 28:36-38) That which is not expected to be holy is, in fact, just as holy as that which is expected to be most holy. Similarly, the common cooking **pots in the Lord's house** or temple **shall be like the** special **bowls before the altar**. Every vessel (or **pot**) in the land will be holy in that day, **yea, every pot in Jerusalem and in Judah shall be holiness unto the LORD of hosts**.

Moreover, **all they that sacrifice shall come and take** the holy vessels **and seethe** or boil their sacrifices **therein**. As with the keeping of the feast of tabernacles (14:16), this further affirms that there will be at least some animal sacrifices during the Millennial Kingdom. Continuing the theme of **holiness**,

Zechariah writes that **in that day shall be no more Canaanite in the house of the** LORD **of hosts**. The **Canaanite** does not mean an exclusion of a particular race but is used idiomatically to refer to an unclean person. As Feinberg comments, "In time they came to be symbolic of all that was deceitful, unclean, and ungodly (for proof note Hosea 12:8 in the Hebrews). God promises that in that day of holiness no unclean [thing] shall defile the house of the Lord."[219] This is fitting since everything in Israel will be characterized by **holiness**, fulfilling God's purpose of holiness for His people. Feinberg again well says:

> In short, what is stated positively in the first part of verse 21 is repeated negatively in the latter part of the verse. God's great object in Israel is holiness; His great aim in the Church is holiness; His great longing for your life and mine is holiness, and only holiness. Our chapter which began in darkness (as did, indeed, the entire prophecy of Zechariah) ends in radiant and transparent light of holiness.[220]

To grasp the beauty of Zechariah's climactic final chapter, we must reflect on Jesus Christ as the centerpiece of Zechariah's ministry. He is the rider on the red horse in chapter 1 protecting the Jewish remnant, the builder that measures Jerusalem for future blessing in chapter 2, the one who makes us clean and fit for service in chapter 3, the one that empowers us by His Spirit in chapter 4, the one that enforces righteousness and removes wickedness from Israel in chapter 5, who in chapter 6 overtakes Israel's enemies and is crowned as the priest-king, the one in chapter 7 that requires true worship from the people of God, who in chapter 8 restores the nation and provides security and prosperity, he is the triumphal king of chapter 9, the provider of Kingdom blessings in chapter 10, the good shepherd of chapter 11, the defender of Israel in

---

[219] Charles L. Feinberg, *God Remembers: A Study of Zechariah*, 205.
[220] *Ibid.*, 205.

chapter 12, the fountain for cleansing in chapter 13, and in this final chapter, the victorious reigning priest-king Messiah of the whole world whose Kingdom exhibits holiness.

The vision ends with the Jewish people finally in a state of security and **holiness** in their Promise Land, a light to the Gentiles who travel there to worship king Jesus. This fulfills God's promises to Abraham and David. It should be noted that the passage gives no indication of an end to this Kingdom. As Daniel wrote: "I saw in the night visions, and, behold, one like the Son of man came with the clouds of heaven, and came to the Ancient of days, and they brought him near before him. And there was given him dominion, and glory, and a kingdom, that all people, nations, and languages, should serve him: his dominion is an everlasting dominion, which shall not pass away, and his kingdom that which shall not be destroyed." (Daniel 7:13-14).

Being the people of God necessarily includes a life lived in view not only of the present, but the future glory of Jesus' eternal reign on earth. It is a life that looks forward to all these glorious blessings outlined by Zechariah and lives now in fervent anticipation. Whatever challenges we may face during our mortal time on earth, we know Jesus will be victorious and we will enjoy the blessings of living in His Kingdom as His people. That hope should comfort and encourage us.

Closing

Holy. How frequently we read in the Bible about "holy" or "holiness." In First Peter, the apostle exhorts, "But as he which hath called you is holy, so be ye holy in all manner of conversation." (1 Peter 1:15) Indeed, God says, "Be ye holy; for I am holy." (1 Peter 1:16) To be holy is to take on the divine nature. Yet because that is so foreign to who we are in the flesh, we struggle to even define holiness. Surely it entails notions of separation from worldliness and being distinct or peculiar or a cut above all that is tied to this decaying world. It is a profound truth that during our Christian lives this side of eternity we are called upon to be holy, knowing that we will soon be in the Kingdom of Jesus Christ that will be holy. If there is something Christians in the United States desperately need, it is to know God better by learning holiness. Living in anticipation of Jesus' Kingdom should stir our hearts to seek to be holy in how we think, what we say, and in every action we take. In a world system antithetical to all that God stands for, personal holiness will make us stand out like a bright light in the blackness of a dark cave. Some people are going to ridicule the light, and even try to dim the light or hide it from others. But others will see the light of a life truly changed and different because of Jesus Christ. One thing is certain, if there is no holiness there will be no light to see. As we keep one foot planted where we are and press the other into the future reality the prophet shares with us, our heart should burn for the things of God, that we may experience the new reality now and impact others by a life that testifies of God's grace and reflects the holiness to which we are called.

Application Points

- **MAIN PRINCIPLE:** In the day of the LORD, while an international force will find initial success when it invades Israel, Jesus will return, making a way of escape for the believing Jewish remnant still in Jerusalem and destroying the invaders. After this, Jesus will implement His Kingdom, which will be holy.

Discussion Questions

1. Why is the international force that attacks Israel in the day of the Lord permitted to prevail at first?

2. In what ways is the Mount of Olives significant in the four Gospels and the book of Acts? How is it significant to Jesus' second coming?

3. How will the Holy Land change when Jesus implements His Kingdom?

4. In what ways will life now be like life in the Kingdom and in what ways will it be different (based on what Zechariah says)?

5. What is the significance of the feast of tabernacles to living in the Millennium?

6. What does holy mean? And if Jesus' Kingdom is characterized by holiness, what does that look like in the daily lives of His people?

7. What is your favorite chapter (or favorite verse) in Zechariah and why?

Appendix

Excursus on Millennial Sacrifices

There are several references in the Old Testament prophetic writings to a future re-institution of animal sacrifices. (Isaiah 56:6-8, 66:21; Jeremiah 33:15-18; Ezekiel 20:40-41, 43:18-46:24; and Zechariah 14:16) By far, the most extensive passage is Ezekiel 43:18-46:24, which is part of the overall description of a new temple and restoration to the land in Ezekiel 40-48. In the broadest sense, the two interpretive possibilities are a literal interpretation—the dispensational viewpoint—and a symbolic or allegorical interpretation, but within both categories there are a number of variations. The question is not academic since many non-dispensationalist see this passage as the silver bullet that destroys the dispensational viewpoint, as Pentecost observes: "An alleged inconsistency between this [the literal] interpretation and the teaching of the New Testament concerning the finished work of Christ, which brought about the abolition of the Old Testament sacrificial system, has been used by the amillennialists to reduce the premillennial system to an absurdity and to affirm the fallacy of the literal method of interpretation."[221] In this excursus, with a primary focus on Ezekiel 40-48, I will analyze the literal and symbolic approaches to interpreting the animal sacrifice verses and argue that the purely literal interpretation is the most satisfactory solution.

At the outset, it should be observed that the interpretation of the portions of Ezekiel 40-48 dealing with the temple cannot be divorced from the verses dealing with animal sacrifices. It would be incongruous to take a literal approach to the one and a figurative approach to the other, and commentators often treat the two together. It is, therefore, helpful to consider the competing views regarding the temple in Ezekiel 40-48 in order to analyze the issue of the animal sacrifices therein. Walvoord concludes that there are five primary interpretations of the temple verses: (1) Ezekiel's description provides specifications for Solomon's temple, (2) the description provides specifications for Zerubbabel's temple, (3) the description is "an ideal which the returning pilgrims should have observed but did not," (4) the description "was intended to be a typical presentation only to be fulfilled by the church in the present age," and (5) Ezekiel's temple is literal and will be constructed during the millennial period.[222]

The first two suggestions must be rejected because Ezekiel's specifications for the temple are substantially different— indeed, they provide for a much larger structure—than either of the first two temples. The third interpretation finds no support in any of the post-exilic writings. The fourth option is really one of several paths that an allegorical or symbolic approach may take, and will be addressed in more detail below. I will not attempt to address in any detail how those taking

---

[221] J. Dwight Pentecost, *Things To Come: A Study In Biblical Eschatology* (Grand Rapids, MI: Zondervan, 1964), 517.

[222] John F. Walvoord, *The Millennial Kingdom* (Grand Rapids, MI: Zondervan, 2002), 309-10.

the allegorical approach have treated the specifics in Ezekiel's descriptions, but rather, will focus on the relative merits or lack thereof within the allegorical and literal approaches.

Representative of the allegorical view, Daniel Block views Ezekiel 40-48 as requiring a rhetorical, non-literal interpretation and offers reasons for rejecting a literal interpretation:

> Nonetheless, Ezekiel's account should not be interpreted as a blueprint to follow in an actual construction project. Although the analytic tone has a ring of realism, with numerous reminiscences of earlier plans, explicit instructions to build the described structure are missing. Furthermore, not only does the design display many idealistic features; the dimensions recorded are exclusively horizontal measurements, apparently without regard for the vertical distances required by architectural plans. Accordingly, the purpose of this temple tour must be sought elsewhere....The precision in the measurements, the presences and size of the gateways, the emphasis on purity, the centrality of the altar, and the strict regulations controlling access to the inner court are designed to shame (klm) Ezekiel's exilic audience for past abuses (43:10). Expressed positively, Ezekiel envisions a day when abominations in the sanctuary cease (cf. 8:1-8), and all Israel worships Yahweh in spirit and in truth (cf. John 4:23).[223]

Later, Block describes the passage in these terms: "...the prophet will be given a tour of the heavenly residence of God, of which the tabernacle and the Jerusalem temple had been

---

[223] Daniel I. Block, *The Book Of Ezekiel: Chapters 24-48* (Grand Rapids, MI: William B. Eerdmans Publishing Company 1998), 510-11.

but replicas."[224] More typical of the objections to a literal viewpoint are those of G. K. Beale:

> Those who see a literal temple structure as the fulfillment of Ezekiel's prophecy usually interpret the sacrifices there to be 'memorial sacrifices' that commemorate Christ's death. In response, numerous commentators have pointed out that this would violate the principle of Hebrews: the Old Testament sacrifices pointed to Christ's 'once for all' sacrifice (Heb. 9:12, 26, 28; 10:10-18), so that to go back to those sacrifices would indicate the insufficiency of Christ's sacrifice for sin (cf., e.g., Heb. 10:18: 'Now where there is forgiveness of these things, there is no longer any offering for sin'). This would appear to amount to a reversal of redemptive history and, more importantly, a denial of the efficacy of Christ's sacrifice.[225]

Rooker likewise states the primary objection: "To support a nonliteral interpretation, one could point out that animal sacrifices do not actually cleanse from sin (Heb. 10:4) and Christ's sacrifice has removed the need for any additional sacrifices (Heb. 10:10, 14). The question is, Why would they ever be repeated?"[226] Along the same lines, Fruchtenbaum comments on the primary objection to a literal approach: "A common argument against taking these verses literally is the question as to why such a system would be necessary since the Messiah has already died. If the death of Christ was the final

---

[224] *Ibid.*, 515.

[225] G. K. Beale, *The Temple And The Church's Mission: A Biblical Theology Of The Dwelling Place Of God* (Downers Grove, IL: Intervarsity Press, 2004), 343-44.

[226] Mark Rooker, *Ezekiel* (Nashville, TN: Broadman & Holman Publishers, 2005), 318.

sacrifice for sin, how could these animal sacrifices provide an expiation for sin? Therefore, some say, these chapters of Ezekiel must not be taken literally."[227]

Those that object to the literal interpretation are asking the right question. As Pentecost rightly observes: "If a consistent literalism leads to the adoption of literal sacrifices during the millennium, it becomes necessary to give reasons why such a system should be reinstituted."[228] While the question is a good one, in my view, those rejecting the literal hermeneutic engage in fallacious reasoning in their analysis. Walvoord is correct in noting: "Objections to sacrifices in the millennium stem mostly from New Testament affirmations concerning the one sacrifice of Christ... While other objections are also made of a lesser character, it is obvious that this constitutes the major obstacle, not only to accepting the sacrificial system but the possibility of the future temple in the millennium as well."[229] Thus, they draw their support from verses like Hebrews 7:27, which states: "Who needeth not daily, as those high priests, to offer up sacrifice, first for his own sins, and then for the people's: for this he did once, when he offered up himself." Also, in Hebrews 9:12, we read: "Neither by the blood of goats and calves, but by his own blood he entered in once into the holy place, having obtained eternal redemption for us." And in Hebrews 9:26, we read: "For then must he often have suffered since the foundation of the world: but now once in the end of the world hath he appeared to put away sin by the sacrifice of himself." From these verses and others, non-dispensationalists find support for their primary objection to the reinstitution of animal sacrifices, namely that Christ died once for all time and any further sacrifices would have no expiatory value and, therefore, it would not make sense to reinstitute the levitical offerings.

---

[227] Arnold G. Fruchtenbaum, *Israelology: The Missing Link In Systematic Theology*, 810.

[228] J. Dwight Pentecost, *Things To Come: A Study In Biblical Eschatology*, 518.

[229] John F. Walvoord, *The Millennial Kingdom*, 311

To those rejecting the reinstitution of animal sacrifices, a number of answers are appropriate. First of all, dispensationalists are not suggesting that the Mosaic system will be reinstituted, but instead, a new order that relates to the new covenant of Jeremiah 31. Indeed, there are several important differences between the Mosaic offerings and those detailed in Ezekiel: (1) the physical temple dimensions are different from the first two temples; (2) the priests who conduct priestly functions are not taken from the entire Levitical line, but only from the sons of Zadok; (3) many of the components that had a high place in the Mosaic system are not mentioned, including the Ark of the Covenant, the pot of manna, Aaron's rod, the tables of the Law, the cherubim, the golden candlestick, the shew bread, the Holy of Holies, and the High Priest; (4) there is no evening sacrifice, the measures for the burnt offerings differ, and while some of the feasts are mentioned, Pentecost is omitted and those things necessary for the day of Atonement are lacking; (5) there are not only omissions, but additions, such as the living waters from beneath the altar and the trees of healing; and (6) there is an emphasis in Ezekiel's description on "the prince" who has both royal and priestly prerogatives.[230] From these differences, Pentecost concludes: "The system to be inaugurated in the millennial age will be a new order that will replace the Levitical order, for there are too many changes, deletions, and additions to the old order to sustain the contention that, literally interpreted, Ezekiel teaches the institution of the Levitical order again."[231]

In further response to those rejecting the literal reinstitution of the animal sacrifices, it must be said that the sacrifices have nothing to do with expiation from sin. Typical of those that conflate the issue of the sacrifices with expiation are Beale's comments:

---

[230] J. Dwight Pentecost, *Things To Come: A Study In Biblical Eschatology*, 519-24.
[231] *Ibid.*, 524.

Those who see a literal temple structure as the fulfillment of Ezekiel's prophecy usually interpret the sacrifices there to be 'memorial sacrifices' that commemorate Christ's death. In response, numerous commentators have pointed out that this would violate the principle of Hebrews: the Old Testament sacrifices pointed to Christ's 'once for all' sacrifice ..., so that to go back to those sacrifices would indicate the insufficiency of Christ's sacrifice for sin... This would appear to amount to a reversal of redemptive history and, more importantly, a denial of the efficacy of Christ's sacrifice.[232]

But dispensationalists are no more arguing that the reinstituted sacrifices will expiate sin or in any way add to the finished work of Christ on the cross than they would argue the same for the Lord's Supper. Obviously the future sacrifices will not expiate sin, just as many of the same commentators readily recognize that the Levitical offerings under the Mosaic system did not expiate sin: "For it is not possible that the blood of bulls and of goats should take away sins." (Hebrews 10:4). If those Mosaic offerings did not expiate sin, but looked forward to Christ's once for all offering, then there is no logical inconsistency with future offerings, without any claim of expiating sin, looking back to Christ's once for all offering. Pentecost is right to conclude, "What folly to argue that a rite could accomplish in the future what it never could, or did, or was ever intended to do, in the past."[233]

Some lesser arguments against the reinstitution of the sacrifices is that it violates Ephesians 2:14-16 in that the barrier between Jews and Gentiles is removed. This objection fails to distinguish

---

[232] G. K. Beale, *The Temple And The Church's Mission: A Biblical Theology Of The Dwelling Place Of God*, 343-44.

[233] J. Dwight Pentecost, *Things To Come: A Study In Biblical Eschatology*, 525.

between God's dealings with Israel and the Church, and in particular, fails to realize that God's purpose for the present age is different than in the millennium. Moreover, just because the position of Jews and Gentiles in Christ in this age is the same does not mean that their positions in the Kingdom must be identical. Another argument is that Ezekiel's prophecy cannot be literally interpreted because what is described is geographically impossible. The short answer to this objection is that it overlooked the topographical changes Jesus will institute in the millennium, as recorded in Zechariah 14. Still others argue that the role of "the prince" in Ezekiel's prophecy is in competition with Christ's reign. This objection should be rejected because the Scriptures confirm that while Christ will reign, He will also delegate authority to others (e.g., Luke 19:17). Finally, some find the idea of sacrifices, with the blood and the stench, repugnant. Walvoord answers this argument well:

> It would seem that [these objectors] have temporarily forgotten that the entire sacrificial system of the Old Testament, while perhaps incongruous with western civilization aesthetics, was nevertheless commanded by God Himself as a proper typical presentation of the coming work of Christ. If such sacrifices were fitting in the mind of God to be the shadows of the cross of Christ, what more fitting memorial could be chosen if a memorial is desired for that same sacrifice. Obviously, a memorial is not intended to equal or to be a substitute of the real sacrifice, but as a ritual it is to point to the reality which is Christ.[234]

Turning now to the dispensational answer to the question of why the animal sacrifices would be reinstituted, there is general agreement among most dispensationalists that the sacrifices will act as memorials of Calvary. John Walvoord explains:

---

[234] John F. Walvoord, *The Millennial Kingdom*, 314-15.

Those who consider the millennial sacrifices as a ritual which will be literally observed in the millennium invest the sacrifices with the central meaning of a memorial looking back to the one offering of Christ. The millennial sacrifices are no more expiatory than were the Mosaic sacrifices which preceded the cross. If it has been fitting for the church in the present age to have a memorial of the death of Christ in the Lord's Supper, it is suggested that it would be suitable also to have a memorial of possibly a different character in the millennium in keeping with the Jewish characteristics of the period.[235]

Pentecost likewise comments: "There is general agreement among premillennialists as to the purpose of the sacrificial system as inaugurated in the millennial age. Interpreted in the light of the New Testament, with its teaching on the value of the death of Christ, they must be memorials of that death."[236] And the explanation by Arnold Fruchtenbaum is particularly helpful:

What will be the purpose of these sacrifices in light of Christ's death? To begin with, it should be remembered that the sacrificial system of the Mosaic Law did not remove sins either (Heb. 10:4), but only covered them (the meaning of "atonement" in Hebrew). Its purpose was to serve as a physical and visual picture of what the Messiah would do (Isa. 53:10-12). The Church has been commanded to keep the Lord's Supper as a physical and visual picture of what Christ did on the cross. God intends to provide for Israel in the kingdom a

---

235 *Ibid.*, 311-12.
236 J. Dwight Pentecost, *Things To Come: A Study In Biblical Eschatology*, 525.

physical and visual picture of what the
Messiah accomplished on the cross. For
Israel, however, it will be a sacrificial system
instead of communion with bread and wine.
The purpose of the sacrificial system in the
kingdom will be the same as the purpose of
communion of the Church: In remembrance
of me.[237]

The strongest support for the view that animal sacrifices will
be reinstituted is that that is what the Bible says. Opponents
take on the burden of proof to demonstrate that the text must
be spiritualized. And while a number of objections have been
raised, several of which were addressed above, the objections
are not sourced in the actual text of Ezekiel 40-48. Indeed,
there is no indication that the passage should be taken
figuratively. Grasping at straws, Beale places great emphasis on
the fact that Ezekiel was taken to a high mountain (Ezekiel
40:2) and that there is a city on the mountain.[238] He concludes
that since no literal mountain presently exists that fits the
description, then Ezekiel is seeing the heavenly temple and
not a future earthly temple. This argument approaches the
ludicrous since other passages indicate future topographical
changes in the Holy Land, and moreover, the same argument
completely undercuts the literalness of Jesus' temptation,
which he surely would not deny. In Matthew 4:8, we read:
"Again, the devil taketh him up into an exceeding high
mountain, and sheweth him all the kingdoms of the world, and
the glory of them." What mountain existed in the first century
from which Jesus could see all the kingdoms of the world? And
yet, the kingdoms and their glory were real! We must conclude
that the literal approach to the Ezekiel 40-48 passage is to be
preferred because there is no textual reason to abandon it. If

[237] Arnold G. Fruchtenbaum, *Israelology: The Missing Link In Systematic Theology*, 810-11.
[238] G. K. Beale, *The Temple And The Church's Mission: A Biblical Theology Of The Dwelling Place Of God*, 336-40.

God wanted to convey to Israel that during the millennium the sacrifices would be instituted, what more could He have said to bring home the point? Fruchtenbaum is correct when he states: "Therefore, some say, these chapters of Ezekiel must not be taken literally. If not, Ezekiel gives a lot of detail that would suddenly become meaningless. Furthermore, if all that detail is intended to be symbolic, the symbols are never explained and the non-literalist is forced to be subjective in expounding them and must resort to guess work."[239]

If we apply a literal hermeneutic to Ezekiel 40-48, as well as other passages like Zechariah 14, it is inescapable that during the millennium God will reinstitute the animal sacrifices. In view of the once for all nature of Christ's work on Calvary, as confirmed especially in the book of Hebrews, the purpose of the future animal sacrifices cannot be expiatory. For these reasons, and consistent with the purpose of the Lord's Supper during the Church Age, the view that the animal sacrifices are memorials is the most reasonable.

---

[239] Arnold G. Fruchtenbaum, *Israelology: The Missing Link In Systematic Theology*, 810.

About the Author

HUTSON SMELLEY resides in Chappell Hill, Texas with his wife and children. He holds advanced degrees in mathematics, law and Biblical studies, and is an adjunct professor at the College of Biblical Studies. He can be contacted at: proclaimtheword@mac.com

www.proclaimtheword.me

www.ingramcontent.com/pod-product-compliance
Lightning Source LLC
LaVergne TN
LVHW051726080426
835511LV00018B/2908